Beginning in the Middle

Beginning in the Middle

Caroline Bailey

Quartet Books
London   Melbourne   New York

First published by Quartet Books Limited, 1982
A member of the Namara Group
27/29 Goodge Street, London W1P 1FD

Copyright © 1982 by Caroline Bailey

Phototypeset by MC Typeset, Rochester, Kent
Printed and bound in Great Britain
by Mackays of Chatham Limited, Kent

For my Mother, with love

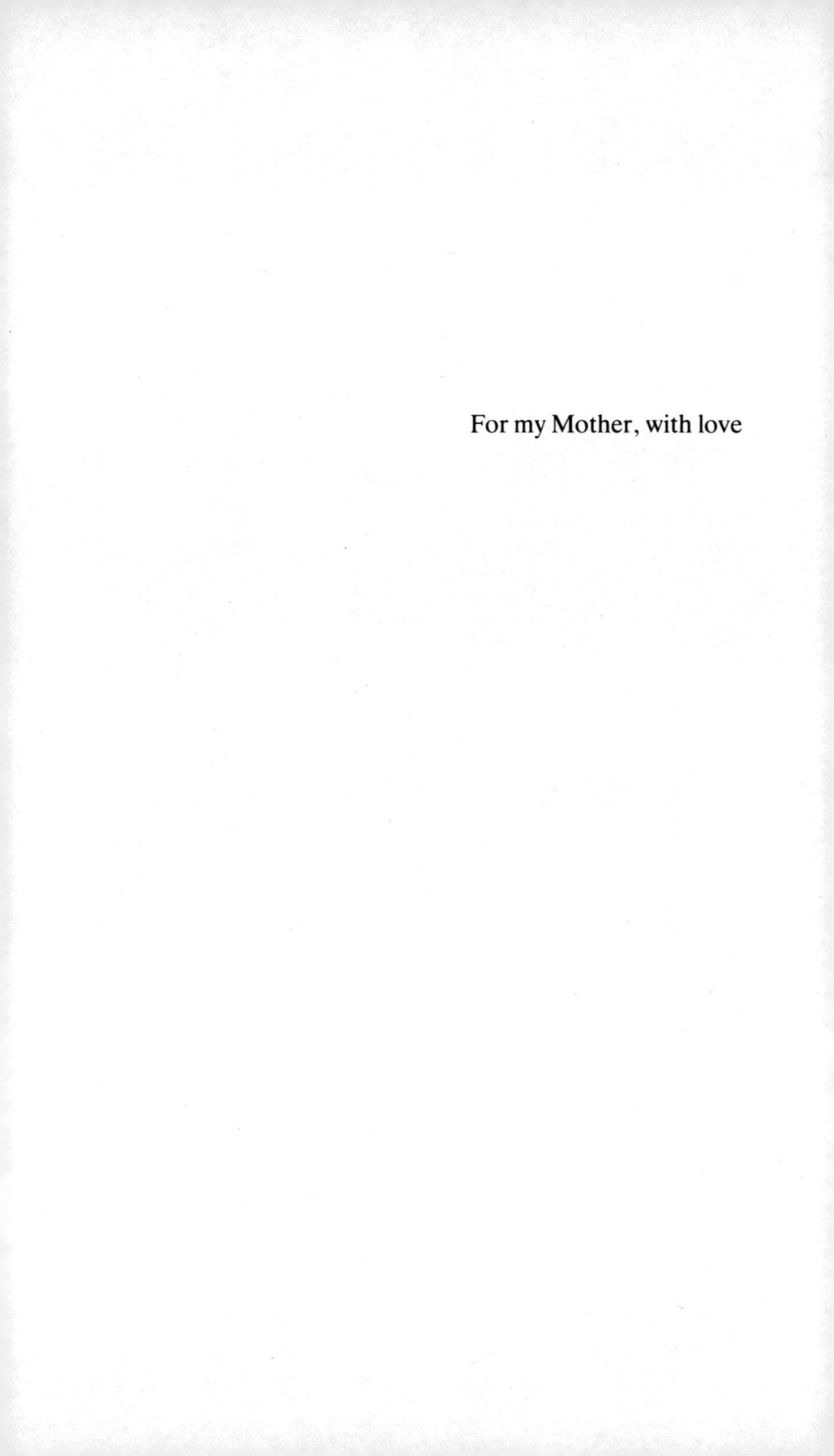

Contents

	Acknowledgements	ix
	Introduction	1
	Autobiographies	9
1	Before and After	108
2	Time	122
3	Ageing	129
4	Society	142
5	Individuals	153
6	Why Change Can Be Inhibited	163
7	Marriage	169
8	The Family Game	185
9	Work: Women's Two Roles	201
10	Education	217
11	Love . . . Sex	229
12	Effects of Change on Partners	242
13	Friends	253
14	Being Alone	260
	Postscript	267
	Bibliography	269

Acknowledgements

It goes without saying that this book could not have been written without the help of all the women who consented to be interviewed. My thanks are due to them for the time and trouble they spent talking with me which I found very rewarding. I am grateful to them for giving me the opportunity.

Without the help of the following, I would not have been able to contact many of the interviewees: Liz Ahrends, Bridgit Baker, Clair Chapman, Jude Craven, Mary Dilworth, Jane Dunn, Christopher Hope, Debby Hyams, Pippa Isbell (The Industrial Society), David Jockelson, Adah Kay, Tom Kay, Irma Kurtz, Nancy Roberts, BBC Woman's Hour, *Guardian* Women, Fawcett Library.

Joe Bailey and Cathy Crawford gave invaluable help with the manuscript and offered much encouraging and critical advice. Also to Jean Maund and Janet Law, my editors, who gave similar help at a later stage.

Finally, without the support of Joe, Anna and Josh, I would not have stayed the course.

Beginning in the Middle

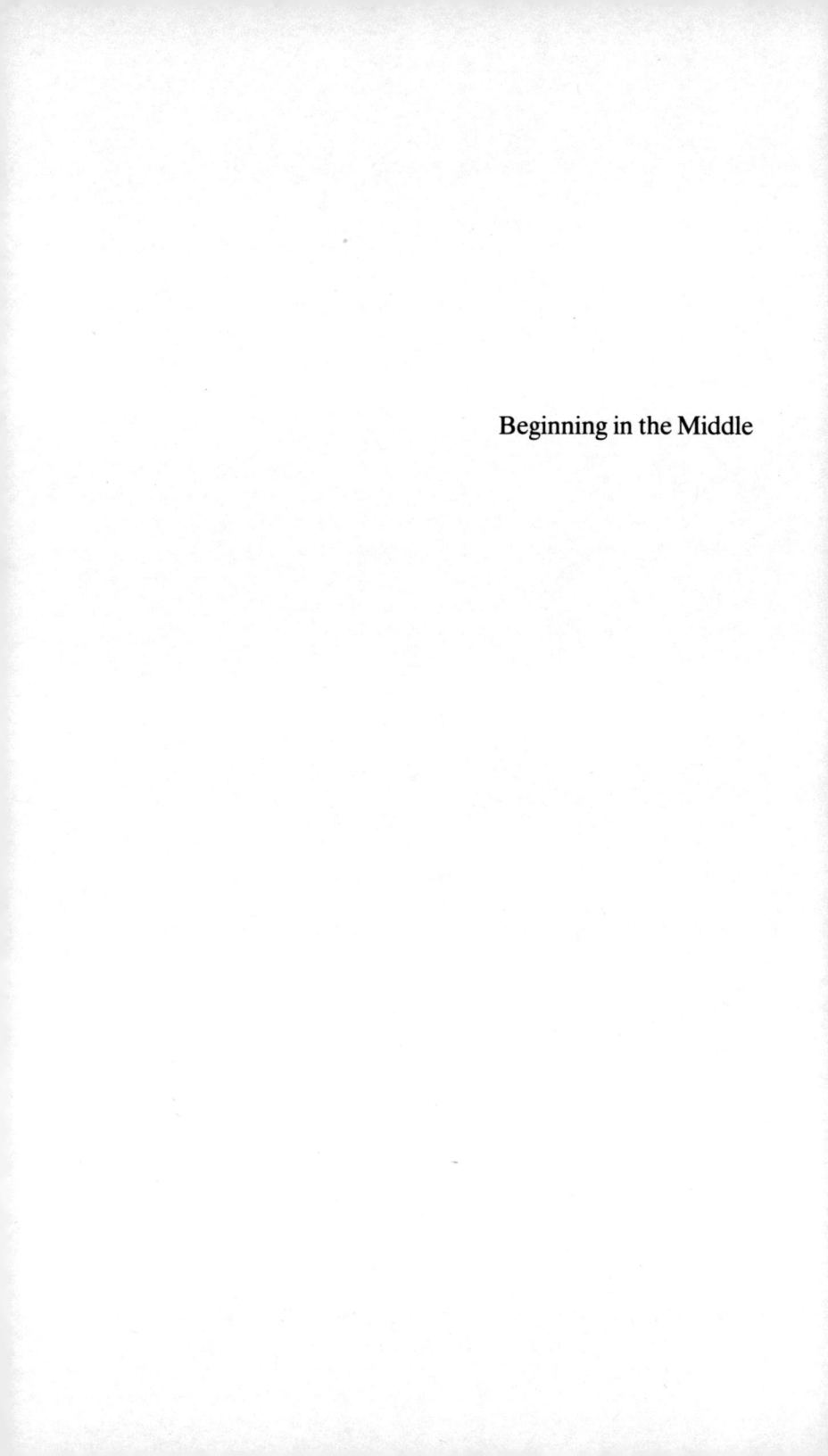

Introduction

> Holding one hand out, groping, and the other out backwards, linked to the security of what was known. Straining like that.
>
> Paul Scott, *The Raj Quartet*

> Midway in our life's journey, I went astray from the straight road and woke to find myself alone in a dark wood.
>
> Dante, *The Inferno*

Middle age does not have a good image, which is one of the reasons why the clumsier sounding alternative – middle years – has been used instead. 'Age confers a kind of authority on men but doesn't treat women so kindly,' Irma Kurtz said, which puts the issue in a nutshell, for until recently women have largely contributed to this negative picture of themselves during the middle years. We need only look at romantic fiction to see that middle-aged (professional) men are presented as having a certain distinction about them while middle-aged women are seen as 'past it'. Admittedly romantic fiction presents an unreal and narrow viewpoint but nevertheless it reflects to some extent the popular image of middle-aged men and women. The conventional picture of a middle-aged woman is not a kind one: usually depicted as either a sagging has-been or a tartar bolstered in iron corsetry, both images reflect a curiously neutered state. A woman is not so much a woman during her middle years, more of a remaindered being who no longer has a very clear role to play.

This could be something to do with the word 'age' itself: we talk about old age and middle age but not about 'young' age, which suggests that after a couple of decades or so, we start counting and going downhill. Once probably a fairly accurate picture when life expectancy did not extend beyond forty or so, it is no longer that way; we all have an average of at least thirty more years to go from that point.

Of course 'middle' has a rather derogatory ring about it too. Apart from age and Ages – the latter being synonymous with the Dark Ages as well, which probably affects our collective subconscious – there is middle class, middle ground, middle man, middle-of-the-road, pig-in-the-middle and a host of others. All phrases when qualified with middle imply an above or below, a before and an after, so that being or having a 'middle' anything suggests the transitional or passing through one stage in order to reach another. There is an implied better or worse attached to 'middle' as well, being not positively one thing or the other but an unsatisfactory mixture of both. When it comes to age, our society is quite clear about the equation: youth is better than old age, which is worse than middle age.

But what exactly *is* middle age? It is rather like the proverbial piece of string, which perhaps explains why there is a mass of research about both ends of the life spectrum but relatively little covering the in-between. It is all too elusive and difficult to pin down – that expanse of time between the springtime of youth and the winter of old age. For to pursue the analogy, it covers both summer and autumn, say the years between about thirty and sixty.

The state obviously appreciates some of the difficulties of pinning down middle age, because this is the one period of time which it has not considered necessary to define. Although curiously ambiguous about the onset of adulthood, allowing a choice between sixteen, eighteen and twenty-one, it is absolutely definite about the onset of old age. Though again it demonstrates an odd and unequal understanding of the sexes by deeming women old at sixty, allowing men another five years to go. Why does the state consider women no longer employable at an earlier stage than men, even though on average they live longer?

Perhaps the middle years remain swamped in mystery because

they are still a relatively new phenomenon. There was really no time for a middle age when life was one long treadmill from dawn to dusk, year in year out. When you had outlived your usefulness, the only expedient thing to do for everyone else was to die. But as heirs to and innovators of all manner of technical developments – the welfare state, longer and healthier life and peace for forty years – there is theoretically a virtually boundless choice about the way we can conduct our lives. Most of us no longer have to direct all our energies towards sheer survival and there is now time to consider basic questions about who, what and why we are.

Traditionally it is during adolescence that the huge questions about 'Life' are first raised. It seems more than likely that for many women this period of questioning remains incomplete and interrupted by having children. Consequently, the focus of their lives is often narrowly concentrated on domesticity to the exclusion of wider horizons. Later, when there has been time to accumulate a personal history and there is a gradual realization that time is no longer infinite, the questioning is often resumed. The middle years then become a crucial pivot in the life history of an individual – a period of time during which many aspects of life are reconsidered in the knowledge that there is still time to change direction, even though intimations of mortality are now more real.

Talking about change does pre-empt the basic question as to whether it is a 'good thing' to change at all – let alone change during the middle years when it is bound to be more disruptive. Most individuals will have acquired some dependants by then, who will have become accustomed to the person you are and may then find change disruptive and unsettling. What is wrong with habit and letting things stay as they are? Why unleash what could be a Pandora's box of problems when everything was all right as it was? But was it? Even if things were going along fairly smoothly, habit is no guarantee that they will continue to do so. It has always seemed rather pessimistic and extreme to talk about change in one breath and decay the next, given that most of human life exists in endless permutations of grey rather than in black and white. Were *homo sapiens* not innately adaptable, we would probably never have risen from the primeval mud. So change in terms of evolution is an essential part of progress and without it we should stagnate. Change during the middle years is probably the most fruitful time for it to occur; both for the individual who can truly appreciate it against a background of previous personal history and for society which is accustomed to regard the middle generation as a powerful one. Accustomed where men are concerned, that is; women are now demonstrating that this is not an exclusively male prerogative.

Why explore changes during the middle years now, as opposed to a few years ago or not at all? The idea sprang from personal experience and grew from that.

Five years ago I was a six-foot weakling, subject to considerable digestive disorders which were weakening and anti-social. After a lifetime of bilious attacks and subsequent investigations, I ended up at what is known locally as the 'bowel hospital' where I was diagnosed as having coeliac disease. Within six months of going on a gluten-free diet, I felt a new woman, like someone in a magazine story. At thirty-four I felt capable at last of doing all the things which had been such an effort until then. I no longer had to go to bed before I went out in the evening in order to have enough energy to see me through; I was not exhausted by nine-thirty, and if not marvellously even-tempered at least I felt I was more tolerant. Above all I had energy, and I had to learn that not everyone shared my over-developed sense of the work ethic.

This major change in my life, visited on rather than by me, caused me to look more carefully at other women of similar age. Did they take on a new lease of life 'midway through life's journey', not necessarily because of physical changes? How did they cope with their lives during the middle years? Having begun to look, I found the ground was amazingly fertile and bringing about change was more common than not. Time and resources did not allow the possibility of talking with more women, so the life stories on which this book is based are a sample and just a reflection of what is now possible for a great many other women in this country.

Later in my researches I came across something called a 'mid-life crisis'. I had heard of 'empty nest syndromes' and 'menopausal miseries' but never something as comprehensive and awesome as a crisis during the middle years. Eventually I came to the conclusion that crisis was an inaccurate and over-dramatic word used to describe a period of time when a number of factors came together to produce a turning point or a decision. To me, crisis suggested something short, sharp and shocking; quite the reverse of the deliberate reappraisal which thinking, feeling individuals would go through before making a change. It seemed unlikely, too, that anyone contemplating a change would do so with the speed which the word crisis suggests, especially where others were going to be affected by new directions taken on by one person. Women talked a great deal about change when they were interviewed but not one of them mentioned either crisis or, as a matter of interest, the menopause.

The focus of the book is on women. Men are mentioned only in relation to the process of change which various women have brought about, so there is an inherent bias. However, it seemed in the beginning and was confirmed later, that there is more opportunity for women to make changes in their lives than is possible for most men. Oppressed and suppressed as many women undoubtedly are, it is still easier to get out from under the oppressor than it is to correct a distorted vision of the world. Perhaps, too, women are more conscious of change in an everyday, earthy way. They perceive a pattern of change in their children and in their domestic lives, but are only now recognizing a pattern for themselves which is distinct from these roles and functions.

The women who were interviewed for the book were aged between thirty and sixty. They lived between Harrogate and Bournemouth, Penzance and London. The sample is personal rather than scientific, and makes no claim to cover all the ages, classes and differences which exist among women. At the same time, it does try to cover as many different types of individual as possible within the limits of time and money. The story of their lives is illustrative and reflective of women during their middle years at this time in history. It is to be hoped that, in the course of the book, experiences will be recounted which are central to all women's lives and that these will encourage others to reconsider in a fresh light situations which may now seem impossible to alter.

Each woman was interviewed at least once and sometimes twice on tape. The completed transcript was edited by the woman herself, and sometimes this went into three or four versions before the final draft was considered an accurate account of that individual's views. One of the difficulties which some women encountered was the glaring difference between the spoken and the written word. I felt it was important to preserve the tone of the spoken interview because speech tends to highlight individuality which can be lost in written prose. This was discomfiting for some who felt they appeared far less articulate than they considered themselves to be. Any faults in this direction are entirely mine and not theirs, because they allowed themselves to be persuaded to keep the 'warts and all'. Some women have preferred to use pseudonyms to preserve their anonymity in case there were repercussions about what they said. I think everyone was courageously honest and straightforward when they talked, which cannot have been easy with a complete stranger who wanted a life history after only a few minutes' acquaintanceship. The book has taken its shape and structure from these interviews.

In the beginning the structure of the book was very different from the way it ultimately evolved. At first it seemed important to concentrate on as many different changes wrought by as many different types of women as possible. That was how I approached those who allowed themselves to be interviewed: partly through friends, friends of friends, via the press and the BBC and through connections at work. Yet as the interviews progressed, although the different types of changes were fascinating and important in themselves, it gradually became clear that it was not the changes as such which were of paramount interest but the way in which they came about, the motivation behind them and their effect on others. This became the real focus of attention: not so much the 'what changes' but the 'why' and 'how', which is how the book has quite naturally taken its shape.

There was never at any point an intention to develop a new theory or a variation of an existing developmental theory. There are theories enough in existence, many of which seem of little benefit to the laywoman. The intention was always to demonstrate some practical examples of change. It became increasingly important to encourage women, by the example of a few others, to make changes during their middle years: not to give up and accept their lot, but to foster a sense of creative dissatisfaction which leads to personal growth and development. The aim is to boost the female ego and to encourage women to consider that the impossible is rarely as absolute and unalterable as it can sometimes seem. In other words, you *can* change it – if you try.

For me, as editor in effect, it became important not so much to find departures from 'the straight road' but to query the straightness of that road in the first place. Gradually, it became clear that change was the rule for women during their middle years; habit, the exception.

Women who were interviewed for the book

Liz Ahrends: Used to do part-time secretarial jobs which fitted in with the children. After the age of thirty, did A-levels, BA + M.Sc degrees and now teaches women's studies in adult education.
Kelly Anderson: Before having a family did office work. While her children were still at home, took a TOPs course which led on to A-levels, then a Social Science degree at Kingston Poly.
Mary Baker: Married with two children. At forty, she left her job, 'took a lover, rented a room in a girl-friend's house and started a professional course'.
June Barry: Was at home for fifteen years with three children. At forty-two took a part-time type job: within eight months became a manageress and was made a director of the firm within three years of joining it.
Judith Bicknell: Started a rural community with seven other families which is still successful. Completed her Ph.D. and apart from her commune commitments, is a counsellor and training on an AGIP course.
Marion Burman: Was a nun; teacher, then headmistress, for over thirty years. Now retired and recently married.
Eileen Curry: When she was divorced and left with a son, she joined the management team of a firm selling freezers and micro-wave ovens; within six months she was offered the Eastern Region manager's job.
Sheila Dainow: Training officer at a London Citizens' Advice Bureau; lecturer in counselling; three years ago set up a counselling business with four other women.
Pat Hull: Ex-secretary; now a 'late' mother and student at a London polytechnic.

P.D. James: Retired civil servant. Published her first crime novel at forty-two, now highly successful with six others.

Jenny Kent: Feminist journalist; part-time teacher at Holloway Prison.

Elizabeth Knight: Health Education Officer who was divorced after twenty years of marriage and now lives with a man twenty-four years her junior.

Irma Kurtz: 'Agony Aunt' on *Cosmopolitan* magazine; freelance journalist; writer, novelist and mother at thirty-eight.

Lee: Teacher and artist; head of a special teaching unit in a large London hospital.

Penny McGuire: Took A-levels, then a degree when she was nearly thirty, and is now a freelance architectural journalist.

Christine Merton: Was married for over twenty years, then divorced unexpectedly, after which she became a sculptor and teacher.

Julia Mitchell: Is now in employee communications in a large national firm. Was divorced and then married a man twenty-four years her senior.

Helen Ness: Has three small boys and teaches women's studies part-time in adult education.

NOW course at Walthamstow College of Further Education: **Joy, Sheila, Irene, Vivianne, Dianne, Carole, Rosie**

A course for adults who want to return to further education, either to go on to higher education or to change direction in paid employment.

Nancy Roberts: Actress in Spare Tyre Theatre Company; founder member of 'Big is Beautiful' campaign for large women; compulsive eating group leader; broadcaster and TV personality.

Bernice Rubens: Full-time novelist and documentary film maker; winner of the Booker Prize.

Jean Shrimpton: Ex-top model; now running a hotel with her husband in Cornwall.

Linda Thornber: Ex-teacher, divorced. At forty wrote a highly successful comedy series 'Ballyskillen' for television.

Annette Wagner: Ex-secretary and wife; now one of the country's top simultaneous translators.

Jane Worthington: Was a part-time teacher, then took a degree and professional qualifications after she was thirty and is now an educational psychologist.

Autobiographies

Jean Shrimpton

I've found something new that I never thought was for me: all the parallels have come down to running the hotel and I feel very strongly that if we do well, all the people loyal to us must do well also. If you'd interviewed me even two years ago I'd be saying very different things and that's very frightening . . . and exciting because you don't know what lies in the future. I'm reluctant now to say how content I feel. Michael and the baby give me enormous strength. Being loved by Michael is the most luxurious thing imaginable but having found something I treasure so deeply, it frightens me to death.

When things are really bad I allow myself to go to great depths before I come up again. Basically though I'm a survivor, somewhere I'm very strong. I've been unhappy quite a lot; partly because of bad personal relationships in the past but also because I have a problem of rejection which has triggered my whole life.

During the war I lived with my mother in my grandmother's house and was the focus of all their attention. We moved back home when my father came back, my sister was born and I obviously got less attention then. For someone with my sort of temperament, one of extremes, anything less than all makes me feel rejected. I cut myself off from people and threw myself into horses and animals and having shut myself off for years it was very hard getting back.

All this was made much clearer to me when I had analysis a few years ago and I could see that this rejection problem coloured my whole life. It was also why I succeeded because to fail was another form of rejection.

At school for instance, I worked hard and became top not because I really cared but because I had to. I didn't care a damn really; it was the sort of education which kills all imagination. I felt very isolated there and always suspected that friends there didn't really want me. I can remember standing in the playground surrounded by all those people and feeling overwhelmed, almost panic-struck by their sheer numbers. It sounds precious put like that, I know, but it's like a door being closed too loudly which triggers a bell and I expect to be rebuffed. I am aware of that now but it's one of the reasons I don't like any social life because it's just too bruising. Michael understands that and I trust in his integrity which I've never found in anyone else.

I still feel frightened of being used. Fame is so isolating and unreal. I always thought I'd handled it rather well because I never believed in it as such and knew it was a load of bullshit. But once you're taking off there are plenty of people who are ambitious for you. Although I was ambitious myself, in some strange way I didn't need to be to get to the top because you are seen as something which other people can make money out of.

I got to the point when I was twenty-five when I didn't want to go on modelling. I'd done it all and it was getting boring. Each day was so full but none of it planned by me. I was right at the top of my career and very successful; life was quite interesting but I began to realize that I'd reached somewhere and had no idea how I'd got there. It was rather like a case of arrested development.

The first period of reappraisal came when I went to New York around this time. Up to that point I'd worked for *Vogue* which was better work for lower pay and had always refused to appear on English television. In the States I had a contract with Yardley for a great deal of money. As I wasn't living there at the time and other people thought it'd be a good idea if I took the job, I went along with it. It became increasingly distasteful though. I was telling young girls all over the country about make-up when I didn't do it myself. I rationalized the situation for the length of the contract with the thought that once I'd made some money, I'd be free to get out and not sell out any more.

Going to a different country makes you reappraise anyway and New York was so very different I was shocked by it in a way. A new place and a different culture helped me to clarify things about myself and I began to realize there were lots of things I was doing in my work which I didn't really like very much.

I spent two very constructive years there and decided to model less which was probably the first great change I made. I was very insular up to that point, so I started going to museums and reading more. I felt it was a very strong period of time for me. Looking back on it from now, I suppose you could say that marked the end of the first phase in my life; I decided to become anonymous.

I landed back in England and went into a very destructive period after that. With hindsight it was all very predictable – I was well known, had a lot of money and I felt enormously guilty. But against all that, perhaps you need to be destructive if you are going to discover things about yourself.

Home became open house and I spent the next few years with neurotic people. I became quite indiscriminate and gave a lot of money away, swinging from one extreme to the other. In 1972 I went to live in Wales and from that time on I've always lived in immense isolation. During this second phase I made different patterns and experienced different life-styles but eventually I realized I was going round in circles and getting nowhere.

Up to then I'd always resented the very idea of analysis. Basically I'm rather puritanical and not given to self-indulgence and it was a big decision to take it up. I realized I needed help with any self-analysis I was doing and although it was immensely hard, I did find it intellectually very stimulating and interesting.

Perhaps I was attracted to therapy in the hope that by being helped myself, I would be in a better position to help other people. I do believe one should try and help one's fellow man to some extent, life is enhanced by doing that. You can't just take your happiness and hold on to it, it dies. You've got to spread it a little to be truly productive. Running the hotel is important in that respect.

I suppose you could say I'm on the third phase of my life now – though I've no idea how many there'll be. I don't regret giving anything up, though there were times earlier on when I was miserable with the present and I had to keep reaching back into the past to see if I'd been any happier. I enjoyed the travelling and being my own boss from the age of eighteen. The money I earned gave me great pleasure though I never thought of spending it at the time. I saw a lot, went to beautiful places and met beautiful people and generally enjoyed the aesthetics of what it gave me. I'm glad I had the experience but now I know I don't want it any more and am profoundly grateful I didn't milk it any further than I did.

The negative side about my working life then was very bad. You were surrounded by people for whom you were nothing more than a commodity. People made lots of money out of you, a lot of which never came your way. You begin to wonder who you are and inevitably get rather bitter and disillusioned.

I know much better now who and what I am and I feel I have a better chance of accepting myself. What I do find difficult to accept is my ordinariness and the fact that I'm completely dispensable – except to the baby. After you've been famous, that's hard. The more public a life you lead, the more public a persona you adopt. In youth you are far more preoccupied with image and are quite literally more self-conscious. You spend so much time on yourself which is so silly really because in some ways, it's time ill spent. You're ageing anyway and it's a hollow goal – though you don't always realize it at the time.

I'm aware now that I'm gradually becoming middle-aged and I'll never be a bright young thing any more. It's very important for me to grow old gracefully and not to cling to my youth. I do think most women find it hard to accept the ageing process. I've always been a bit scruffy and I'm scruffy now though I find people still look at me to see if I look like the Jean Shrimpton they know from photographs. Now I'd much rather just be Mrs . . .

In general I do think it's hard to reconcile yourself not to be a beautiful person if you once have been. It's been easier for me because I'm not stupid and I'm perceptive and I get a great deal of pleasure from a lot of things. I've always been an inveterate collector. I just can't be bothered about looking after myself though I do get aesthetic enjoyment out of looking at a beautifully dressed girl – or flowers, pictures, so many different things.

Being lazy helps too, I'm glad I'm like that. In spite of what I've said I do think one has a certain duty to look after oneself.

I'd like to be much more physical but I'm very reserved. When I was in New York I longed to be like the warm demonstrative Jewish family I lived with but it's locked away and I find it difficult to show how I feel. It's not that I'm a cold person, quite the opposite in fact, but it's rather like friendship for me, problematical.

To be quite honest I'm not very interested in either sex though I think on the whole I prefer women to men. There have been times, especially when my personal life has not been going well, when I have very much wanted a friendship with a woman; like you do perhaps with a man, which has nothing to do with being a lesbian. I've wanted this friendship to be open and strong and intellectual and warm but so far, it's never quite worked out. Possibly I idealize too much and project what I want on to other people. It's something I'm more aware of now than I was but I know being unrelaxed about it can distort a relationship. I have one friend I've known for about fourteen years or so but there's no one else who goes any further back in my life – except my family and they don't really know me.

I suppose I'm a bit of a loner. I like pottering around on my own, but I'm very dependent on Michael and the baby. I've never been very good at the social frills, chit-chat and gossip and things like that; when I talk, I'd much rather talk intensely and with some depth. I'm neither intellectual nor academic but I've made a conscious effort to better myself. I can stand in front of a picture for instance, which means nothing to me at first until I come up with some sort of answer for me.

I'm not a creative person in the sense of painting or writing, though I would like to be, but the groundwork is rather daunting. I think I live my life creatively and at a level which is satisfying to me though I realize a lot of people wouldn't think so. Creating a home is important, so is music, soft sheets and flowers, all essential to my well-being.

I live my life from day to day now and we don't buy papers, except the Sundays, or listen to the news, it all changes next day in any case. We don't have the sort of control over ourselves or the world around us that we're led to believe. I really hate that sort of arrogance which assumes a mastery which doesn't exist.

No one's told the truth about anything. I suppose behaving like this is slightly irresponsible but it gives one both a sense of complete unimportance and freedom at the same time.

Life is going well for me at the moment and I'm very content. I no longer really care what people think or say about me though once having been popular, the media can still get through to me. I can't be as cut and hurt as I once was, now I just get angry and throw away any unpleasant anonymous letters I receive. You can never quite get rid of the public image, there's always some residue which remains.

Reacting to it, I searched all over the place to go beyond it when I suppose a great many people don't even want to. I think now my intelligence was sublimated until I was twenty-five or so and I didn't begin to think, though I must have absorbed a great deal intuitively. Now I know the boundaries of my life; I've gained strength and comfort from them and I feel secure.

Bernice Rubens

I think everything finds its right time: there's some reason that one doesn't do things at certain times. It isn't ripe. I think one of the prerequisites for creativity is to recognize when the time is ripe. I don't think the right moment in time is related to how old you are. 'If only I had done such and such' is an expression of lost opportunity, is not a chance that has been missed, but a non-recognition of ripeness or otherwise of the time. Things happen and you adjust. You recognize this is the time and either act or not upon it – if you don't you lose out on an avenue of growth. Ripeness is a signal to new growth: the road to recognizing that is the most important thing. I acted as I did when my marriage broke up, not because I was clever but as an act of survival; the alternative to putting my head in the gas oven. If once you decide you're going to survive, you can do it splendidly. Women do it superbly; men don't do it half as well.

At the time when I was of marriageable age, if one didn't get married that was something to be deeply ashamed of, so I went to university as a kind of standby just in case I didn't fall off the shelf. I'm not an ambitious person and certainly marriage doesn't constitute one of life's ambitions. I want to write better and better and I think I am.

I hadn't written at all before I was thirty and it was an entirely new life for me. It is quite possible I started writing late because I was married young so there wasn't time. Two things are needed for writing: obsession and time. You can have the obsession but it helps to have time so I had to wait until the children were at school. Over the years I've alternated novel writing with documentaries. In a way, it was advantageous to write a first novel at thirty. I had experience of many things, I was emotionally rich and I could draw upon a variety of experiences such that I possibly could not have in my twenties.

The novel is a very high form of writing art. I admired great novels, loved reading – read English literature at university, which was a mistake for a novelist. You develop an awe and respect for English language and it is terribly difficult to equate yourself in the same tradition as George Eliot; it requires a certain arrogance to do that. There was no question that I would do anything else but write. People have certain innate predispositions and mine are for words, not being terribly responsive to the visual. I wrote about my family in the first novel, the second was more difficult but if you can finish a second novel, it's likely you'll go on writing. Through words I was able to adjust my respect for the English literature tradition, so that it no longer intimidated me. I always write for myself but once that's done, I want recognition, so a pattern is formed that you write, then publish. When I am writing, I don't think of immortality because that doesn't concern me in the sense of time – as a writer, I have for ever. Just because I write that is enough to make me immortal.

The point at which I liked myself was when I started to live alone when I was forty. I'm hooked on living alone now though it costs a great deal to learn how. I'm not sure it's all that natural to live by yourself and a certain area in me regrets that I'm no longer fit to live with anyone else. The first year was really hard and if I'd found a lover during that year, I wouldn't be alone now.

Of course there was a time when I had to live with someone: the time was ripe then for me to be coupled. I know that is not right for me now, but I don't cut off the possibility that that may change in the future. Living alone has got its own joys which are very difficult to visualize when you are married. Because you are living with yourself you must have work that you love and that has to do with liking yourself. That in turn means valuing yourself and doing whatever is within your reach, not beyond it because that would be to overvalue yourself. In effect, you need to know yourself and like what you know.

If women held board meetings with themselves from time to time – and it doesn't require intelligence and has nothing to do with class, all it requires is an initial bout of dissatisfaction when you look up from the ironing board and wonder whether this is all there is to life; in a way you have then joined the revolution. I honestly feel if women came to certain conclusions about themselves, the whole issue of marriage would evaporate. The logic of it is to live alone, to find one's own instincts and feelings. This kind of independence I have found as a woman is not possible within a marriage. One needs one's own space: man's perception of self intrudes into that space and many women are quite happy to fit around it, but on the periphery. Peripheral living negates self-assertion.

There are lots of exciting things about marriage. Its whole tradition and cult. There is a time when you must identify yourself with it. It helps to have been married and it is necessary to go through it in order to achieve liberation and independence, although women alone can achieve this in a different way. I believe in marriage; it's a beautiful and wonderful experience and it has its own time and place. Trouble arises when the time to end it remains unacknowledged; history and habit is no basis on which to continue a marriage, though it is if affection remains. Possessions are accumulated though and that makes for difficulties in breaking up.

Of course, the ideal situation for me would have been to marry the boy next door and for him to stay next door!

I still feel a neurotic need for male piggery in my life but that's a hangover from my own conditioning, otherwise I'd be a logical lesbian which I'm not. Perhaps I'm too old, but I see a great logic in that. My whole appetites are not conditioned that way so I would have to make a total break with myself to tune into another direction. Men are very different from women in that respect. They wouldn't understand that you can't be alone and live with somebody, though maybe I'm wrong about that and I'm affecting a rationale for the way I live now.

Privacy is territorial and the sharing of space is prorogued when you get married and inhibits growth, especially for women. Women particularly, because I believe they are conditioned to submerge themselves in the process of supporting their men. I began to break from that role and there's no question that that contributed to the break-up of my marriage. I began to question my place.

When we separated the reaction of my friends was one almost of hostility because it began to underline their situations and their own fears, putting their marriages into a different perspective. When people divorce in their forties, it has repercussions all round; now most of my friends are not married. People think in couples, it's convenient, but what kind of people are we that we're reduced to thinking of man, woman, man . . . around a dinner table? It's all very unliberating.

Women are enormously supportive of other women, especially in the forties age group because they're all going through the same experience and because they are ashamed of what they might term failure, particularly if it's marriage failure. These are particularly women who have been conditioned to equate beauty and pleasure with youth – after all, that includes many of us. But children don't equate age with ugliness. Things have changed so radically in the last few years. When women reach forty or so, the greatest thing they can do is to seek other women friends and that's a sure beginning, for the strength of united women is enormous.

Beautiful women have an additional factor to cope with as they grow older and lose their looks. Personally I don't have that burden, but as looks are lost for a beautiful woman, this is also the loss of her main weapon. I consider I'm getting more beautiful as I get older. I remember as a child being deeply jealous of beautiful girls and not liking myself because I was fat and dumpy and all those things you weren't supposed to be, and so basically I didn't like myself too well. You're only beautiful when you begin to like yourself.

Many women are enormously frustrated when they become more aware of themselves and when that awareness is not put to any use for lots of reasons – the men they married, economics and so on. One of the major differences between men and women is that women understand cause and effect. It's a gender difference: men can do things and not envisage the results. But some women, just because they are aware of the consequences of their taking off, refrain from doing so. It's disruptive and troublesome. What gives some women the strength to make boat-rocking changes I don't know.

I think though that energy is directly related to motivation. There's no such thing as not enough time: if you want to do something, you will do it. Bringing up children can provide an excuse, almost become a cult which allows exhaustion to become a legitimate excuse for not doing anything else.

The contentment I have now is not related to age. My appetite for life has increased though my energy has grown less as I've grown older. My expectations are no less than they were; joy, vigour and despair is as great as it was in youth. For me marriage was a school through which I had to pass in order to achieve this freedom. I have never forgotten what my grandmother said when she was ninety-four: 'however old you are, you are always too young to count your blessings'. To count them is an act of abdication.

Elizabeth Knight

I would go through all this again to feel as good as I do now – I didn't know life could be so good. It's fantastic. Financially we've been creased but we've managed although James is still a student. It's all been worthwhile. It's always been acceptable for older men to marry younger women but the reverse is less true, though I think it's becoming more so as women become more liberated. Everyone can say now whether they want children or not. I think a lot of younger men at twenty to twenty-five don't want children and are happy to be with an older woman. Perhaps people are becoming more honest. I think I was born a bit before my time and have always been a bit of a rebel. I've never got into a set pattern and things have changed all along: I try something and then I want to know more.

My family lived in this small village in Somerset for generations and when I was eighteen and just starting nursing, I had a baby. In those days you couldn't complete your training if you were married or had a child, so my mother looked after the baby while I worked as a secretary. When my daughter was four-and-a-half I got married, though not to her father. I had another baby early on in marriage as I felt it was important if we were going to be a proper family, and when my son was fourteen months I started doing my SEN. That turned out to be unfulfilling so I went on to complete my SRN when I was in my late twenties. I thought that would be enough but I went on to do obstetrics, district nursing, health visiting, then health education, which I've been doing now for sixteen months. I can see this will be all right for a while, then I'll want to do something more high-powered again. I'm doing an Open University course at the moment and I've been accepted on the Social Studies course.

Throughout our marriage, my husband had girl-friends which I accepted, I used to play heavy bear about it when I found out, get upset and feel very inadequate but I realize now he needed to have his ego boosted all the time. I gave him lots of attention and he had everything he wanted as far as fast cars and that sort of thing went, but he needed constant conquests. Looking back now, when I was on the health visitors' course for a year in Oxford, I needed the excuse to be away for the week from the humdrum of marriage and return for the weekend. It did wonders for my marriage. We'd been married fifteen years by then. I always had to meet the girl-friends, Ted expected me to. I had to be nice to them because I knew what was going on even though their husbands might not, which made it all the more distasteful. When my husband was going out with an eighteen-year-old widow, I think I had an endogenous depression, which was the first time I'd ever had anything like that in my life. If I hadn't a good friend who was also a GP to see me, I think I would have gone under. I decided then, when the last girl-friend came along, I wouldn't slip back into that state again.

I colluded all the time for years; now I wish I hadn't. I see now it was cowardly but at the same time I felt I was protecting the children, my mother, my marriage and something was better than nothing. I was trying to prove to myself that I was being tolerant and prove to these other women that Ted had everything at home, so why was he needing them? At the same time I often thought what was wrong with me if he needed to have other women? I can remember him one day coming back and comparing my body with another woman's. That made me feel very sick and caused me an untold amount of anxiety. I went through an awful time losing a lot of confidence and wondering what the hell was the matter with me, but Ted obviously needed the excitement of the forbidden and it's unlikely he'll ever change. I don't think he could. We always had a very good sex life because he was a sexual athlete, but I got to the point when I didn't want to have anything more to do with him because I never knew where he'd been before. It put me off after a while although I tried to be tolerant.

To all intents and purposes we were a happy couple. I kept all our problems from everyone in the family. When we went out, my husband used to treat me super in front of people but we never had a deep conversation at home. For years I tried to talk, reason and communicate with him but I always ended up frustrated because I couldn't get through to him. It took twenty years of married life for me to realize there was nothing underneath. It was quite a shock because I'd always thought he was thinking as deeply as me and it was a real jolt to realize he wanted to skid along the surface. I don't like giving up easily and I felt I had failed in giving up my marriage, perhaps I could have tried harder.

We were growing apart and the gap was becoming wider and wider. I was getting more education but my husband stayed as a driver and never progressed as he was happy doing that. I needed more stimulating conversation and he was content to sit in front of the television. I think my competence made Ted feel inadequate. If we had a row he had to make love to me as it seemed the only way he could meet me on superior grounds. The more I did, the more inferior he felt. He used to brag about me to other people and lived through my glory. I'm not a snob in any way but he used to embarrass me in front of other people because he had to be the centre of attention, no matter how. He had a need to impress and I had to watch what I said about work or he'd use a snippet of information just to make himself important. To most people he's very kind but he's got no long-standing friends and he used to resent me having them. So I tried not to let them intrude by meeting them when he was working or he'd be very jealous. The crunch came when I went to do a health education course.

I don't know what the course did but it made me assess my life, sit back and survey the scene. I thought to hell, am I going to put up with this for the rest of my life or am I going to do something about it? It's very easy to sit back and do nothing – rather frightening to do anything else. Home, family, everything jogs along gently. It's a big thing and very traumatic to suddenly break up a marriage and be completely independent. Sometimes it's better to have somebody than nobody.

When I went on the last course, Ted had lined up a girl to have an affair with before I went. As usual he felt the need to tell me about it, like he always did. Many years before, I'd told him that I'd wait until my son was sixteen and then I'd do something about it, but I just went on. When I went to do the health education course, my son was twenty. Having found out that Ted was having an affair with this girlie, I discovered too he had used my knowledge and position because she wanted to be a nurse. I felt very angry, very used. I'd not felt as angry before. It was probably the course, because I'd started thinking very deeply about things and assessing my life. After finding out about this latest girl-friend, I didn't go home every weekend as I used to because I no longer wanted to.

We had a confrontation around Christmas time. In February we had a very bad one and I thought then I didn't want to go on with the marriage. I didn't say anything to anyone on the course or my flat mates about my marriage being on the rocks. I kept it all to myself. But my husband drove up one day and made a scene in front of lots of people. He stayed overnight but I said I was sorry, I couldn't go back to him.

I met James one evening in the hall of residence. I had seen him about during the previous few months. He was getting over a broken engagement and I was smarting from a rocky marriage – it was like a bit of sugar on the lemon; we were good for one another. I didn't know how long we'd go on together so I never mentioned him to the family. He's twenty-four years younger than me and so many people at that time gave me good advice about the risks I was taking. I can honestly say, no man has given me as much as he has: he's mature beyond his years and a very strong character.

Towards the end of the summer term, James moved in with me. Ted made a great fuss although we were parted, he couldn't take it. It was the first time I'd ever challenged him on his home ground and taken a boy-friend. Ted sent James a solicitor's letter demanding his marital rights and saying he would sue him for costs. He told my family I was living with a long-haired, lay-about, drug-addict student. When eventually I took James home to meet them, they were shocked because there was nothing they could dislike about him.

Right until the end of the last term of the course, I was not going to get too involved with James. I wanted the relationship to go on but as James was so much younger, it had to be up to him. Now he thinks it'll be long term. We have a fantastic partnership as we are now, except we're going to have to do something to cover ourselves legally. That end of term I was devastatingly unhappy because the arrangement was we'd both go our separate ways. It's so very different living your own life away from home, from going back to your own environment with a new love and I felt I needed the love and support and approval of family and friends, so we split. My ex-husband was still in the house but when I came back from holiday with my family, he had just gone and left a note. He left me to sort out everything and I filed for a divorce on 7 August 1979.

I wanted a clean break. I've got the house and everything in it although I didn't ask for anything. In a small rural village it was a nine-day wonder. I always tried to be honest about what was going on but when you meet people it can be very difficult. Men friends from my marriage days felt very threatened by James: he's such a young man, they wondered what he'd got to hold my interest. There are always all sorts of anxieties when you start a new relationship, aren't there? There were times when I felt my age was a great obstacle. I had terrible feelings of insecurity, wept and cried, did so much crying the last few months at college. I went through quite a bit with James's peer group: girls were very difficult. Some of my own peer group were difficult and told me I was being totally unwise and James was taking advantage of me. It's amazing how your own contemporaries can moralize yet make out they're so open-minded and liberal. The truth of the matter was I needed James more than he needed me at that time. He was so protective and outspoken and stood up to my husband. I get little barbs from 'friends' about James which I'm now able to rise above because I've got confidence.

I was convinced our relationship was the right thing and whatever happened I wanted to be with James. So after eight weeks' separation, we got back together after much soul-searching. I'm not sure he was as certain as I was about what he wanted and he went through a time of not wanting to be tied down. It's been completely different since July last year. Suddenly James has become more confident about what he wants: he doesn't feel trapped any more and wants the relationship to continue. I have always tried to make him feel as free as I could, now I feel he doesn't want to go. I couldn't have said that a little while ago.

I always felt that everything I did in my marriage was for us and the children and I wouldn't allow myself to think any other way. The children were the most important thing to me and I didn't want anyone to think that things were less than perfect. It was my main motive for us at that time and I made myself believe it was true. I never imagined I would become divorced until I met James, but I felt I couldn't live with Ted any longer knowing what I knew through James. Possibly we'd still be rubbing along if James hadn't happened.

It's a gut feeling I have for James: it's too dynamic a reaction and too moral a commitment I have, ever to have gone back to Ted. Instinctively I knew my relationship with James was right. I've never found anyone else ever who could have made me go through such upheaval. I knew I had to file the divorce papers, even though to all intents and purposes we had split that summer. I felt the affair was very one-sided initially, I had to hold back and not be too demanding or possessive. At the time I was too frightened of losing him to realize the enormity of divorcing Ted.

I felt when I was married, maybe I had missed out a little because I always felt I had three children. Ted never helped to make decisions about schooling or finance or anything like that. I adored the children, especially when they were younger. It was good to be able to do things for them and they compensated for a lot. I'm not sure I was that good a mother though.

My mother has been an absolute gem in my life. She always accepted everything I said and never delved for deeper reasons. If I needed a boost, she'd be there to supply it and encourage me. I've got great pride and stubbornness, I'm persistent and a stayer. I hate failing at anything. I'm the sort of person who, if I was drowning, would probably come up for the third time with a smile on my face. I'm so proud anyway, I wouldn't let just anyone see I was feeling miserable.

I'm aware now that throughout my life I've evoked jealousy in some female friends, maybe because I'm so enthusiastic, it makes them feel guilty. I think perhaps when you're thirty-five to forty, you're meant to knuckle down and be sedate. I don't believe there's anything I wouldn't tackle now. If I want to do something, I'll do it. I don't really feel the age difference with James – not like I did with my husband who's forty-four now – probably because we're more compatible.

I don't feel myself to be forty-five: I see myself as me. I've got more energy now than I had at twenty. The worst period in my life was between eighteen and thirty: I had such a lot to do and I was so tired working, running the home, caring for two children plus the emotional stress. I felt very old then. The best time for me's been since I was forty, yet when I thought I was going to be that age I was devastated. To think in five years' time I'll be fifty! I don't believe it! I don't relish getting old and not being able to do what I want. Age is relative, I feel, and very much an attitude of mind.

Thank God I've got the confidence now to be what I want to be and be myself and sod everyone else. I feel I can cope with anything as long as James is around. Sometimes I feel I'd be fine if he went but only sometimes. Yet I know I'd be devastated if he went, but I'd cope, I'd have to. I sometimes feel guilty about demanding so much from someone so young and feel perhaps he would be better off without me, but then I console myself with the knowledge that he knows exactly what he wants and I am not conning him in any way. If we were to finish, we've had a marvellous relationship but I think we'll go on like this for a very long time, it's so good now. I need reassurance all the time, sometimes I ask it of him, tongue in cheek. James is not glib and he sticks absolutely to what he says – I can't get used to that after living with a man who needed so many other women; that's taken its toll of me and I do question a lot.

I wouldn't see marriage as a greater commitment than we have now. I am totally mentally, emotionally and physically committed to James. Marriage would be tying up a few legal ends.

I'm more committed to James than I ever was to Ted. All the time I was married, I almost felt it was necessary to chat to the most attractive man in the room at a party, just to feel I wasn't a piece of luggage. If we'd gone on, things would have become messy I suspect. I've become much more relaxed now and see life in a very different way. People coming to the house say how relaxed it's become now the tensions have gone from it.

I would say to anybody to do what they want to do. The only person you can please all the time is yourself, with regard to other people and their fears. You can only do what is right for you. Life is for living and you only have one of them.

Julia Mitchell

I think a lot of women don't realize they can cope on their own. I was on my own for a few years and it was a bloody tough haul – society makes it tough in so many ways. Some women take a cop-out decision and remain in that state. They can see their values being compromised all along the line but are driven by fear. It takes them a long time to realize they could cope on their own and the so-called damage to their children might not be as drastic as they think. Some women never ever realize the extent of their compromise, which is even sadder. I've got a lot of sympathy for women who do realize it but can't take the hassle of breaking out on their own.

There are more opportunities now for women to do things which were unthinkable in my mother's time. More are masters of their budgets, Child Benefit goes direct to women, there are retraining schemes, night schools and so on, but there's still an enormous amount of prejudice about, more than there should be today. Attitudes haven't changed as much as is sometimes made out. The Women's Lib. movement has put the clock back as much as forward in its extremism – the aspect which is most publicized. It disguises the real movement and the real work and puts a lot of people off the important issues.

For instance, where I am employed, out of about 560 managers, thirty-eight are women. At my daughter's school, I'm appalled at the attitudes expressed about careers for girls which immediately place limits and parameters on the available possibilities. I think it's antiquated to suggest careers at all nowadays – it's outdated, given the nature of work now and in the future. Pursuing careers will have nothing to do with it. A person will have an ability, talent or skill which will be used part-time with other developed skills. Society is not preparing children to face the new world. It's almost facile to talk about career opportunities for women now: we're into a whole different ball game. I'm saying to myself, as the mother of a daughter, what talents has she got which will be useful for gainful employment in the future?

There's still an attitude among some women that men must be the bread-winners. The man must be expected to pursue a career, tie himself to a job for n amount of years in order to be the material provider. There's no question of his changing within the 'normal' institution of marriage, yet many women have the choice as to whether they should work or not. To a great extent, many men get a raw deal out of marriage, condemned to some sort of drudgery in jobs which they often hate, for people who belittle them, with no choice to get out. I deplore the attitude which so many women adopt that the man should be the stable provider. I think it's rather immoral and I expected there to be more changes in that attitude. When they can make arrangements for their children, women do have the choice to work. There's an enormous amount of literature about working mothers which can induce unnecessary guilt.

Men aren't automatically asked about the sort of work their wives do, but the reverse is true. We've discovered there are more people reversing traditional roles than we thought. Some people find this hard to accept and make those who do reverse, freakish. Women do have choices, but at a cost, not just to themselves but for their husbands also. A lot of women could do a hell of a lot more than they do: they bleat but remain where they are. Sometimes it's fear, sometimes not enough *nous*, sometimes they don't know how to go about changing things – perhaps they don't read enough. Traditionally men have made it their business to acquaint themselves with the business of wider issues. Once women have children they often seem to forget the whole of the outside world except other mothers. They incubate themselves and if they do this for a few years, they aren't able to cope in the world outside the home. There are things you can do from home. When I had young children I organized a folk club and sang. I made enough to pay a babysitter and a little more. But there's been no movement on the part-time job front. How many jobs can you do like this?

I recognize the constraints put on me by having children but to some extent we are masters of our own affairs. We can shape our lives and mould them to change, often more than many people do. I've tried to shape my life within the constraints and responsibilities I have. The most significant decision which I made was to leave my husband when I was thirty-three and the children were seven and five. We were married five years before either of us recognized that he was an alcoholic. We went through everything you could go through to help the situation. The children were young and I recognized the effect it was having on them. He was a very kind person when sober but one day we had a fight because I poured two quarts of cider down the sink. He was so angry he chased me all over the house and he all but strangled me. The fear is still with me. It was 1 January and in my mind I resolved to give it six months and then I'd make a decision. On 1 June it was clear the alcoholism was here to stay and I kept my word to myself and asked him to leave. I said if he didn't I'd get him evicted. It was a conscious decision I made, largely because of the children. If it had been just me, I would probably have kept the *status quo*. The children questioned me for a long time afterwards about why I'd sent away their Dad and from that time on, I've changed because it was such a hard thing to do, to boot someone out. I can't say today that it was the right thing, probably about eighty per cent right.

When he was sober I loved him. He was a brilliant person and we shared a lot in common. I did more music and writing with him than at any other time in my life because he always encouraged me. Along with booting him out, I booted out a lot of myself as well and it's probably only now, ten years later, I'm beginning to develop the need and confidence to start doing these things again. It was a very, very traumatic experience having to get my husband evicted, especially as there was a great bond between us. The result was devastating to me personally and brought about changes which are still with me. I've not been able completely to overcome that experience, not been able to control my destiny as much as I would have liked because of it. I had to take a strong hand in the divorce anyway. It was difficult, hard, ridden with guilt. I can't say now I'm free of that guilt and if you live with those sorts of feelings, it influences so many things you do and choices you make. It closes a lot of doors because I still haven't straightened all this out.

For a year afterwards, I went totally within myself and threw myself into the children and the home. Although I was working, my interest in it completely waned even though, up to that point, I was fanatically interested in pursuing a career. Then I went to the other extreme. I am a fairly moral person but I became totally immoral, almost wild, after living within myself. It was a devastating year during which I threw most of my personal values out of the window and one which brought about changes that are with me now. The net result of the whole experience was so frightening I sought shelter, need and comfort. Entirely consciously I made a decision to marry a man twenty-four years older than myself because he was the only person of the only age group who represented totally what I was looking for. I felt afraid, bewildered and disillusioned about all the things that had happened to me. I couldn't face coping on my own, yet I know today, in retrospect, that I could and would have coped and still can. I sought a prop and married Charles, who is undoubtedly the surest emotional support I've ever had in my life. Yet I can still say it was maybe the wrong thing to do, because the inner part of me has been the exchange. That's what I've given up, that was the trade-off.

When I was at school, everything was music. It was my ambition to teach it. My family were high achievers and when I took seven O-levels and passed in only three, I felt a failure. I acted out a failure role and to a certain extent that feeling of never having achieved what I could have in their eyes, has lived with me ever since. I feel now I've achieved things that are satisfactory in my eyes. I went into the dummies' Sixth and did a secretarial year, leaving school with the idea that I couldn't achieve what I wanted, so I would work and pursue music outside work. I had classical guitar lessons and sang in the Bach Choir while I worked in a solicitor's office. For a time, I got it into my head I wanted to continue being a solicitor's clerk. It had a semi-professional image and wasn't demeaning as secretarial work is seen to be.

I met my husband when I'd left school at eighteen. We courted (on and off) for five years and were married when I was twenty-three. We were utterly devoted and had great respect for one another, but we didn't have the capacity to learn about ourselves in living situations. We went out two or three nights a week but never slept together before we were married, so had absolutely no sexual knowledge of one another. Any sex in my life was reserved for diversions from that courtship when we had break-ups. I managed to find situations when I could organize anything between the relationship but neither of us could organize anything between the two of us. I was living at home then and my parents were very strict: no kissing on the doorstep, no lights out in the living room, in by ten. When we did get married, we began to learn things about one another which were not pulling us together but very definitely pushing us apart. The strictness and formality in my own upbringing resulted in my going totally 'hippy'. I chucked the solicitor's job and started writing in an in-house journal. For the first time in my life, I was able to make decisions about what I wanted to do and be able to learn about myself. I feel very strongly about this in relation to my own children and try and give them some freedom now.

There were a lot of evolving changes over the next ten years. Sometimes I thought during that period maybe I shouldn't have got married, maybe it was not men I wanted but women, maybe music was thrust upon me and shrouded a lot of other possibilities. Roles are thrust upon members of families. One is often disbarred from doing other things as a consequence. I've only begun to see this clearly over the past few years and I'm forty. I've got to start now defining my real self which seems incredible.

Ten years ago my life-style was such that I rarely did anything without music on. I love all sorts of music – to listen to, to make and play; it's part of my life. Since I've married Charles, I've lost that because he doesn't respond to it. I've lost a really deep part of me: it's there in my children and I can share through them but it's not enough. The trade-off I made represents a drastic change which came about because of all the emotional upheaval I went through over the divorce and after.

Nearly two years after the divorce, Charles moved in with us on a part-time basis. It was essential he got to know the children and it was convenient for work. At that time we had no plans to marry at all and we were happy to leave things as they were. It was a very good time for all of us. All the battles I'd gone through had worn me down. It was comforting and so good to be serene and cosy. It was so new to me after years of emotion and drama. That's not to say there wasn't a lot in it for me because I needed and still do need that stability. I chucked my job in, sold the house, and moved to Charles's house with the children – which was an enormous change. Seven months after we'd settled down, we formalized the relationship and got married. The main motive behind that was the children. We were happiest up to the time we moved. After that, his mother was ill and had to be looked after for two to three years which was a distraction from the relationship we had together. We were very relaxed up to this point and then suddenly, things changed and the relationship between us changed. Very good and dear friends who have lived together for years, put the success of their relationship down to the fact that they didn't get married because they say you lose something. Charles and I did lose something from the day we got married.

For the next two years, I was not formally working. Charles and I did business things together, buying and selling anything really, living reasonably well. I was using my mind less and less, becoming mentally lazy and domestically obsessed. I could feel myself playing out this role which wasn't me. I was suffering a lot of internal anguish at not satisfying my mental processes. I became depressed and suffered from psychosomatic illnesses, put on weight and so on. Friends said they didn't recognize me. I made the decision that it was no good for me and decided to get back to where I thought I was, motivated partly by my own need and partly by money. I felt there were things I needed to provide for the children and couldn't, though sometimes I think I needed to make up to them for booting out their father. Perhaps I was trying to do this by too much material lavishing.

When I was thirty-seven to eight, I did a year at college in personnel management. I'd made up my mind that the area I wanted to work in was employee communications, not in PR as I'd previously done. I needed some personnel training which eventually led me to my present job. The year at college had given me aspirations to pursue more training and I got into university to do an M.Sc in Management Science. I did the first term, amongst people who had A-levels and degrees, none of which I had. I was about middling but I was torn by so many conflicting demands, I chucked it. The whole of last year was of enormous regret to me because of that. I do attempt to keep up the academic/intellectual impetus in an informal way through my work here. I deeply, deeply regret passing up that opportunity because I'm fairy certain it won't come again. It's not often that an establishment is prepared to take on someone with no qualifications and had I pursued the degree course and obtained my Master's, I'm fairly certain it would have opened up further changes. But – there were considerations, like developing the job, and I couldn't compromise the situation at home any further.

I am a very forceful person. There is an inner drive in me that would be motivated to achieve regardless of failures at seventeen or not. My sense of failure then probably thwarted certain directions I might have taken for many years and my aspirations were dampened for a long time until I got the confidence. My confidence still needs constant regeneration. Most women are confident in the home because they are bred and expected to take the lead there, but not in the outside world. It's terrifying sometimes to be at a meeting of all men and to know that one's credibility is on the line. I have to put on a cloak of confidence which is unnatural, a lot of it. It's unnatural because of the translation process. I have a natural dialogue with women but have to be very, very careful with men. I have to say what I need to in a way that men find acceptable; in their language with their values, almost playing the role of a man. It's disgusting having to do that but if I don't, I'm regarded as a simpering little woman, work-wise. I tend to develop supportive relationships with men in the organization, so that I can turn to them when my confidence gets sapped.

In some senses, years were wasted but they can always be made up at different times in my life and in different ways. I wouldn't describe myself as ambitious but I do have aspirations. If I had ambition, I would set goals: say in this job. But 'going to the top of the organization' appals me. What I want to do, I want to do here, in this office. I have aspirations to achieve something of my own; whether in the field of employee communications I get that recognition is highly questionable. I want recognition as a person who has contributed something, however small. It's the same drive which makes me want to write. When I'm on the train, I'm thinking about things which I want to translate into thoughts for other people, to be able to identify things for them.

I've spent a lot of my life indulging in whims which wouldn't further ambitions. I'm a very self-indulgent person, but I pay for myself not at someone else's expense I hope. A lot of women are self-indulgent at their husbands' expense. I have a very honest relationship with Charles. When we got married I said that I couldn't be sure that it would be for ever. How can one say that? You can't be tied for ever in that way, it seems unrealistic to me. We have an unspoken agreement that something could happen, though the reality is such that as the years go by, you depend more on one another. I don't know – if an opportunity presented itself which I felt I had to take and which meant parting from Charles – whether I could actually do it. I really don't know but I feel I'm quite likely to. I could cope with my relationship with Charles much better if I had a close female friend but since our marriage, it's a matter of great regret I don't have any. Prior to 1975 I always had close female friends but they've moved away or gone abroad. It's an enormous gap in my life which I must fill.

Happiness comes in snatches. Situations are ones of compromise all the time, it's a system of trade-offs. I like having the 'upper hand', running things for myself, for Charles and the children: nevertheless, what has happened because of the trade-off is that we have effectively swapped roles. By becoming the bread-winner, I've become the decision maker. It's a great pressure sometimes and therefore I increasingly view Charles differently. It's an odd situation really: he was the oak tree, the rock, he now does most of the domestic bit at home. He tries to take over the mothering role but that's difficult because of the age gap and the different values of different generations between the children and himself. Because of swapping roles, the dependency is purely emotional now, maybe it always was. My view of him now is very, very different from what it was and his of me I expect. This change has had a pretty drastic effect on our relationship and in my heart of hearts, it's probably not one which will last for ever. Perhaps he and I are compromising and we'll have to come into the open and make some decisions. Neither of us would stay together if either of us was unhappy.

I've set a target for myself: to work as long as it takes to put the children through the educational process. When I feel I've done what I can in about seven years' time at most, there should still be enough left in me to chuck it all. I've always invested in the real accumulator – houses – and moved to bigger and bigger ones. When the time comes, we'll sell that, give what money the children need or invest it for them. Then I'll say, now's the time to do some of the things I want to do.

Christine Merton

I can understand why women deliberately make the move to opt out or make changes in their middle years: I did not make the initial move, it was forced on me. It came late, after twenty-five years of marriage. During all those years I thought I could have had my inner independence and do my own work within marriage, but it didn't work out like that.

Divorce and being alone were the two main factors which made me finally harness all my energy and direct it towards my art, never thinking at the time that I could ever make the grade professionally. While I was married I had spent as much time as possible on my art after the initial study period at the college and when the children were established at school. But my lack of freedom and inner confidence in what I was doing and a belief in myself presented many difficulties in developing my work and myself in relation to my work.

I am the sort of person where parental background domination had been strong and lingering. Difficulties had been further magnified by political segregation and persecution which reigned over most of my childhood and teenage years. This brought a great deal of isolation. It also affected my education most drastically.

However, the three years of serious study at the art college were a vital step. It was a terrific effort to launch and do this – my own thing. I found I could not concentrate. Having children, doing housework and having constant interruptions had made havoc of my ability to do this and structure my work. It was hard to learn and it took time to discover my own rhythm of work in relation to the study.

It was to me as if women's work during their thirties was a sort of muddling through. A lot of relearning had to be done.

Thinking back, when I was married I did not want to do my own thing at first or build my own life. I loved my children; I liked being a housewife and being married. Although I struggled, once having got to college, with the efforts of discipline and adjustment, it seems now that I was still cushioned by the feeling of security inside the family. I remained primarily in the position of being a mother and a partner to a man and did not emancipate myself into a fully fledged individual person or artist. That was still easily the secondary role especially for someone of my times.

In the first part of my life there were so many hurdles and factors which hindered progressive development, yet I feel more conscious of them now. It's easy being over fifty because by that time so many troubles have fallen away. I'm physically more fit, the sex drive seems to go a bit and I've more energy more clearly directed. I'm no longer thrown about and buffeted by drives and urges which kept on getting in the way – to which I was once quite susceptible. There had been prejudices and manipulations by others which I could not identify and which often misled and confused me. I now find better insight and understanding in these matters and the earlier they are developed, the better one can manage later on. There had been no friends or guiding person to talk to and I carried on being inwardly isolated. My life had to take a certain course which made me a late arrival.

By now I don't mind this but sometimes I get in a panic, feeling that I must put as much as I can into my work. I get restless if I don't. Once you start on a career, it takes over. You worry about harnessing your energies but you become wiser and learn all the time. It is much more difficult to make your mark when you come late in life into a profession, since others have been climbing the ladder from an early start onwards. Often one is not even given the entry at all because of one's age, and that can act as a big throwback and be frustrating and disillusioning.

I've got a capacity to bloom out of catastrophic situations – I've proved that. I'm half-Jewish and lived in Germany and was six when the Nazis came to power. There were no other Jewish families living in this part of the country and I didn't know that I was different from the others around me. At school as in everything else, I was the odd one out. I was singled out because I didn't belong to the [Hitler] Youth Movement and I realized then there was something different about me. There was an atmosphere of fright. Fear crept around. When I was ten, I was taken to a school of the kind like Gordonstoun where there were others like me. My parents then told me that my father was Jewish and I began to understand our whole situation. I remember thinking, 'I'm not going to be beaten, it's not going to get me down.' Bit by bit I got used to the deprivations.

In 1938, during the wave of persecution, my father was locked up. There was great chaos in Germany and we had to leave our country property. Life began to be really dangerous and one could not speak freely or say anything which would suggest one was of Jewish descent. Fear was everywhere, fear of being put away especially stayed with me a lot. I had no further schooling but stayed at home in Berlin with two old teachers, which was no life for a teenager and I was totally isolated. I grew bonkers over this and I still remember thinking it wasn't going to get me down and through it I developed an enormous strength.

At sixteen one had to work in a household for no pay. It was dangerous to say who I was because I never knew if I could trust the people I worked for. I couldn't speak up or say anything: never, never, never. In general, I had to find a way out so I withdrew and never mixed in. It lasted for so long, the fear didn't leave me until the war was over and I was nineteen. I'd spent all my impressionable years in that atmosphere. My father had left the country and was caught by the Nazis in Holland. At that time my parents were already divorced to protect my Dutch mother. When she died, I was really alone because all my relations had left the country, all except my sister. We belonged to a well-known family and had social status and so could have been taken to one of the labour camps for reasons of reprisal. These periods toughened me up when things went from bad to worse. I had lost everything and was nobody. But I followed my principle that there is, in every situation, something from which I could learn and, since I was deprived of education and coherent upbringing, I made the most of even the worst opportunities.

After the war I came to England to marry and thought things couldn't get any worse, only better, but they didn't. I married a man of a different social standing from the one I had known. When I came to Yorkshire, it was so grey and dreary, there was no response or understanding, no comprehension at all of what I'd been through. It was immensely difficult to get through the years in my twenties: it wasn't easy to make friends because I wasn't in a situation to meet people easily, as the influence of the past lingered and gave me almighty depressions.

When I married and had children, I was immensely happy and thankful, though I would rather have waited for my first child until I'd found myself. I always made them the main focus of my life, over-compensated perhaps and later paid the penalty for this when they were teenagers and opted out. You may think you have your career or have developed an interest but all the same it threw me when they left, especially so as it coincided with an early menopause. Life seemed to derail then because all the liveliness the children had brought with their friends and the sense of being in a complete family, disappeared. This can be a very crucial time for many women; even if they've been developing as people and have been thinking wisely about careers, still much is lost. It has something to do with being a female and making a nest; men go to women for that. It hurts when the children go. When this being all together gets dispersed, it leaves a big emptiness. It helps to have a career built up but it's still a factor – there is more understanding of that now, life is more accommodating.

Women who haven't had children don't know what sacrifice is, it's such a total thing having to be there with them. It's such a vital experience and such a demand, it gives an insight into the ups and downs of life. Yet if you cherish the family unit it can take longer to come out of it. You're more sluggish at coming forth and there's more conflict when you do.

To become a mother is a change made for ever. In order to put up with the sacrifices, the constant pulling and tugging and having to be there for 'them', it is vital to develop one's own personality alongside as best one can, so as to have this thread in hand when the children leave later. During the middle years a mother and daughter may come together again more closely. When the daughter herself becomes a mother, she can open up new understanding between them.

It's a pity women feel they have to make an identity for themselves outside the home and cannot do so, in most cases, within it. We should be able to take the generosity of feeling free whatever we do. But how can you be free if you stay at home? Sometimes women pay too much perhaps for being independent and doing their own thing. Maybe things have to swing to the extreme as they are doing now before reaching a balance. I'm not sure.

When I was divorced in my late forties, I felt totally stripped. I felt completely unprotected and almost physically in the street because I was so used to being with a partner who was protective of me. Suddenly I lost my status. I felt totally unprotected from other males and in order to avoid being gobbled up by them, I used to keep my eyes down to the pavement. I felt tremendously insecure and took about seven years to heal. I didn't know how to cope because I'd never had to take a job before. I had to learn to write business letters and take care of all matters, all sorts of things, and finally I learnt how to be precise and not to fluff around. All this took all my courage.

The hard times in my life have toughened me up to the extent that people said to me during the period of my divorce, 'You are very strong, you can take it, have some more!' When the pressure builds up, I jump in. I don't risk too much, I start slowly because by doing that, you get courage. After the divorce, for instance, I started teaching and the exhibitions came gradually. By standing up to the outside world I managed to cope with different situations from the ones which faced me before and during marriage. Somewhere inside me there's an inner pride which raises its head, as it did after the divorce. It was difficult when I was by myself and I had to move forward on my own and not be manipulated. Afterwards I'd go and collapse at home. I cried a lot for several years. As a child, I remember, crying wasn't 'convenient' because it didn't fit into the accepted social pattern and was messy. But it's easier now, I've come a long way since then.

The period over the divorce and the loss of my home was an immense welter of emotional collapse which eventually exhausted itself. By weeping, I sluiced it all away. I think it's very important that women accept the need to weep. It's a good thing even though the outside world doesn't want to know it's going on. It is important to feel yourself from your innermost being, being drained clear by giving total acceptance to the situation you are in. I learned to accept and, in the end, did not lose the energy you spend fighting and resisting the agony. If you can accept the enormous pressure and hold on with your back to it, you can accept total and drastic situations, let them be and recognize they can go on for years. To learn that can be a tremendous help in bad times. You learn not to fritter away your time and energy in useless spurts of justification but to adapt. The whole bad spell during and after the divorce took about seven years and I still feel a lot of insecurity. I need to talk to friends a lot. If I didn't have them now, I'd be very miserable.

I need a balance of friends and loved ones. There are areas where I need to talk with friends of my own sex. It is immensely important to nurture friendships. I had discovered that my husband didn't have friends in this way and was aware of the pressure that built up in him. In those days many men were afraid of being pushed in the category of appearing homosexual. Wives should try to help friendships come about – as well as encourage fathers and sons to be companionable.

I like men as people but I didn't understand how very different men are from women until after my divorce. The whole structure of society, being largely built up by men, presents us with a biased attitude which is so hard to break down in order to be heard. Competitiveness is one important point where difference lies. Although both sexes have it in their own way, the method, kind and area of action are often very different. The scale of success is still male oriented and many times a woman is put out of the running because of the unequal condition and non-recognition or -acceptance of a female way of progression, capacity and quality.

Women have to understand their values and be assured of them. We need to acknowledge the difference between men and women and be aware that they each approach things from a different angle. What is needed is to be paid on an equal basis with men and to have equal rights as citizens, but it is a very difficult area because it is all tied up with sex and that is such an animal thing.

I'm consciously happy now and have said so at other times when I have been interviewed. I experience a feeling of totality and am very conscious of when this started to happen. After the divorce, I took up studies in ceramics and sculpture and grew from that. Once I got going, I had a searching time sorting myself out and found confidence in myself as a human being. A combination of many things – awareness, confidence and so on – made me become a more total person than I think I was before. I'm happy now and, if I can carry on, that's fine. I don't want any more.

I think perhaps the vision I had of myself as a teenager has come true to some extent. I always saw myself as a distinct individual even though I was part of a family and maybe, because I had this clear concept of self, it caused my husband envy and insecurity – I'm not sure. What I'm doing now suits me perfectly, fifty per cent physical and fifty per cent intellectual. I can't just work with my brain, I need to use my arms and legs as well, employing physical cunning in my work.

The middle years involve finding out what one is and where one's path lies. One discovers how to direct one's energies into activities whether they have status or not and it makes one a better person which, in turn, feeds into those around one. It can be a creative process whether one is scrubbing floors or writing a book. One learns to get round things one hates doing by disciplining oneself because the rest of one's life is well spent. Resentment takes up a lot of energy and can cause aggravation and poor health, all the result of doing unfulfilled work. The middle years mean maturity when many things come together in life, but it requires honesty to stand by what one does and not be worried by status. Our society is so status oriented, it's a real enemy in the camp. You recognize too the importance of being aware of your limits because if you don't that too can cause misery. In art this comes out in your work, for art is the most regulating activity, always needing to come back to the core of your being to maintain its quality. During the middle years, one must recognize that to overstep or over-drive oneself will undo one's creativity in the end.

Irma Kurtz

I don't remember any moment in my background when I had a moment of conscious decision. They seemed to make me in a way. Like I'm an expatriate and I don't know any moment I decided I didn't want to live in America – I just knew I didn't want to. I've never been on the horns of a dilemma – maybe morally or about work – but not about my own life.

When I decided to leave the flat where I'd been leading a cosmopolitan sophisticated life, I knew I had to buy a house and I guess that was the beginning of wanting to get pregnant. I had to have a roof of my own, a small garden and a washing machine. It wasn't exactly a decision, more of a recognition of the moment as the only possible course. It's a sort of inward thrust: there comes a point when you reckon you're paying too much spiritually for this life and it's time now to change.

I've got friends in their early forties who've made a conscious decision not to have children but I think the impulse is to have them. I think it's a *decision* not to. I think we're driven to do it one way or another.

I had been broody before, not necessarily when I was in love. I can remember feeling it for the first time intensely just before my thirtieth birthday, when I went to visit someone who'd just had a baby. I'd never liked babies or looked at them very carefully and it really was a physiological drive to have a child. It was fierce but it went away.

I can remember going away on holiday with my son's father and making lists of names, not even being pregnant at the time. We'd already decided the child would have his surname but that was all rather abstract sitting there on the beach in Samos. Soon after, I went to Japan for six weeks and if there was a moment of decision, it was there. I was on the fifth floor of a large department store and it happened to be in the children's department and I thought, yes, I'm going to get pregnant. Then I went to get the escalator and I couldn't. I had to take the stairs down and during my entire pregnancy I had a phobia about escalators.

I think until I was thirty-six it was a decision not to have a baby – that's what we have contraceptives for. So the decision to have one wasn't a decision, just going with the flow of things. I don't really know why I had a child except that I knew I'd be good at it and I knew I could mother. So I thought, hell, there are so many around who're bad at it, one or two who are good should have a try. The only thing I regret is that I haven't got two of them, having one is a great luxury and that makes you greedy for more and I'm only sorry I couldn't. But that wouldn't have been possible in any way – time, money, everything. It's so much harder, more compelling, obsessive than you can ever explain to anyone else.

I've waited so long to have a child I've had time to have a really adventurous life. I've gone round the world a couple of times, hitch-hiked across India, been to Vietnam during a war, been to Australia, had tons of lovers, been well fed and pampered, down and out as well. I wasn't being cheated out of anything: on the contrary, I'd actually come to the end naturally and then it was natural to have a child. I might well have resented having a couple of children by the time I was twenty-eight or so, having been trapped into marriage at eighteen or nineteen, but that wasn't for me.

From the age of about eighteen, there were certain things I knew: that I wasn't going to live in America, wasn't going to read sociology which is what my parents would have liked me to do. And, by the way, I knew I wasn't going to get married. I feel like I was born knowing that. Maybe I was brainwashed by my mother who used to tell me that marriage stinks and men always get the better deal, in which case I'm enormously grateful to her. Frankly, I've not liked the look of it and I can't stand the feeling of being trapped in any position. Last week for no reason at all, I went to Hastings for a couple of days just to remind myself that I'm a free agent. I stayed in a guest house, walked around, went to restaurants, visited the castle – just as a reminder that I can wake up in one city and go to bed in another, out of choice. I've always felt the world was mine. No one's ever stopped me from doing what I wanted to do except my son and as I wanted him beyond all things, he can't.

I knew I could never have a lasting relationship with any man. It would be impossible. I'm so dominating! I run my life and a man must dominate his woman, somebody must dominate somebody else in a household and I would hate to dominate a man but I'd kill him if he tried to dominate me. The marvellous thing about a child is there isn't any domination because he's growing away. There's progress and he's changing and there's no stagnation like there can be in a union with a man. He can't stop me from doing anything I want to do and I'll only stop him from doing anything dangerous because he's only eight. As he gets older I'll stop him doing less.

Next to Mark, writing is the most important thing in my life.

No male writer would ever say that but we're earth creatures and I don't mind it a bit being bound to earth by my son. But I didn't have the guts to try and publish so much as an article until I was thirty-one, and that's from someone who's been a more or less free agent since eighteen and knowing there's nothing I loved more than writing but afraid to do it. I've been a late developer in everything – I don't think I got my periods until I was about sixteen. With writing it was total lack of confidence and I still lack it. I'm terrified of the blank page and terrified of getting a commission. Every time I'm asked to do something I think, oh God! I can't! I'm not at all sure men go through that; it's something women have to struggle with and I'm not sure, God damn it, it's not hormonal or physiological.

It's too easy to say that it's because some man's been putting you down but no man's ever put me down. Male society, perhaps you should say, but it's treated me quite well and I've hardly noticed it. I've gone about doing what I want to do. It's the getting the confidence from inside and I still suffer from that terribly. It takes ages to get it anyway.

I think it was desperation at another awful job which I had to commute to right across London that was the final spur. I had terrible jobs, really terrible, writing ad copy. Not only was I not a good copy writer but it bored the hell out of me. At the same time I didn't think I could do anything else. I had such a poor opinion of myself and such a high and mighty opinion of what 'good' was.

I had written a piece for *Queen* which they sent right back to me. About that time a new magazine called *Nova* started up, so I retyped the article and sent it in. They bought the piece, and gave me a job on the magazine. I thought it was all a fluke but once a man had confidence in me, it all got easier. I didn't write a book until I was forty-three, and now looking back you could say I had been wasting my time and I should have been writing books all along, but I don't regret it at all. It was being me.

You get a philosophy as you get older. If you keep your wits about you and your eyes open that's the only thing I can call it. You can accept loss, looks, youth and so on and even make something of it. I think it's marvellous that a middle-aged woman is going to take a chance which she wasn't offered before, that she can see she's missed the opportunity once and is damn well not going to let her life end without knowing what it's like to be a liberated creature – whatever it is. I think it's terrific. For older women who are contemplating changing their lifestyle radically it's the same sort of thing as me deciding to learn to drive after the age of forty. It's using your imagination and that makes it scarier – and more thrilling. Much more wonderful. Sometimes we do things in order to have done them, not because we really want to do them. Someone said that about writing books.

Age confers a kind of authority on men but it doesn't treat women so kindly. We have to take the authority, we don't get it naturally or automatically the way men do. Age does bad things for women if we lead a totally feminine life because it does nothing but take away our sex appeal. So I suppose the only way you go about doing things late rather than in due course is to be willing to tackle them in a slightly eccentric and original way.

I think a forty-year-old who decides she'll make a go of a career and change the nice, stable home her husband's been coming home to for years, is going to be in deep trouble, eight-and-a-half times out of ten. Deep down what's she's rebelling against is that union and that's part of her pattern of revolt. She's going to pay a price for that thought and however bitter and neglected she felt, her husband's going to miss the old person she once was. The man's been going his way and he can't expect to have to live with a new person in the house.

Many women have never been alone: never actually had a bed-sit or a flat without a flat-mate, partner, husband, lover or children. They've never been in the position of closing the door and being alone in that space. It's the most painful and important thing to have done, to be absolutely on your own with nobody who needs, wants or calls on you. You learn a lot. I was always confident of my mother's love and that's an enormous help when I was living on my own in Paris years ago. Being on your own is the most strengthening thing there is; recognizing if anything's going to happen, you're going to have to make it happen, there's nobody else. You can't sit in a room and do nothing, you just get older.

It's a good time to be a woman now and be able to take advantage of it. But it's also a time when if you haven't taken the opportunity before, you could feel bitter and regretful you haven't got into the liberation thing. Possibly you could be put off. I could imagine a woman between, say, forty and fifty regretting that very much. Against that, women are free to find the support and friendship of other women. There are more choices around for us now, a network and a sisterhood, a practical down-to-earth advantage which wasn't there a few years ago.

P.D. James

I think quite a number of women do still see marriage and children as the ultimate fulfilment and of course, in one very important way, it undoubtedly is. I think what can happen is that as children get older, women realize there are other forms of personal fulfilment they may have missed; then they can go and seek these forms, sometimes with startling success. I feel with many women, the drive towards marriage and children is probably a biological urge and it's very important if the race is going to go on at all. It may be only when this is fulfilled that women look, even at a happy marriage, and say, 'Is this everything? Is this all I intend to do?' For many women, I think they would say, 'Yes, it is.' They are perfectly happy and fulfilled within it and for them it is absolutely right; it would be deplorable if we made women who find their fulfilment in this fashion, feel in some way odd or inadequate. If this is right for them, they have just as much right to it as the career woman has to hers. What I feel very strongly is that we ought to have a choice, that we should know ourselves what kind of life we want and what things are important to us. It's not for society or other people to dictate what form that should be.

I don't think for myself I would have been fulfilled doing nothing else but running a house, but I don't undervalue the skills which doing that properly requires and for many women this is undoubtedly the way they reach their greatest happiness. It's awful the way people ask 'What do you do?' and these women look terribly apologetic and say, 'I'm just at home', or 'I'm a wife and mother', as if they're somehow confessing to something that's inferior. We're now seeing some of the results of inadequate parenting. If we undervalue parenthood we do a great disservice to our children and ourselves. On the other hand, I do want a society which allows women, if they feel they want to do something outside the home, to seek and be able to find it. I think there is and must be a danger in seeking all your fulfilment wholly in personal relationships. Everything is invested in personal relationships and when children grow up and move away, this can leave a woman feeling very bereft. Some women then do apply their intelligence and latent gifts into making some other kind of life with great success, but many others by then, even if they wanted to do this, do not have the self-confidence or the training.

These are problems which, because of my personal circumstances, I've never had to face myself, but I've seen them in other women and I think they're aggravated by this awful 'ageism'. We may be overcoming sexism but undoubtedly in recent years particularly, there's tremendous importance attached to youth. This means that the woman going back to work, perhaps into an office or into business life, feels doubly at a disadvantage. It has become an unfamiliar world as it's one she's not been in for some time and additionally, she is at a disadvantage because of age. I deplore this tremendously. I think it's extraordinarily short-sighted of employers. I think that a middle-aged woman is probably much better value than many younger people, much more responsible, harder working and capable. I have been surprised to see in those women among my friends who are well educated and remarkably capable, this feeling that there's almost a jungle outside the home: they haven't learnt its laws and are going to be slapped down and beaten. Age shouldn't be a barrier.

I think a lot of women feel, particularly about those in business, that these people are endowed with extraordinary qualities of mind and body, training and intelligence, financial and other skills which make them almost super-gods. Yet once you're in that world, even briefly, you see that many of them are ordinary people and in no way outstanding. An intelligent, sensible woman need have no fear, though I think this may be difficult for many women to realize.

There is a tremendous waste of potential amongst these women. After all, if you're going to organize a church fête or a school bazaar, you have got to be capable and they are capable.

It's a very cruel waste. For those people who do not want to step into this very different world, they certainly shouldn't be compelled to because if you start pressurizing women to do two jobs, it may result in this situation which I understand obtains in Russia, where women are the most overworked section in the community. But for those who do, it's an absolutely crucial waste of human potential and skill that they should be ignored the way they are ignored. It's a very difficult time at the moment because of the recession; it couldn't be a worse time. I think women themselves may be in the forefront of suggesting that they stay at home and look after the children because they see their husbands' jobs threatened. I think particularly in the North of England, women have been the bread-winners for some considerable time because of men's redundancies. It's all too easy for Londoners to think that England stops at Watford.

I have worked for almost all my life though there was a break during the war. I was the eldest child, there were three of us in the family of a fairly minor civil servant who worked in the Inland Revenue. We moved around a lot probably because I think he and my mother were fairly restless but also because within the Inland Revenue, it was perfectly possible to get moves relatively easily. Luckily we lived always in very agreeable places. I was born in Oxford, moved to the Welsh borders and then to Cambridge where I went to the High School. I knew from a very early age I wanted to write but I was a very late starter. I think there were a number of reasons for this. I was nineteen when war broke out, married when I was twenty and moved back to London. There was every excuse for not writing because of the problems of getting a new novel published and also, above all, uncertainty about whether one would survive. My husband qualified as a doctor and went into the Royal Army Medical Corps and came home at the end of the war mentally ill. As his mental illness was not officially ascribed to his army service, he received no pension, so that meant obviously I had to support myself and our two daughters. I needed a safe job, which meant I couldn't rely on writing even if I'd achieved anything by then, which I hadn't.

This was soon after the formation of the National Health Service in 1949 and the new Regional Hospital Boards were advertising for staff. Of course, at this time I was hoping my husband would recover and was looking then for a temporary job. We were living with my parents-in-law and I wanted to contribute to the housekeeping and to my daughters' education. So I took a job with Paddington Hospital Management Committee and as the years passed, it became obvious it was very unlikely my husband would ever be able to work again. I went to evening classes and passed examinations and obtained a Diploma in Hospital Management and in Medical Records, both of which I thought were necessary if I was to obtain promotion and compete in a job which is very male-dominated. I did get promotion and reached a fairly senior post.

In my late thirties, I realized that unless I made an effort and wrote my first novel, I would eventually be a grandmother and telling my grandchildren what I always wanted to be was a writer. So although it was difficult with a full-time job and travelling from Essex to Paddington, I felt I must get on with it and I did. It took a long time to write because if my husband became worse I had to put it to one side. I had periods when I was very busy at work and hadn't the energy to write. When it was finished, I was extremely fortunate because the novel – it was called *Cover Her Face* – was accepted by the first publisher my agent sent it to. At least I was spared the disappointment and trauma many other writers have endured through perpetual rejection slips. In fact, my two small children, knowing I was working on a novel and worried that I would be disappointed, said that I must realize if it was to be any good at all, it was bound to be rejected. I think they were full of the most frightful doubts when they heard it had been accepted. So that was the beginning of it.

I wrote a crime novel for a number of reasons. I enjoyed reading them. Dorothy L. Sayers was a potent influence in my girlhood. I thought I could write one. I thought a crime novel might have the best chance of success because it was a popular art form and there might be a demand. I didn't want to write an autobiographical novel, which a first novel often is. I was fascinated by the structure of an orthodox English detective story and construction has always interested me. I thought too it might be a very good apprenticeship for someone who was really setting out to be a serious novelist. And of course, as I went on with the genre, I did realize there was something which I could do and do really quite well. It was perfectly possible to be a serious novelist within the constraints of this particular form. There was a progression in my writing and at the same time, my professional life continued. I passed my examinations and earned enough to support the family. Then in 1968 I went in the Home Office and became a senior civil servant.

This was a very big change and there were a number of reasons for it. My husband had died in 1964. When he was alive, I did not think I could have changed jobs because I felt it was important I did jobs I knew I could tackle and had experience in. But after he died I did feel I wanted a change from hospital administration. This would be something new. I think this is the time of life possibly (I was then forty-eight) when women who work ask, 'Do I really want to go on doing this until I'm sixty?' Those last twenty years of working life stretch ahead. By their late forties, most women in jobs and professions have got the measure of the job and themselves, they can do the job competently and possibly fairly easily, so it doesn't represent quite the intellectual challenge it may have done when they were younger. There is too this sense of there's still a long way to go and what am I contributing to the job and what is it doing for me? I was certainly keen to make the change, so I took the examinations for the Civil Service and was successful and this opened new vistas for me.

I worked first in the Police Department, then in the Criminal Policy Department, concerned with the law relating to juvenile offenders and those considered by the court to be in need of care and control: largely this meant I was concerned with very controversial legislation, the Children and Young Persons Act 1969. It was fascinating to gain an insight into how government works and how policy is made and to see something of Snow's *Corridors of Power*, even though I wasn't seeing it, as it were, from the higher echelons.

I retired in December 1979, having reached the stage when I had had enough of doing two jobs and generally feeling it was time for a change. Basically what I wanted was more time for writing. By then I'd written *Innocent Blood* which was the first book not purely a detective story, much more of a straight novel. It was so successful that I've spent a lot of time since, travelling in the States and doing promotions, so that it seems that since I've retired, I've had less time. I haven't written another novel though I am just beginning another one now. I spend my time thinking next week will be clear and I can start writing, but when it comes, there is no time. It might be an example of the old truism that the less time you have, the more you manage to do. When I was working I would get up in a fairly disciplined way and manage to work before breakfast because I would be too tired to work in the evenings.

I've often wondered whether the fact that my first novel was accepted by the first publisher to whom it was submitted, may not have been because it did take so long to write and I was comparatively mature when I finished it. Perhaps, had I started writing in my teens or early twenties, I might have had to go through this process of discouragement. There seems to be an optimum time in life for all enterprises and changes and perhaps one of the skills of living successfully is to recognize this time, as Shakespeare says, 'There is a tide in the affairs of men . . .' It is not altogether a question of just female intuition: I'm sure it is true of both men and women but whether women feel it more keenly, I don't know. It certainly happens in the writing of a novel. The planning period with me is really very long; during that time I'm almost in a sense living in the world of that novel and living with the characters. There comes a right time to begin writing, almost as if the book were ready to be born. I think there may well be, I'm sure there is, a time when it's right to make certain changes which we ought to be able to recognize. You can begin certain enterprises either too young or too old.

One shouldn't grab at life or grab at experience; perhaps there's a tendency to do this which may be the result of living in such very uncertain times. I suppose for the human race, all times have been uncertain but there can be ages when people feel that time is short or could be short and they are under threat and everything must be crammed in. And this is probably a mistake: just ordinary living, experiencing and growing are very important processes. Maturity comes and you know when the time has come to take a definite step and really change the direction of your life.

When we are talking about valuing human potential, it is those women who do not go on with their education but perhaps take jobs which are not emotionally satisfying before marriage, who are not encouraged to feel they can compete with men in the professional field. I think there's a great deal of ability wasted here. These women are forced into a kind of maturity and whether in middle age there comes a different type of maturity, I'm not sure.

I think also there can be a reverse change of direction taken by women in their thirties. We are seeing now an interesting phenomenon of career women, now deciding rather late in life that they will have children. I wonder really whether this may represent some disillusionment with their jobs and professional life, whether in fact both men and women can feel this in a highly competitive world but for women, as it were, there is a way out and for men there isn't. For a woman who has a high salary, her own flat and car, possibly a husband, she may think there is something missing and have a child and change direction in this way. This kind of change is governed by biological laws and is a decision that can't be put off beyond a certain point.

I think this is a very interesting and very difficult decision which faces women: do I or do I not want a family and when am I going to have a baby? A decision which after all, was one which our sex for generations was not in a position to make. It is an immense freedom which has brought with it immense problems and its own tensions and anxieties. In this age, when women have the choice, it's the most difficult age of all for women to find help with young children. Our mothers really had no choice between a job or a family but even in a fairly poor household, as mine was, there were always girls who helped. I think women now are even more responsible about the kind of upbringing they want for their children. I'm sure many women who want to carry on with their jobs and yet don't want to be deprived of parenthood, are worried about the kind of day-to-day care they can provide for the child if they go back to work.

I wonder to what extent most women do recognize their own sexuality and what in fact their own needs are. Women are conditioned to feel that the world outside the home is a difficult, alien place and are loath, I think, to lose the security of a home and a marriage even if, in part of their minds, they know it isn't a wholly satisfactory set-up for them. I feel that group of women who have married young, after perhaps not very much education, and who have done jobs before marriage and feel they want to fulfil themselves outside the house, possibly overlook the strength of the need they had for the marriage and the family. Had they stayed in their office jobs, perhaps for the local authority or the bank and had missed the husband and marriage, they would possibly be feeling much more frustrated. This isn't to underestimate the extent of the frustration they could feel in the home, and of course, it is a very lonely job and in modern society, made even more lonely. Women in this position, seeing only other women with young children, make an artificial intellectual and social life for themselves.

It's very easy I'm sure for people to feel, 'Once I'm working, I'm not going to be bored.' But much office work is by its nature, boring. But what it does offer I think, is this change of companionship, another world, other people and the economic independence of feeling, 'This is money I have earned.'

I think that many men do see the fact of their wives launching out into a job later in the marriage as a threat and it suggests, doesn't it, that many men do prefer their wives to be totally economically reliant on them. They see it perhaps as a double threat: for the woman who is meeting people outside the home is in a world which the man cannot share, any more than she can share his working life. Sexual jealousy may be involved also. I think it is vitally important that a woman has money which she has earned, to do what she likes with. I think too, privileged women who are highly educated and married to highly educated men, do not appreciate this as a problem for women in different social and economic groups.

One thing I've noticed about married men and happily married men, when talking about domestic matters, it's seldom in terms of 'we'. They talk about 'my house', 'my car' and so on, almost as if they are the centre of this little universe and somewhere, tucked away there, is this woman to whom they're devoted, who does the cooking, cleaning and provides a comfortable background for them.

In a sense perhaps, we all create a kind of fantasy for ourselves and live within it, don't we? The recognition of the reality can be incredibly painful. I wonder how many women being totally honest, might look at a husband they've been married to for years and decide they don't like him. If it seems to them there is no alternative but to spend the rest of life with him, this is a very painful and traumatic thing to accept and possibly many women do not accept it. I think that women who do face the alternative and who divorce, may in a sense regret the change because the subsequent loneliness is so great. Women on the whole have not learnt to live with themselves, and I think it must be tragic for a woman to realize that certainly she wasn't happy before but at least she was married and with a home. The world is so aggressively organized for pairs, the orthodox couple, and the divorced woman can feel herself the odd woman out. I think for many women the effect of a divorce is so intolerable that it might have been better had they remained married. I suppose it all boils down to the fact that women are so conditioned to see themselves as one of a pair, the prospect of being alone is something they never face or train themselves for, either psychologically, physically or economically. Therefore it is all the more terrible when this happens. The same thing happens to widows but for a divorced woman, she is also lumbered with a sense of inadequacy and failure.

I do believe it is almost essential for human beings to feel that there is one other human being in the world to whom they are necessary for his or her happiness. The real loneliness must be for women who haven't this and it must be very real and very frightening. I don't think it necessarily need be a husband or a child. It may be a best friend or a parent. The ultimate loneliness is to know there is no one in the world who really would be very much worse off if you didn't exist, no one who looks to you for their needs. So that in a sense we are organized in pairs. I think it is difficult for any human being to live entirely alone and if he does, it can be a rather selfish existence. Maybe many women, knowing of that loneliness, are inhibited from changing direction in middle life since they see this as threatening their basic security.

I do very much enjoy living on my own. As a writer it is almost essential and I'm not lonely but there again, I have children and grandchildren and it's easy to live alone when you have friends and relations who are there. I think having someone who is necessary for your happiness is part of human experience, perhaps particularly for women. Usually I think we do recognize our needs because subconsciously we work towards them. I think one of the characters in a C.P. Snow novel says, 'You can always find out what you really want from life. It consists of what happens to you.'

Perhaps women who fall very deeply and very romantically in love are lucky as they never have to make the decision whether to marry or not, these decisions are more or less made. If you have this ability to fall absolutely in love, you don't have this question of 'Am I going to love this man when I'm forty?' You're just so obsessed and want his children. What I think is very interesting are those women who postpone marriage and usually have a succession of lovers and then have this decision to make, 'Do I marry?' By then, they seldom fall in love in the way I'm describing and they do look at relationships with a more dispassionate eye. Obviously they are not needing to marry for sexual fulfilment. In this sense the Victorians may have had life a little easier than we have in regard to choice, because there was none. It was the same for me when I was a girl. If you wanted to have a sexual life, you married. Marriage is now separate from sex and the decision may now be, 'Do I want children outside marriage?'

I still feel that it is better for children to be brought up with two parents. If I believe this, I think that women are being selfish if they say they want the experience of parenthood but don't want a husband. What they are saying is, 'I'm risking the happiness of this child for my own fulfilment.' A great many people would say I have no right to make that moral judgement. There are all these additional choices about marriage and children which earlier generations did not have to make.

I'm fascinated by the fact that many educated, successful, intelligent and attractive women complain bitterly that they cannot find a man: either a higher proportion are gay or all the eligible men are married. I really think there must be a dearth of eligible men once a woman has decided to postpone the decision to marry. As far as I can see, quite a number of marriages occur from relationships which have developed while at college or university.

I think people still see marriage as their greatest defence against loneliness, against a world which they may see increasingly as being an aggressive, a violent, a dangerous and an unhappy place. I think this is reflected in the tremendous interest that people have in the environment in their homes. I suppose they always have, but one does get the picture that this is the door we close on the outside world and within this relationship, we will try to defend ourselves against all the dangers which threaten. At least inside here, we can be understood and understand.

Nancy Roberts

Spare Tyre Theatre Company came along for me at a very fortuitous time in my life. Basically what had happened was that I'd read *Fat is a Feminist Issue* in April 1979. I'd read it and thought, my God, isn't this unbelievable! Here was a woman, an intelligent person, who was saying dieting doesn't work, dieting is bad for you. I'd been on diets on and off all my life since I was six years old when I was taken to my first diet doctor. All of which set up terrible syndromes of guilt and self-loathing which compulsive eaters know so well. It was no news to me that I was eating because I was unhappy – I'd also been going to shrinks since I was eight. I had that real identification of which Susie Orbach speaks between what you eat and how you feel about yourself: whenever I was on a diet I felt noble, self-righteous and absolutely terrific. Suddenly here was this woman saying it doesn't work. I read that book in one afternoon; I couldn't put it down as you can imagine. I immediately rang the Women's Therapy Centre and tried to get on a compulsive eating group but they said there was a six-month waiting list, so write back in September. I thought, oh my God, how am I going to wait that long? This is impossible.

A couple of weeks later I saw an ad in *Time Out* on the theatre board which I'd never read before, asking for women interested in writing a play based on *Fat is a Feminist Issue* to write in. I dithered around and finally wrote, got a reply asking me to come to a workshop at the Round House. I went along with a lot of misgivings, having no idea it was going to be an audition or anything like that. I thought I'd be licking envelopes or doing some of the basic garbage work. Well, we had to do impressions and I was terrified! All I wanted to do was get out of there as fast as possible. We talked a bit and I did my impression, then they fixed up to meet the following Sunday night, and I thought I wasn't interested in this. I wanted something to fill my days, not something on Sunday night which is the last time in the world I want anything filled up.

I came home to Uwe, my fellow, and said this stinks! I don't want anything to do with this. But the next day Claire called and said I'd been chosen and I didn't have the heart to tell her I wasn't interested. Uwe said go, go, go, you can always pull out once you've seen what it's all about. And that's how it was for the first few meetings. I was really very hesitant and I think I was just terrified. I kept going and we started to write the show together and after about a month, one of the characters started to emerge as me. And that's how it happened.

Now the irony and what makes it all so interesting is, that I come from a theatrical family. My brother is a big actor on Broadway and TV and my father is a TV announcer and was *the* voice on radio in its early days. It was in the blood but for various reasons and lots of insecurities, I'd never gone near it. I'd never trained or voiced the feeling that perhaps I'd like to be in the business in some way. I was terrified of it. I think my feelings about acting and show-biz were coloured by my feelings about my family. Basically I felt very rejected, second-rate and alienated from them and therefore anything to do with the business also made me feel that way – even though in the back of my mind that was for me, paradise. I always wanted to be somebody on TV.

As a child I had this terrible weight problem which was obviously a symptom of other things in my life. I had this nanny until I was six, whom I absolutely adored but she was dismissed because my parents thought I was old enough to do without her. That to me was like losing a parent and that's when I got fat and miserable. My own mother was, and is, an undemonstrative woman with terrible problems about her own mother, who was a monster! And so there I was at six years old left with this woman who didn't seem to want any part of me.

I'd gone through this life until now with a parent who only wanted me to be thin. That was all she ever talked about. I was brilliant at school. Yet I never was encouraged to go on to college; I did go but it wasn't 'What are you going to be?' but 'When are you going to lose weight?' I went to a school in New York called Music and Art where you specialized. My brother went there too. I was pretty talented as an artist. That was never encouraged. Just 'When are you going to get thin?' with the ultimate aim obviously to be beautiful enough to get married – to someone good.

And I had a string of losers. One after another of my boyfriends were, in various ways, losers. Either gay, or just not going to make it any way.

I always thought of myself as the crazy one, always going to the shrink. I made a couple of abortive suicide attempts when I was a teenager. I was always very unhappy, yet very bright. But all I felt was nuts. My earliest shrink said to my mother, 'Why does she think she's crazy?' When I was a little girl, my mother would grab me by the cheeks and say, 'Oh, you're so crazy!', which was meant to be endearing to her but I thought I really was. Everything revolved around my weight. When I was dieting my mother loved me, and when I wasn't she didn't. I now realize my whole weight problem was my way of being involved with her because it was the only level on which we communicated. So the more we focused on it, the more of a relationship we had.

My early life is what feminism is about, because there's no denying that a terrible wastage of human potential was allowed to exist just because I was a woman. They lived through my brother's success and his career, even to this day they're deprecating about me and my success. They're frightened of it because it means too many negative things to them, particularly to my mother who said after my first show, 'Everyone in the family's a star, except me.'

After working as a PR in a theatrical office, we all came to London for my brother's wedding and I knew, I don't know how, I wasn't going to come back to the job; maybe I saw the trip as an escape. I met my new sister-in-law's brother and fell madly in love with him: he had a lot of problems. I lived with him for four years and never went out once with him anywhere.

I always had the fierce conviction I didn't want to be a secretary, though my mother urged me to be, pointing out all the successful women who'd started out that way. I just couldn't do it. To succeed I would have to remove myself from the area of their approval; it's still happening, because a part of me is tempted to go back and be a failure but I've got that practically beat now. So I did part-time jobs here, started a business with

Keith. It was a nightmare working together and living together, so by the end of four years I knew I had to get out. Oddly enough, my parents acted as a catalyst and I remember thinking when he left, thank God that's over. I felt like I'd been let out of prison.

Then I went through a more relaxed period. I slept around a bit, went out all the time. One of the things I wanted to do then was become a therapist but it was a very long course, so I opted for teacher training which was a little shorter, at Sidney Webb down the road. Unfortunately, I was unable to get a job as a teacher due to the huge cutbacks in education spending which were implemented during my first year at Sidney Webb. During this time I met Uwe who I still live with. He's six years younger than me and at first the difference in our ages put him into my 'loser' category. We went through some rough patches but our relationship has become steadily better over the years.

I got involved with a couple of people in the fashion business after I left college and for a year made quite good money. Then both firms went out of business and I found myself working a few hours a day at a record store, having dropped all connections with the rag trade – as I'd dropped other things before. Then I saw this ad in *Time Out*. When I really got excited was in rehearsal and I found myself singing and dancing, because all my life my brother had said I was tone deaf. Yet here I was on stage and it was like having uppers shot in my arm twenty-four hours a day! I was beside myself with joy. I was so excited about the 'specialness' of the project, which was entirely new for me, that I thought the whole world ought to know about it, so I wrote to everyone in the media.

There were incredible reactions from the media and the audience to the show and concurrently with this success, my compulsive eating problem ceased to exist. Once I'd read Susie Orbach's book I stopped dieting and I stopped weighing myself. I eat now because I'm hungry and for me, that's a whole new thing. I lost weight during the rehearsals though I've stabilized now. After twenty-seven years of misery, my fat has become a positive thing for me – an asset. I started enjoying food and stopped worrying when I did compulsively eat. It was such a relief to be free of constantly thinking about food. It's a release from that hell, so liberating, so strengthening. The last thing I think about now is that I'm fat, though I'm still about five stone overweight.

I'd always dressed to hide, always loved clothes and dressed like a band-box but I was embarrassed if I wasn't covered up – jeans with a long top and that kind of thing. Now I often wear jeans and a short T-shirt in public which seems to inspire other women and give them a good feeling. My favourite line in the whole of *Fat is a Feminist Issue* was 'Don't be afraid to tuck something in!' Suddenly people were listening to what I've got to say. My friends always did because I was something of an amateur shrink but over the past year I've come to appreciate my own mind. This is an incredible feeling. I'm able to talk to all sorts of different people about what we do, convert them to our way of thinking without alienating them. All these things come from Spare Tyre – a rebirth on so many levels. I went home before the summer last year and stayed with my parents and realized that my mother was obsessed not only about my eating habits but about everyone else's as well. I'd always thought before that it was my problem – I now realize it was hers.

I think the main thrust of Susie Orbach's book and of our compulsive eating groups, is you have to begin to live now. You can't continue to put off into the mythical, thin fairyland future, all the things to do with your life as it is at present. By putting things off, you create a kind of schizophrenic existence: the disgusting life now and the wonderful other self, when you're thin and life gets better. One of the things women put off is the way they want to look. When they're thin they'll dress how they want, but for now they'll find the biggest tent-like garment they can. One of the things we do in the groups is say get rid of the clothes that don't fit, throw away the scales and stop dieting and gradually start wearing what you want to. But where the hell do you find it? You don't – hence 'Big and Beautiful'. It's only when you see the weight problem in this context that it becomes politically viable, for a woman who feels like shit is not a powerful, independent person. And forty-seven per cent of women are size sixteen and over. What gave me hope about clothes was going to the States where I could buy jeans, sky-blue pink if I wanted, and that's a big, big step.

A group of women from the Women's Therapy Centre met and thought it was a good idea to promote Big and Beautiful clothes. So now I'm trying to get money to put on a big fashion show to get the kind of coverage we want. If the fashion show doesn't work, it's just as viable to talk about it in public because it'll only happen if people make demands and someone can see money can be made out of it.

All this made me realize something which is very satisfying and comforting but also the most terrifying thing I've ever experienced: that you really can make things happen for yourself, you really can change your circumstances. I still feel that however trapped you are, you can still make changes. I think it was the day I saw my picture in the *Observer* that I realized this was true and it certainly applies to other women in my situation – middle-class, middle-aged, who never had any aspirations or money for themselves. I think it's very, very frightening, because it lays a tremendous responsibility right at your feet. I do think women have to help one another and do believe in the 'network' situation which is happening in the States. If we help one another, we can make it at any age; it's never too late. We're very lucky in that it's become possible for us to do this. But we really have to think about what we're doing and the choices we have – it's hard. I think in some ways, our generation is a generation of guinea pigs.

I'm finding myself all right but I'm very much dependent on someone supporting me and that's not equilibrium. I don't think there are many great neurotic Jewish enjoyers of life. This planning ahead, I've never done this up to now and it's difficult and exciting to do it now. I don't really believe I'll ever work again, yet two high-powered agents want to take me on and I've made money before, so I guess I'll do it again.

There are two sides to being supported by Uwe. For the past year and a half, what I've been doing hasn't been financially viable. I didn't have the time to do other things because of all the behind-the-scenes stuff I did with Claire and I don't think I could have managed that anyway. At first it was very difficult for me to accept that the flat and everything in it's mine, so Uwe moved into a home without having to pay for anything. Finally I was able to relax and allow him to pay for things and realize what I was doing had other values beside monetary ones.

I've never been a loner. I've been emotionally dependent and have always seen this as a drawback because I thought I should be able to live on my own. The few times I have, I've been amazingly productive and I've enjoyed it, yet when Uwe came along we formed a constant kind of relationship very quickly. Then I thought, why should I have to learn to live by myself? There were circumstances in my childhood which made me feel very insecure and unsupported and I'm happier now with someone around all the time. You constantly seek to overthrow some basic thing in yourself, why? Now it's as if I'm finally sympathizing with myself and can stop criticizing myself all the time.

There's something about having another person there that allows me to relax and be someone; maybe I feel I've achieved a goal set way back when – a partner. My shrink once said to me, 'You'll really be in good shape when you can do absolutely nothing and be happy.' This was all tied up with my parents and having to do, do, do. I suddenly had the blinding insight a while ago that I could win the Academy Award six times and I still wouldn't get the kind of approval I was looking for. Up to then I'd always done the kind of things which would make them love me. It was shattering to realize this but also very liberating. It allowed me to relax. The first time I did a big TV show, I didn't call them because I knew they'd bring me down from this big high and that was a turning point for me.

Parents' influence? If you imagine a pint measuring jug: it's full up when you're a child. Pour out half an ounce and that's what's left when you die. My brother's favourite quote (I think it's Woody Allen's) is, 'To not become one's parent requires eternal vigilance.' The older I get, the more like my mother I become. I feel threatened by her lack of health. I've lived away from them for eleven very important years and yet it's kind of sad, they could die any minute and I'd miss this family togetherness. Then I think, no you wouldn't, it's never been there.

There're so many things I want to do, like put a Spare Tyre Cook Book together; write a TV series . . . And after all these years, having made my foray into show-biz, I don't want to leave it. I want to be up there singing and dancing on stage. I'd like to have my own chat show and comedy series, that's what I really want and the way to get that is to capitalize on what I've done already. It's a way of thinking I've not done before, maybe because I'm a woman. Men have to think that way all the time.

Marion Burman

My family was not Catholic and it was chance and the war which sent us to a convent school when my own school was evacuated. I was absolutely taken up with the convent, having been very non-religious previously, throwing everything out at home and wanting nothing to do with the Church of England. The convent belonged to a French order so when France was invaded, and everyone was in a very emotional state anyway because of the war, we used to go to chapel and pray in the colourful, rather emotional and to me, mystical way of Catholicism. I was extremely happy at that school, far more so than I'd been at my previous city grammar. I began to say I wanted to go to university but my mother, who was a teacher with an external teaching certificate, really pressed me to go to the Froebel Educational Institute. She was determined I should go there as she had wanted to do but didn't realize I wanted to do a bit more – which I did eventually. While I was at the Froebel Institute I decided I definitely wanted to be a Catholic, but somehow knew my mother would take great exception to this, coming from a very low Church of England family who did not approve of Catholics. I was the eldest of the family, and in a way it was my form of rebellion. If my mother had taken it like my father did, much more calmly, I would not have stuck to my guns so strongly. I had been very close to her and she had always ruled my life. We went through very difficult times, partly I think because she was so terribly bitter.

I had a series of boy-friends, as one did. One of them, a bomber pilot, was killed; one of my cousins was killed in the raids on Liverpool, another during the invasion of Caen; another boy-friend whom I quite liked, in the Navy, came back married. I think I began to wonder whether I was not meant for marriage and I must therefore do something else. The feeling was very strong during the war that life was precarious, you didn't know how long you had and you must make something of it. I decided what I probably wanted to do was enter a convent. I suppose I had a very glamorous view of it but it seemed to represent the only way I could ever do anything with my life – I wanted to be a saint, I think!

I had kept in touch with the nuns at the school and used to go and see them. I was twenty-two when I entered the convent but quite immature and in many ways an adolescent. The sister nearest in age to me was very bitter, but it was my mother who suffered a nervous breakdown because of me. She wouldn't have anything to do with me once I entered and would neither write to nor visit me. My father reproached her and pointed out that I would perhaps never have entered if she hadn't been so bitter. I think I might well have gone home if it hadn't been for my mother's bitterness, but I just couldn't face that.

Once you enter a convent, you're inside an institution and don't really look at it as you might from the outside. It becomes a normal life for you and like marriage, you don't constantly examine it. In the beginning, I wasn't at all happy and might well have gone home if it hadn't been for my mother. I think all through my convent life I knew – deep down – that either I should never have entered or that now I no longer believed in it. Nevertheless, I settled down to a routine and tried very hard although it was all rather alien, still hoping that I was moving towards becoming a saint. There were a few rebellious times when I felt all this was too good to be true and wasn't normal, but as soon as I worried about leaving the nuns were very quick to persuade me that these thoughts were tricks of the devil and temptations which I had to fight. In the end, I didn't know where I was and felt this was the sort of thing you had to go through and suffer in order to become a better person.

I went through the novitiate in England but wanted to go to France as it was a French order, but it was 1945 and the war had only just ended. I did go in 1951 and had a second novitiate and thought it was marvellous. I was in an active order doing teaching, nursing and social work but run on somewhat monastic lines. The habit we wore dated back to 1703 when the order was founded and was never changed by a pin until I'd been in the convent for a long time.

I had a very good career as a nun. I was eventually sent to university to read French and obtained a first class honours degree, was top of my year and won the modern languages prize. In effect I had a professional life within the religious one, which was successful and fulfilling but in a way prevented me from realizing how out of harmony I was with the spiritual side of things – though again, I was quite caught up in it. In one school I helped with 'Young Christian Students' for many years and enjoyed that, as I had the opportunity to meet a lot of people including priests of the more intellectual variety. I also worked with the Catholic Marriage Advisory Council and because of my somewhat freer upbringing in these matters, taught sex education. I became head of modern languages in school, then effectively deputy head, then headmistress of a school under the local authority in my home town.

When I came to my home town a lot of things happened. My father had died the year before I came and I'd already begun to feel there was something shoddy about the religious life I was leading. I'd not seen a great deal of my father because of my mother, though that relationship had improved a little over the years, but when he died I was allowed as a great privilege to go home. Many things were changing in the Church and convents at that time – you were allowed home if there was a real necessity. The old habit had disappeared and became more like a dress. I was allowed to stay with my mother for a week because my superiors thought this would help but I couldn't help thinking, 'It's all very well now he's dead, how much better it would have been if I'd been allowed to visit more often when he was alive.'

At the time, I was having difficulties with my career which was uppermost in my mind. I had expected to be made head of the school where I was deputy as I'd more or less been doing the job anyway. But I was thought to be too much of a rebel and not suitable. I went to the Superior-General, who was a man – convents are very male-dominated in some ways, because priests have a say in what goes on – I said I thought I should have been made head and he agreed . . . If he hadn't, I would have left then, which was just as well as it would have been for the wrong reasons. He got me an appointment as head of a school under the Education Committee. This meant that I was effectively in charge there, rather than the Reverend Mother who is seen in the convent as knowing by some divine inspiration, as opposed to professional experience, what's best.

The Encyclical *Humanae Vitae*, on marriage and birth control also came out around that time. We'd all been working towards a more liberal attitude within our work in the Catholic Marriage Advisory Council and then this dreadful document came out which was so reactionary. I began to question authority and wonder whether this man in Rome had any right to make such a statement – not so much concerning contraception, but whether the Pope had any right at all to interfere in the sphere of methods of birth control and so on. I felt that the Church could make *general* statements regarding our duty to act lovingly, respect others and so on but no *particular* ones about methods and means and this sort of thing. I went to meetings and discussion groups a great deal around this time and began to think more clearly about my spiritual situation because I was more or less satisfied with my career.

Then my mother began to die of cancer and my Provincial Superior said I shouldn't go and see her too often because my first duty lay with the convent and the school. I'd often rebelled in speech before this but invariably gave in, but this time I didn't. I said my mother came first and I went to see her, but I should have done even more and it produced the most terrible conflict in me because I thought if I had not been so obedient, things would have worked out differently. I reproached myself terribly on the night my mother was dying because, although I couldn't be sure, I felt instinctively she was at the end, yet I returned to the convent instead of remaining with her. She was buried on my first speech day as head. After she died, I had what must have amounted almost to a nervous breakdown without knowing what it was. I began to question the whole set-up. How stupid I was to take notice of what other people said, all the bitterness of the past came up. My father had left me some money in trust in case I should ever leave the order, but my mother cut me out of her estate. The money didn't matter at all then, but it made me feel bitter that she should still feel like that after so many years. I'd tried to be reconciled with her and even disobeyed the convent to do so. My mother, who wanted me to leave the convent so much, did nothing practical to help me to leave and still wanted a sort of 'revenge'.

During the period I was headmistress, which was also the period leading up to Vatican II, a lot of things began to change in the order. Four of us decided to live in a flat in a poor district where many of our pupils came from. It was a form of experiment living among poor people, so we wrote to Rome for permission. From that time on, I never lived in the convent again as I moved on to a presbytery and eventually to an ordinary house. I began not to wear the habit so much and eventually we didn't have to wear religious garments at all. As head of a school I was also on various committees and as a nun, became a member of the council or committee which actually ran our order in the British Isles.

For a while, I had strong feelings that although the whole religious thing was not right, was an institution and uncreative, I could reform it from the inside and might be able to change it. There was this idea of democracy within the order which allowed nuns to be elected on to the council. I took it all very much at face value, knowing I was not the type of person who'd be elected without the assistance of the grass roots. I worked very hard for my three years of office trying to push through some very practical reforms. The convent didn't pay national insurance for the nuns who weren't employed outside it, though those that were obviously got pensions. At the time, a lot of sisters were leaving the order, many in financial difficulty, and some did not leave because there was no way they could afford to live. There were several incidents of nuns leaving to get married, often too fast, just in order to gain some security. I wanted to see nuns in the position of either having their national insurance contributions paid by the order or the convent setting up some type of pension scheme, so there wouldn't be this lack of choice or the wrong choices made.

After three years I was 're-elected' and I decided I could not, in conscience, continue to serve on the council. Then I took the time to look at things very carefully and began to question my faith and felt I was wasting my time. I knew I had some money behind me and I could remain at the school because I was employed by the LEA. I thought if I'm going to be able to do anything with my life, I must leave now or I'll be too old to make another life. I really didn't believe in it any more, not just authority, but God. I felt the whole thing had been a big con. I did to some extent voice my doubts and discuss them but as I was now further up the hierarchy, I was more resistant to the pressures I'd not been able to withstand thirty years before. My departure wasn't a sudden process. I'd always read a lot (a great deal was written about the Church at the time) and thought about the matter very seriously.

I felt the hierarchy in the convent was unreal and not based on merit but Reverend Mothers were thought to be divinely inspired. I was also living outside the convent and more able to see it objectively. From the time I'd entered the convent, I'd always got on well with men, although it was in a protected environment. I had a lot of friends and knew a lot of people with whom I could talk who were not involved with the convent.

Authority was one of the things I questioned. Poverty was another. We all made vows of poverty, chastity and obedience when we entered the convent but in some ways these were rather false. We didn't get married because the choice wasn't there in an environment which offered little opportunity. As for poverty, in our particular order we had a right to keep any property we had, though we had to ask permission to use it for what we needed. The concept of poverty within the convent was a made-up thing because although you weren't supposed to have anything of your own, you could have anything you liked, depending on your needs and how clever you were in getting round the Reverend Mother. We had good clothing and were fed well. It wasn't poverty at all because it wasn't a case of living within your income. We had more security than most people usually have, whereas real poverty contains an element of insecurity. I was far poorer when I left the convent because I could only spend what I earned and had no job at times. There was an awful lot of talk and not nearly enough helping the real poor of the world.

I felt too that nuns were 'non-people'. The ideal seemed not to develop each individual's potential but to make each conform to a set pattern, a very submissive one at that. If you conformed, you were a good nun: in other words, you had to toe the party line. Quite a lot was written at that time about repressive regimes – fascist and communist ones – and in many ways, a convent is like that too. I definitely had this feeling I wasn't a person at all but a cipher and that was equated with being a good nun, not necessarily with being a good person. I decided I was living a lie, presenting an exterior which people interpreted as being representative of a way of life which I no longer believed in. It was even worse than that, in that what people thought they saw was not in fact what a nun really was – an empty chrysalis.

I'm not sure what it means to lose one's faith. I think faith is often a belief in other people, that there is good in them and therefore good in the world. I think that is as far as I would go now in stating a faith. I still think the Christ in the Gospels was a very great man, many of whose ideas I'm prepared to accept, like loving one's neighbour and trying to forgive enemies. I certainly think most organized religions do more harm than good, I don't believe the Church is a good institution and I'm getting married in a Register Office because it would be hypocritical of me to do otherwise.

I had the advantage of being able to do something about my situation – that is, some financial backing, qualifications and contacts – all that gave me the courage to walk out in my early fifties. When I first left I was very lonely, a feeling which many people have to put up with. It was hard being a woman on her own, because I no longer fitted into a safe category nor did I fit in easily with a lot of social life. Another sister left at the same time, so we shared a flat in a house whose owners were extremely kind to us. I kept on as head for a term after I'd left the convent but I could never be anything there but a 'sister'. I could see I could not go on in this way and it was for this same reason that I left my job and moved away. I thought it would be easier to go and do something completely different away from all the associations I had with the convent, so I went on a TOPs course in business and secretarial studies. That cushioned me to some extent because I was back in an adolescent situation as a pupil and I was meeting new people, though I'd kept in contact with all my other friends and not cut myself off completely.

My first great shock after the TOPs course was the difficulty I had in finding a job. I had the illusion I would find work fairly easily, as I was well qualified and had extensive administrative experience, but no one even interviewed me. I kept this touching faith that if once I could be interviewed I would be able to get a job, but my qualifications on paper were perhaps too threatening and the image was too peculiar as an ex-nun. I wasn't able to state my case in person and dispel the illusion. Anyway, Gingerbread was prepared to take the risk and I enjoyed working there very much as an administrator. I'm at the moment chairman of the trustees for Gingerbread. Unfortunately, the pay was so lamentably poor, I couldn't afford to go on working there, so reluctantly I had to go back to teaching. I'd managed to get a house because of my father's money and a mortgage, but it was difficult making ends meet while working at Gingerbread. I was never happy about going back to teaching, but I thought it wouldn't be for too long as by then I was fifty-seven. And then I met Harry.

It had been very difficult at first to find an identity for myself. I wasn't sure how to dress or even behave and was always afraid of appearing as 'mutton dressed as lamb'. My sisters and friends had some difficulty in adjusting to my new circumstances when I left. That first year was all very exciting: people gave me lots of advice and I was busy setting myself up, but the next two or three years were far harder. I tried a number of things and had some short, rather unsatisfactory affairs which were rather shoddy somehow. They didn't mean very much to me but I felt I had to have the experience of what it was like to have a close relationship with a man.

That's the marvellous thing about being engaged now. I know I can be attractive to men in the normal way and establish a relationship of both body and spirit. I think I did know I was attractive to men while I was in the convent, but you repress any feelings like that. I knew some men were attracted to me, sometimes beyond ordinary friendship, but I was not in the position to explore it: that is, I knew by intuition I was normally attractive but I desperately needed that to be reinforced. I had an awful fear when I left the convent that I would again be nothing. I had had an identity as a nun which in itself was a problem. Roman Catholics tend to put nuns on a pedestal, so the girls at the school and many ordinary Catholics automatically respect you, but whether it was the habit you wore or the person beneath it, I wasn't at all sure. I went through various periods when I could see myself ending up as an old maid, living a half-life and not being at all fulfilled.

I have always felt quite strongly that if you want things to happen, you must do what you can to make them happen and not rely on fate to do so. I tried one or two friendship agencies. Gingerbread had provided some social life too, but the school I went to had an all male staff rather younger than me, so I wasn't in a situation where I'd be likely to meet anyone. I decided what I really wanted and needed was marriage, so I joined Prestige Partners in London and met my first introduction who was

Harry. We got on very well from the first moment and have a great deal in common. I feel terribly fortunate now and realize some of the things I missed. I have companionship and the love of someone who cares about me in a special (sort of) way. It's a tremendous boost, even though I sometimes feel very inadequate in my efforts to show all the love I have for him.

There are moments when I have tremendous regrets that I have no children of my own. I have felt that I've missed out on one aspect of a woman's potential and have not made my own contribution to a human being, but in my more rational moments I feel quite strongly that all life consists of choices and I've had a successful and fulfilled life. A great many children have passed through my hands as a teacher and maybe I've influenced them for the best. Maybe I've made some small contribution to the world. There's no point in any case in looking back with regret, because it doesn't help much and convent life wasn't all misery; in fact it was mostly quite happy.

If I'd made the change earlier, it would have been a different one. If I'd come out during my novitiate I would probably have reverted to living my life of young womanhood as I'd done up to then. There was a period in my early forties when I very nearly did leave, because it was the last chance if I was going to have children. It was round about then that I knew I would leave eventually. Instinctively I knew I would come out, but I probably did it at the right time as things have worked out. If I'd left in my forties in order to have children and then not had any, I would have had nothing left. The decision to leave when I did was made far easier because another sister left at the same time. It was her support and that of others before her, which gave me the final strength to act on my decision.

I did have a very strong conviction that I was right to leave the convent. In a way it was a reversal of what had led me into it in the first place. Then I entered because of my mother's opposition to the idea and I left it almost to show the convent I could, since I no longer believed in that way of life. I didn't have the same romantic illusions any more, and I knew it wasn't going to be easy though I suffered terrible disappointments when it wasn't. I have a very optimistic nature. I always think things will turn out all right for me. I came out with the idea I could manage, even if others couldn't, so now that I have I feel like a contented pussy-cat. I'm very happy as things are. I don't feel there are things I want to prove and I do believe you get the courage to face what you have to: that's the nearest to faith that I can get.

Kelly Anderson

When a boy-friend of one of my daughters was killed a few years ago, the girls, Philip (my son) and I all had a feeling of the inpermanence of it all. I resolved then that I would grab whatever came along, so when the chance to do a TOPs course came up, I took it because anything could happen. We've tried to do this ever since.

My parents managed through the Depression and I went to a grammar school in Middlesex and was in the first term of the sixth form taking English, French, German and Latin – they'd probably have driven me mad eventually – when I left. My parents had heard of a job in personnel at J. Lyons and were looking for a 'safe' job for me, remembering the Depression experiences. Nobody at school talked about further education, you were just there, filling up time between exams; it was unusual, looking back, that nobody there encourged you to stay on or to think about the future. I thoroughly enjoyed the office job – wages, tax, insurance and that sort of thing – until the family came.

I was married when we were both twenty and had my first child at twenty-two, eventually three girls and a boy. My husband had been a boy entrant of sixteen in the RAF. I led two lives really, one at home and the other on my own. As the girls grew up, I felt one day I would do things because I felt I had missed out, not gone anywhere or done anything. I always read a lot, and as a family we've always looked things up, but I never had any direction, there was no one to lead me.

I'd started evening classes twelve years ago, studying Russian which shocked my mother: 'What does a housewife want with Russian?' she'd said. My father was interested though and has always been supportive. During the second week of the evening class, my husband said he didn't like me going out because he wasn't used to the idea. I hadn't been anywhere for years and years on my own, always having the children with me. I said I was going anyway, which was the first time I'd done anything he didn't really want me to.

I didn't feel I would be useless when it looked as if the three girls would all leave home more or less together, but I didn't want to be a perpetual babysitter to my grandchildren. There's more to life than that. While the children were all still at home, I started on this TOPs course – audio-typing and book-keeping – for eighteen weeks. After the course, I knew I didn't want to type other people's work but be a bit original myself. I asked the tutor there if she thought I was capable of doing A-levels and she assumed I meant full-time, so I went on and took English Literature, Economic History and O-level Maths. The money I'd 'earned' on the TOPs course paid for the A-levels. Having started that, what was I going to do next? I'd still no direction in mind. I wanted to do a degree course, not just for personal gratification but with the intention of being able to use it to get a better job. It was embarrassing I was accepted at so many places, but eventually I settled for Kingston Poly because it was near home. I read Social Sciences as it covered all that I was interested in. I did like Portsmouth Poly, it had a lovely view and I felt very happy there, but I just felt it was too far to travel each day.

To start with, my husband took the view that if I wanted to do it, then I should go ahead. I hadn't worked at all while the family were at home so it wasn't a case of missing out on money. My husband never said anything to me, but a couple of years after I'd started at the Poly, I gathered from my brother-in-law that he was afraid I'd blossom out into an intellectual woman and leave him behind. I think I must have felt that, because I never talked about college work at home. It was a disadvantage living in two worlds as I didn't get any discussion which the youngsters had. They were able to talk in the subject language but I went home. I missed a lot, which was unfortunate. I had a marvellous time at college: the youngsters were very encouraging and helpful but teaching at school was nothing like at the Poly.

My main worry was whether I could keep up the course work and everything else. My mother had died ten years ago so as the only child, I used to go and see my father a lot. I didn't spend enough time in the library, because I went home and cooked meals which were eaten and there was no achievement in that. I did resent that. I worked hard at not bringing home college worries and that could be traumatic. During the first year, my eldest daughter had a baby and there was a wedding in the February of my finals year: while I managed, I couldn't do it again.

If my husband and I were reading in the evening, he would imprint on me what he was reading – even now he tells me. What should I do? Say no, I'm not interested? I just used to listen to him and think I'll read what I have to tomorrow. Whether, to him, to read is not a legitimate occupation, I'm not sure. My husband didn't regard my going to college as profitable although all my grant money went into the house; it was just something I was doing, something to amuse myself. I knew it wasn't, it was desperately important to me. It did irritate me. When I got my degree, he was thrilled to bits and bought me a gold necklace, but it didn't mean a thing because I needed help and support over the three years, not now. Then I thought, how ungrateful.

During my second year at the Poly, I saw a prospectus from Surrey University about a course there on women's assertiveness. It was fantastic. I found out how lacking in confidence even the most confident people are, which absolutely amazed me. I'd recommend the course for anybody. I learnt how to say 'No' and not feel guilty and that did a lot for me. I realized all the confident people I'd seen around me were beset by the same doubts I had. We learnt to talk to one another and cope with simple situations. During the course I began to understand that I'd been allowing people to lean on me for years and not allowing myself to be my own person, while being wife to my husband, mother to my children and daughter to my parents. I am still discovering me and am not sure whether I'll like me at all. It was very exciting but when I'm indoors now, everything starts to come in again, that's why I keep coming up to town to keep the impetus going, otherwise I'd quite happily slip back.

The course was fulfilling as a starting point for many things, such as discussions on television because I knew more about what was going on. I did feel I'd missed out on the social life in the sense that I should have done it when I was younger and learnt more from the experience. My criteria for its success would probably be whether I'd recommend someone else to do something in my position and I think I'd say yes, go ahead.

I'd had it in my mind to be a careers officer after the course because I'd met such marvellous people who'd helped the girls, but I knew by the end of the first year that my degree wouldn't be good enough to get a grant for further training. The course was at either Reading or Maidstone, which was also impossible because it was just too much hassle to be away from home four nights a week and I couldn't face commuting, so I abandoned the idea. I'm still at a loose end. I need someone to point me and make me work at something because everything I do has to be by myself and that's very hard to keep going.

I worked for five weeks at a wholesale model shop in the early autumn which I thoroughly enjoyed. Going to college gave me the confidence to do that, otherwise I couldn't have. Now I feel I can go anywhere and do anything – at least, I would have a try which I would not have before going on the course. Now any problems I am given, I try and work out.

My husband would like me to work round the corner with him at a local aircraft firm. He's always telling me about the job vacancies they've got and he even brought home an application form about three months ago, which I haven't filled in because I want to do more than that. Apart from which, I don't want to work where my husband can keep an eye on me and he would. I'd have the feeling of being watched from a distance. Anyway, I could have worked there without having done a degree.

I've sent an application to the British Museum for a job I saw advertised in the *Telegraph* for a temporary assistant. It combines all the things I'm interested in. I don't want to be in the commercial world. I thought on the train of all those people writing memos to one another and that's not productive enough for me. At the British Museum, I'd be doing something for posterity. I don't want a job where I'd be at somebody's beck and call, I've had too many years of that. I want something I can work up myself, make a place for myself in which I can become an expert. I must settle on something and make a success of that. I would like to work at the airport to help people go off to places even if I can't go.

It would be dreadful if I had to stay at home now because I couldn't get a job, having seen so much of the outside world and the interesting and boring jobs people do. I have the ability to stick at things – I stayed the course at the Poly, which everyone said was so admirable at the end of it all. It's a pity they didn't encourage me earlier on. It's sad that people can't talk to one another more.

I can't talk to my husband, I never have. He's a good provider and a good, loyal husband but I feel I've missed out on something because I haven't had his support over anything I've done. I try to support him and I think I do. I can't see any future way of life at the moment. I've got to start work and then see. My husband's very clever at making things and I think he feels that to think is not an occupation really. We're in different worlds. I didn't realize for twenty-seven out of our twenty-eight years of marriage, that he might be resentful of the fact that I had the opportunity to go to the grammar school and he didn't.

I feel a bit lost now. I can't see a way. We don't share anything. Some years ago, he was quite appalled when I said at a party that dad and I have nothing in common except the children. At the time I couldn't go back to that and explore it further and now it's so far in the distance, to bring up again. He thinks I'm awkward because I change my opinions over the years. Perhaps with children growing up and gradually pushing them out, I'm more used to change than he is. I've had more opportunity for a very changing life.

I think I'm really a bit afraid of my marriage going by the board. Before we were married my husband used to come back on leave every two weeks or so and I was very happy to see him, but I think I got a false impression of what he was like and what life would be and how I felt about him. Perhaps I was not wholeheartedly committed to him at first though I made myself be. It was probably not what I really wanted to do. I am a very restive sort of person and that's perhaps why I still am. I travelled a lot with my parents during the war and that continued while my husband was in the RAF. We've been in the same house now for seventeen years, but it's not really where I want to live though we probably won't move now. I have rarely been anywhere socially with my husband since we were married, partly because RAF sites are so remote and that sets a pattern of not doing things together. We don't know how to get into a new pattern. At weekends now, he's always so busy doing things that I'm thrown back on my own.

I still feel very constrained by family commitments; this is my own attitude, not theirs. They are completely independent. I wonder whether I'm not looking very purposefully for a job because my daughter's expecting a baby in the New Year. I never felt the children were my property but I was looking after them and helping them grow up. I don't really like children; I always got on well with mine but it had to be worked out. I felt social work was not for me because of that. I don't feel their world would fall apart if I wasn't there, but I just feel very guilty when I do something for myself: am I always going to feel like that? I bet I am.

I feel I could be of enormous help to somebody somewhere but can't find the direction or the person. There is definitely a job somewhere for me, but I just can't spot it. I'm very up in the air and don't know what to do. I feel I could tackle anything, I know I could since I've been to the Poly. I've gained an enormous number of little things that make up a large bundle of confidence.

Linda Thornber

That's a bad time, Christmas: it's bloody shitty. I hate Christmas and I hate my birthday. They're the times I miss my mother. She was one hell of a lady, my mother. Her sole object in life was that we weren't to go to 'the Mill'. She used to go into the chip shop and ask them for the crosswords off the newspaper and she'd do *The Times* crossword with no bother. Then almost the day my sister got her SRN, she turned her toes up and had the stupidity to die six weeks before David was born.

I was born in Bolton in 1940 and my mother worked in the mills, spinning. She was a doffer, which means you take off the tubes, put them back on and they fill up with cotton. My father was a professional soldier, killed in Italy in 1944. My mother remarried and I have two half-sisters who I never see, so I've no family apart from my kids. I went to school for seven years and did absolutely nothing but I was always the child who got the prize for writing; all I could do was French, English and Scripture and imitate people. I've always written, it's always been there. Then I went to college and did absolutely nothing for some more years and came out with a teacher's diploma. I taught for about four years, then I got married in 1965 which was my first accident.

I didn't like being married because I discovered I didn't like him after we'd got married. I think I loved him but I didn't like him. You had to get married then: I'd been engaged and unengaged so many times I felt like a public lavatory. This ring got worn out passing round. I knew him for about seven years and I decided as he had a degree and prospects and there was a very strong chemical attraction between us – I wanted to go to bed with him all the time – I might as well have that one. So I did. We bought a little house and I had my first baby and suddenly the marriage was over because I already had a baby and that was him. I didn't realize that until I got my second one which was really my first and it was all downhill from then.

I deliberately came off the pill and had John because I didn't want to be left alone with just one child, I wanted to be left alone with two. I threw him out on Jubilee Day. And that was it, but he made sure he had someone to go to. They always make sure they have a thick mattress to fall on. And now he's married to someone who looks right and says the right things to the managing director and doesn't object to wearing dead animals. I'm very, very against killing animals simply to wear them. I used to give lectures in lavatories about that. I was the most awful bloody wife for a company man. As far as looking after a man I couldn't organize a piss-up in a brewery. I ran his diary very well and made sure he was always in the right place in the right suit at the right time, that side of it fascinated me. But as far as saying the right things I couldn't do it. I don't bear close inspection.

I waited so long to be free of the marriage because you just go on and there was nowhere else to go and it isn't something which just happens to you. At the end of one of those days, you can't stand any more but you've just got to wait for that to come. You want out and you don't, because he's part of the structure of your life and there's still something there at the end of all that because you've been really close in a lot of ways. Mentally and emotionally we weren't just parallel lines, we were going off at different angles and our tastes were very, very different. I couldn't sit in a room if he was playing his modern jazz and he didn't go a bundle on my Prokofiev. We lived completely separate lives.

I was led to believe I was ill after I'd had David, my first. I was depressed, so I started going to head shrinkers and polling around various hospitals saying, 'I'm not happy; I'm very depressed; life is a long tunnel and there's no light at the end of it' and sort of silly things like that. The first fellow put electrodes on my head and I went off him. Another one said there was nothing wrong. I was great but I got worse. By this time I was expecting a baby and Frank said I'd finally flipped and took me off to Walton where I saw a lady and talked for hours. She said there was absolutely nothing wrong with me and I wasn't really neurotic but what was wrong with my husband and my marriage? I said there was nothing wrong with Frank but the marriage was a separate thing and a lot was wrong with that. And I was seven months pregnant. I made up my mind, no matter what happened, it was over. And I had the baby by caesarian section in a private hospital and that night Frank was in a hotel in bed with Dorothy Houghton, to whom he is now married, and he didn't know I was dying or the baby was dying. I think the hatred set in then. I knew there were a lot of women but that didn't particularly bother me.

I joined the Liberal Party and had various other illnesses and put all my energies into charities like the NSPCC so that I didn't have to be in the house when he was there and vice versa and we split the babysitting lark. But I still like him. He's done very well and I admire that. Then I got rid of him in 1977 and spent about six months sitting very still thinking about what I'd done. John was about twenty months when Frank left. Then I sold the matrimonial home because I thought it wasn't fair for me to sit in large detached splendour and he had nothing. So I bought a little house round the corner, moved there and continued to sit very still, mostly because my foot was broken at the time!

Anything was better than living with Frank because we were just so far apart. All we did was get on one another's nerves. I was working all the time I ever could, travelling all over the place to teach, taking David with me. I spent all my money on things for the house and I wasn't getting anything back and I think he felt the same. He was putting a lot of time into his job and coming home to a non-person, each to the other was a non-person. My favourite day was Saturday because he went off then to see his mother and took David with him. That kid up there, he's my life now. I worship him and him five years old. I made up my mind to have that one. David's like me with his father's brains and that's an impossible animal. He needed his dad so I sent him off down the road back to him, for the best.

When I was on my own at first, I couldn't see very far and my main worry was would the alimony keep coming? Would I or would I not be able to pay the gas bill, things like that kept me alive. I just lived from day to day. I thought one day I might have to go back to teaching when John was five but I hoped not, because although I liked teaching, I didn't want to do it any more. I knew there was something else I wanted to do but I didn't know what it was. I thought it was acting.

It was hard on my own, the social life was just gone. I tell you, when it hurts is when your little one realizes all these dads are coming home and he hasn't got one. I feel guilty about that. I hadn't been out socially from June 1977 to September 1978 when everyone persuaded me that it wasn't in my best interests to stay in the house all the time. I didn't look like this then. I was very pretty. It's awfully sad this, really. He'd been the managing director of the only industry in the village so everyone you met knew who you were and wasn't it a shame? I got to the stage I felt *de trôp* and didn't go to dinner parties any more or the Ladies' Circle. Anyway, they dragged me out and I was stoned out of my mind at ten o'clock and I didn't drink but this was to get me to the village hall. A chap took me, a beautiful looking bloke and he was single, so it was all above board. I fell through the door and saw this man and I'd been in a play with him years before – *When We Were Married*. I looked at him and I thought, I want him and that was it and that's the reason I write, just because of that moment.

It only happens in Mills and Boon, doesn't it? So I walked past him and thought, sod him, and two hours passed and when it was chucking-out time, a voice said, 'Are you going to put down that cigarette and dance with me?' As I was stoned out of my mind, I had to cling on to him. All those things happened that should have happened when I was sixteen or seventeen and I was thirty-bloody-eight! And I felt I was right over the bloody hump. That was it, all the road downhill from here. But it was a lovely feeling. I was in love for the first time in my life and I was thirty-bloody-eight and divorced and he was married with three flaming kids and she was standing there. He got my phone number out of me because I was stoned and he just never stopped. It was murder! Poetry on the phone, bottles of Guinness with the milk, gave him a key and he'd be in and out, just as he pleased. Then he told her he was leaving her for me. First of all he told her he had a mistress but she didn't care. It was like wading through custard. Then he told her it was me and he was leaving the following July after Henry had done his O-levels. She said you either go now or you stay, so I made him stay. And then I started writing this very sad stuff which immediately turned to comedy and that's why I write because I gave him back and I shouldn't have done that. I should have taken him, but I don't think I could have written all those sad things which turned to comedy, if I had.

It was a severe reaction, writing, to a total nervous breakdown. I think it's a symptom of a deep-rooted psychological disorder of which I won't recover – I'm pulling your leg now. I did start to write because I couldn't face the village. I was apart. I stayed in the house. Everywhere I went, I saw him. It's a difficult thing to live in a village so I moved here, only fifteen miles away. So now I'm frantically losing weight for when he comes back and then I'll jump in with both bloody feet. That's what's behind it all. I've had a lot of men since and I've put on a bit of weight but I can't do it now, I've forgotten. Life is so sad you've got to turn the coin over and make it funny, otherwise you're just finished.

And I had a very sad childhood too, absolutely tragic, but I was brought up by Irish people who always laughed all the time no matter what happened. So, it's in the blood, this hilarity. But I cry a lot as well, on my own at night. I don't like it on my own at all but I won't take second, third or fourth best or anything else. It would have to be someone like that next time. I don't like the idea of staying on my own, I don't belong on my own. I just had one bad marriage and I'm hoping I could have a good one and that it doesn't mean I don't just plain like marriage. I'm hoping I just didn't like that one and I'll be able to get married again, because I don't fancy sitting in that damn chair working at the typewriter when I'm sixty.

I wouldn't advocate this loneliness. I wouldn't say to a woman of thirty-eight, go on and try it. If it happens, that's OK, but don't force it. Being alone is an art because it's very depressing and writing has been an antidote, because I sit there killing myself with laughing. With 'Ballyskillen' at some stages I just had to leave the room picturing Frank Carson doing it. I don't know you could do this with another adult in the house, or get up at three in the morning because you've thought of something. I think some women like being married and all that and more power to their elbow. We need them, otherwise society would collapse. I really do believe in marriage: it's a sensible unit to work from if you can stabilize it. Unfortunately, I wasn't very good at the management: managing the day-to-day, I couldn't be bothered because I was too damn lazy. I was a bad wife. The writing would suffer but I'd love a man of my own that cared about me; it'd be lovely, that's what it's all about. But I don't want another bloody marriage like that one, so I'm twice as frightened at forty I suppose. I don't go much on this on-your-own bit but it helps my writing and there are other little freedoms.

I love being with him. I always thought it was in books that you saw someone who's the other half of you and the tragic thing is, it does just happen once and it's too late. It's too late because Amanda's only ten. If the time ever comes when he's walking out of there, I'll pick him up and bring him here but I can't carry him out of there. He's got to walk across that bridge on his own. I won't even encourage him at the moment. I want him to come because it's finished there and he thinks there's something here. I still feel the same way and I haven't seen him for two years. He's made me feel more joy and more misery than anyone's ever done. Knowing him has jolted me into doing what I should have done before.

I started to write at the end of April 1980. From the end of 1977 I didn't do a lot. One of the first things I did was make a lot of tapes in Lancashire and 'Scouse' because I always wanted to do my own stuff. I wanted to do something purely creative, using nothing except my mind and things I remembered and that's what I'm doing. Everything's triggered off by some memory or something you've read, nothing's fresh. I'm just using myself. I'm very proud of that, using no tools. I think that's what I wanted to do, but I don't really know yet, there may be something else. The pieces I wrote were getting funnier and funnier and I wrote my famous novel in longhand which is sitting in the cupboard over there. Then I stopped writing when I moved here. One day my friend Lynn who's an author in Rainford, was being filmed by Granada. The director who came to measure her up asked if she knew anyone who could write Liverpool comedy. Within twenty-four hours I sent in a script and I was phoned and asked to 'finish it and for God's sake, learn to type'. Clive and I worked on them until I'd done about five, then he showed them to Stephen Leaky who said could I do one about a theatre in Ireland with Frank Carson as manager. I didn't go to bed for the next twenty-four hours and turned in a script which was competing with eight other writers. And I got it. So it was only four months between actually being asked to have a go at TV to getting the commission. I was very lucky. It's not all talent because it's where you are and who you know at the right time. Now I'm chasing work, touting for business, that's the worst part of being a freelance writer. The thing about teaching, although you have to put up with the little buggers from nine to four, you do get paid. This way is unsure, insecure and very exciting and I wouldn't give it up for the world. I would be nice to have a regular commission, 'Coronation Street' or something like that, and time to do my own stuff as well.

As for the future, I want to be Carla Lane again but not just in comedy. It's a lovely present when you do get a commission, it's part of the game but unnerving. It gives you a sense of being in charge because you've done it yourself and you don't have to thank anybody either. My drama's fairly heavy. I enjoy it because it gets something out of the system. I'd like to write a book some day, to dramatize something that's based on fact and give it my own bit of salad cream. I'm not very good with facts, as I tend to shoot off on my own.

But working on television's like a drug. I love it. It's a real 'upper' being in the studio. 'Ballyskillen' was one of the most beautiful things I've ever seen, though I've reservations about the finished product. They bought this old theatre from Oldham and took it to the studio. I watched them working and all because their lines and actions came out of my head. It's not exactly power, more a sense of wonder it's all happening. That's why television's magic. I listen to people breathing life into my flat pieces of paper, but it's terrible when you have to come down after it's all over, the two worlds don't belong. They took a hammer to my theatre and knocked it down and I cried. I'd never shown any emotion up to then except to thank them all but when it was all over I cried and cried. When it was on television, I used to feel terribly ill, going through all the lines the night before. It was hard watching, but I want to do it again but better next time.

I don't think you could do anything like this suddenly without being forty. I've sat and thought why the bloody hell didn't I write ten years ago, silly cow, and I could have written all those books. But if I look back to when I was thirty or thirty-two, I had things to say and I was finding things out, but compared to now I was bloody adolescent, a complete bloody kid. I hadn't really lived through anything worth talking about or worth comparing with anything else. It's only when I really suffered, and I have suffered over the last five or six years, really suffered – life has not been pretty – that I started to see anything funny in it at all. But suddenly, and it was suddenly, my attitude changed; I'm talking about the last eighteen months or so. I didn't see life as plodding along that dark tunnel any more and you had to get to the end of it. Seriously, there were days when my older child was younger, I hoped I wouldn't wake up in the morning. I couldn't have killed myself because that's not in my nature, but within the last couple of years I've begun to realize there's black and white and a hell of a lot of shades of grey in between. I don't know whether it's because I'm getting older or it's maturity or what. By turning something over and looking at it from another angle, somebody's suffering becomes someone else's enjoyment. Broadly speaking, comedy is just drama without death. I love comedy because if you can make people laugh you've cracked it. As long as you can make them cry as well. In the last episode of 'Ballyskillen', I hope there wasn't a dry eye in Ireland or the whole of the North East.

And that's another thing, you get loved. It's a way of getting loved without being touched. You have a sense of value and people respect you. But to get all this straight in your head, you've really got to be older. If it happened to me like it's happened to Victoria Wood, at her age, it would have blown my mind instead of being in control as I am now. I still see the black side. I couldn't write comedy if I didn't. I cried a lot more when I was young than I do now and really you're crying for yourself, though it's nice to be able to pin it on something all the same. I think you have to be really old in the head to be able to see the funny side of things.

I want to be a successful writer and at whatever else occurs. I'd no staying power at thirty. I'd take up something like the Liberal Party, then drop it. My doctor says I put on blinkers and keep on going like a great big carthorse. And it's not just when your kids are grown-up either: it's something that happens on a day which isn't in any way controlled by your conscious self but you make a decision. There's a trigger sometimes – my particular one was falling in love at thirty-eight. It would have happened anyway because it was always there. I would have been annoyed with myself if I'd gone to my grave without ever publishing anything, and I think it's been a matter of letting it surface. You haven't got it when you're young: ability's one thing but acquiring purpose is another.

One of the things that happened in the last few months was losing David. I couldn't have coped a few years ago, giving up a child, but I knew it was better for him to be with his father and I made up my mind and came to terms with it. I think about him a lot but the sensible side of me says it's got to be done. There's no way I can offer anyone stability or predictability. I'm too lazy to be firm.

I don't put a lot of effort into relationships. I like to watch. It's like a nice piece of china which you pick up and look at, then put down and go on to the next item. I suppose I'm rather cold and that's why it was so shattering when I was thirty-eight because I don't do things like that. I don't feel things about people as individuals. I just theorize and categorize and walk away. I think there's something lacking in me when it comes to personal relationships.

I am fond of Carol. I do feel something for her and if anything happened to her, I think I'd curl up and die. She gives me a great deal of strength outside of me. We support one another. I don't think I'd develop a relationship like that with any other woman now, but she was there at the right time and the right place. I'm probably closer to her than I ever was with Frank, though in a completely different way. I suppose it's like having a sister. I know people but I have no friends, never have had. I pretend not to mind but I think I do, being so lonely. As for men friends, I don't know what I'm looking for in other people, but I have this strong sense of superiority which must be misguided for me to feel so different from other people.

I would like to need other people enough to go and find them and go to those clubs. I would like to be able to communicate with other people on all levels: I can't. I'd be bored out of my mind in ten minutes. I get through the day-to-day but I'm not sure that's self-sufficiency. I've done all the sorts of things that single people do, like going to singles clubs, but I stopped that when I found I was becoming social secretary.

I couldn't come to terms with being fat because I'm not fat underneath and besides, it's bad for you. I've always had a weight problem but it became worse after I had David and I went to Weight Watchers and lost about forty pounds. After Frank and I separated, I actually lost weight, then it started to creep on. I have a theory though, that after I met Ted, I must have made a decision it was safer to be a fat lady because no one expects much of you. You just sit around all day and nobody sees you as a person. It's very safe. Men don't want you if you're fat and they think you don't want them. So I didn't have any trouble after Ted left because I've been fat, but I've decided not to be. If I'm going to be rich and famous, I'm going to be rich and famous and thin. I want to be on the other side of the camera, but I won't while I look like this. I wasn't bothered until all this happened but they're all so slim. I don't like my physical image at all, I find it disgusting – that's come with the writing and working desperately to be a success. I don't want to be a success and be like Hattie Jacques, basically I'd like to present a nicer-neater image. The doctor has no doubts I'll do it – and I will.

June Barry

My childhood was a very happy one, fairly ordinary and I was well adjusted; my brothers and sisters contributed greatly to that. Because I was so much the youngest, it was almost as if I had three fathers and three mothers. I left school with no great aspirations: I've never been the kind of person to pursue academic qualifications. I love life and everything which contributes towards making a well filled life. I found a job as an assistant in a pharmacy and a mentor who helped me tremendously – a 'gardener' as the Industrial Society would put it. I never became a qualified pharmacist because I didn't like all the things which went with that but I enjoyed the work and had a great feeling of satisfaction helping other people. This was in the North East and Don and I weren't yet married. Then he had to go and do his National Service.

During the war, I'd lived in Cheltenham with one of my brothers and liked it very much, being very different from Sunderland. To some extent my decision to find a job in Cheltenham while Don was on National Service, was a sign I was beginning to do things my way. It was the first time I'd left home and I was a very, very immature twenty-year-old. I'd never been encouraged to do anything for myself and the first thing I did was to send my mother some flowers, recognizing just how much she'd put into the job. I was there four to five years, very happily: I've always been lucky in enjoying the work I do. Then Don applied for a job anywhere but in the North East and we went to Huntingdon. I got a job. We were married and we found a flat. We'd been going out for seven years on the basis we'd have more money put aside to get married, but we ended up with fifteen shillings between us. From there we built our first house in a beauty spot near Cambridge.

I worked for six years after we were married and I very strongly wanted a family by then. Don felt I'd be a better woman if I had a family, so we embarked on Lisa, Joanne three years later and finally Graeme three years after that. At this time Don had to qualify for a second time in order to become a chartered surveyor, for it to be possible for him to become a partner later on. I stopped work when we started a family and enjoyed being a mother and being part of village life. I always thoroughly enjoyed my children and I think we've been very successful in achieving a happy family life generally speaking. My great boast at this time was that I had no problems; I would have been hard put to present one. Then Don was offered promotion in Leeds. I have always believed firmly that you must support your husband whatever your own personal views may be, on the basis that because he has looked after you, you owe him that support. We opted to live in Harrogate rather than Leeds, and at that point I found difficulty in settling down. I was just coming up to forty.

I'm not sure why it was so difficult for me but I did feel the children were growing away from me. They had new schools, Don his new job and I had no one somehow. I made a friend after two or three months and I got in the way of going to the pub at lunch-time and generally doing awful mundane things like coffee mornings and women's groups, with no real satisfaction gained from any of it. I had never been a frustrated female but I began to feel I was becoming one. I was less easy to live with, finding myself at screaming pitch and then wondering why. It slowly dawned on me that I wasn't happy because things were so different. Don found it difficult because he felt as if I was blaming him, that he had failed in some way – and Barrys never fail! I desperately needed someone to relate to. Someone who could see me as me and who could sympathize without being emotionally involved.

At that point, I thought we must do something about this and I saw this part-time job advertised, applied and got it. I think what really pushed me into getting a job was standing at the sink one Sunday morning, with the children and their friends going in and out, in and out, not seeing me. I could have been anyone standing there and I realized I had to take stock. I had become used to being needed and assumed I'd always be, but the children were no longer of an age when they could be channelled in the direction I wanted them to take. Don objected to his time with me being encroached upon: all men are babies and need to feel needed but if you run a democratic household, it becomes increasingly difficult to find a place to be in alone together. Don began to go through middle age and I think men are much worse than women during that period. He continually needed his ego boosted. It was like having four children instead of three and in the end, I found myself thinking I must find a space for me to be me. I had this great urge to be me. Death seemed very close. I'd become more aware of it when my mother and father died within a month of each other. I thought if I'm going to achieve anything in my life, I've got to do it now. No one's going to look at a fifty-five-year-old bag; I'm more likely to get a job at forty-two.

When I was put on the short list for the job, Don was very pleased that justice had been seen to be done and we could all go back to how we were before. The children were amazed anyone would want to employ me and every day for the first month,

Graeme asked me if I'd got the sack. They thought I was playing at it as being part-time, it didn't obtrude too much although I was a wee bit more bustly. I think I am a very good mother but I know I've failed deplorably in some areas. I've never insisted upon the children doing household chores too much. I probably should have done this with my husband as well but at the time it wasn't important to me; though it would have been very good for him.

One of the things I discovered on going back to work after fifteen years' absence was difficulty in taking orders from younger people. I hadn't thought of this as a problem at all. It never occurred to me, but I knew instinctively I had to get rid of the situation. I wasn't aware of working towards that, but I knew I had certain assets in terms of maturity and experience of working with people, so I began making inroads into the hierarchy. I made myself pleasant and noticed. It was probably devious of me but having been in charge of a family so many years, I was not used to taking orders.

The firm was a photocopying bureau, an off-shoot of a printing company, and business began to expand and opportunities occur soon after I joined. The management was very liberated and tried hard to be democratic, making its employees part of the decision-making process. At the time of its expansion, the company decided to change its image. The opportunity came when a second branch was opened in Leeds and they were looking for a new manageress in Harrogate. I was distressed a new manageress was not going to be taken from existing personnel and dreaded the thought of another bright young thing in charge. I told the managing director why I was upset and said I could do the job better. Bob told me if I would come full-time, the job was mine. So eight months after I'd joined the firm, I became manageress.

I discussed the situation fully with Don and said he would have to make adjustments as I couldn't do the job unless I was fully committed to it. I had enormous guilt feelings about apparently rejecting my family after they'd all been so kind and whether it would be fair to them to come back to an empty house. Don didn't care too much about my part-time work but I knew there'd be repercussions if the meal wasn't ready on time. The children coped beautifully and were very supportive. The first thing I bought was a deep fryer and a slow cooker and they learnt to cook over the phone. As the business expanded and became more sophisticated, inevitably it began to infiltrate into domestic life.

Don didn't really know what had hit him. It was a more salutary experience for him than me, yet he seemed to be losing all round, except for the money, which he did like. There were times when we were friends and could meet on neutral territory. He admitted I was more interesting, but he was disappointed it needed more outside influence to make me put on make-up before nine in the morning. He was fascinated in spite of himself, amazed that anyone could consider employing me, take me seriously and regard me as worthwhile. He's never really taken me seriously, always working hard academically himself and finding it difficult to accept that I had no time for this and so thought I had nothing in my mind. I didn't want to know about household accounts, he saw to that. Holidays were arranged and bills paid and I never knew how he did it. He was very happy for me and I tried very hard not to neglect him but he had to adjust because as an only child as well, everything's always been done his way and he's never had to step back and let someone else take the limelight.

One of the problems I had, I think, was that I took an awfully long time to mature. I had been cosseted for a long time as the baby of the family. When I left home, I'd never even washed a pair of nylons for myself or cooked a meal, though I knew how from school. When I left the family, Don took over. My first experience of 'real' life was having a child. When I was told I'd have to have a 'caesar', I thought it was the most awful thing which could happen. I should have begun to make a stand earlier in life because it would have made the last five years far easier if I had. I was pre-conditioned that wives run after husbands.

The strange part of making a change like this is having made a step forward, there's no way you can go back. I've found strength in myself I didn't know I possessed. I didn't know I could be so hard or fight so hard. And it got harder as we went along. Don still felt responsible for me and insisted on picking me up from work which he hated because, without realizing it, he objected to these new interests in my life which he wasn't part of. He disappointed me when he behaved like this. I felt resentful towards him because it was so humiliating. I'd always supported him, and began to think he wouldn't do the same for me. There were times when I found myself on the front doorstep and I'd have to force a smile on my face, sailing in as if I'd had a great day. Even now Don can't see me shattered. He gets cross if he sees me upset, but he can't find words to say he's upset on my behalf, as what comes through is 'I'm upset with you and why are you making me upset?' That still has to be dealt with. He's trying very hard and it's coming. But he still objects very much that my work is very important to me and obtrudes into his time with me. Emotionally I still need his approval and it's important to me, so if it really comes to the crunch and his life was shattered because of my job, I would give it up – but I'd fight hard before I did that.

It's taken about two years for Don to come to terms with this. I had to keep reminding him at first that we had discussed my working full-time. He always treated my work as a trifle, but over the past year he's seen that other people think I'm doing a good job. In some ways, I think he thinks I've achieved more in my job than he has in his, because for a time I think he felt he hadn't got the recognition he either wanted or deserved. He felt very vulnerable because I was achieving that recognition and he wasn't, a lot of male pride came into that. Basically he was very pleased and he always told other people how good I was, but never me. Now he's become a partner, things have become easier. I think there is some professional rivalry and jealousy because he doesn't like me to have more perks than he does.

A further difficulty lies in the fact that ninety-five per cent of our customers are men. It's not easy for Don to come into the office and find me in close proximity with other men. It was difficult for him to share me with the children when they came along and it's hard now for him to share me in some senses, professionally, with men at work. Don doesn't really like me to do anything but relate to him, which is flattering after so many years together but a bit claustrophobic as well. We're lucky to have a marriage where we can talk: it takes an unusual or a very weak man to cope with a wife working full-time.

We did reach a point when I said I'll give up my job. At the time I felt resentment towards him that he'd put me in that position. Don is accepting much more, though I have to be careful and not let things get out of proportion. I'm still in the early part of my working life, only three years altogether. I have little time for my house now. Don thinks I don't care, but I have to sort out the priorities continually.

It took me quite a long time to become a good manageress. I did it intuitively, running the girls as I run my house, like a second 'Mum' to them. I am really very fortunate in having a good boss who's also a 'gardener' and never hesitates to tell me when I go wrong. I put everything into it because I'm determined not to be beaten. I had had thoughts about becoming manageress and had formulated my thoughts towards that point, but when Bob told me they would like to make me a director, I was overwhelmed. I had no thoughts at all of going any further and still find it hard to think of myself in that way.

Whereas four years ago I wouldn't have accepted every challenge, I do now. The Industrial Society ran a course for the firm which was very instructive and then I went on a finance and accountancy course and learnt a lot about big business and trade unions, though not a lot about finance. Then I went on a three-day Pepperell course run by the Industrial Society for women in management. It was the most fabulous experience. At the end of the course, eighteen Maggie Thatchers went off to conquer the world. It helped with the girls at work and with the children at home too. My first action note after the course was to the effect that I'd aim to become managing director – not altogether facetiously. I've done great battles since I've been on that course and as the only woman manager in an aggressive man's world, I have to fight like a man. I now accept that no quarter's given because I'm a woman. I still don't find it easy and have learnt to speak at meetings as soon as possible and to prepare a good case beforehand, never be tentative. I've never had the worry of having to keep my job because I'm doing it because I want to, not because I have to, and this gives me a more casual approach towards money. In those areas, men take advantage of women because they don't tend to stand up for their rights as men do. Men think in black and white and you have to stop being a woman, muddling through. It's necessary to have training courses for women, because they help you stand up for your rights and think things through and have more faith in yourself. Now I quite enjoy doing battle. It's generally a disadvantage being so small, but big men are very receptive towards me and by the time they take me seriously, the battle's won.

I think our marriage is on quite a different standing from five years ago and that's probably the biggest reaction to the change. I do believe in myself now and if, for instance, I don't go along with Don's suggestion, I say so. I never used to. He's not used to me fighting, but I do it without thinking now because I do it at work and it spills over into private life. Don does feel threatened by my changes because he doesn't make friends easily and he felt I might grow away from him. I am his best friend, almost his only friend and he is mine. My going to work and becoming a more self-sufficient person has helped him. We've been able to discuss things more because he sees me as more of an equal, though he's not taken kindly to the change. I am an entirely different person from the one he married. I know my strengths and weaknesses more. I've had to take stock and become more confident. Don's had to get used to living with a different person in many ways.

Sheila Dainow

I think the quality which privileged women like us have and which makes us change our lives, is a feeling of dissatisfaction. I've never been satisfied in a total way, nor do the women I identify with feel satisfied. There must always be something else. The worst condition to be in must be to feel dissatisfied but not to know what to do about it and that's where people like us could have such an enormous influence. We can help people realize you can change if you want to, show them it is possible. I've no interest in changing someone who feels satisfied with him- or herself and then becomes dissatisfied as a result.

There are two main points in my life when I've changed most: the first was in my twenties when I got married. What happened then was that I realized I needn't always be the same person. I found marriage very freeing; being with someone who really valued me, which I had never felt before, with someone who had no vested interest in me becoming the sort of person he wanted, and this allowed me to develop. In my twenties, I felt I could change and I began to be more confident: the age-old maxim that in discovering someone loves you, you can then begin to love yourself, was true for me. I worked for six or seven years in the Youth Service which was also a freeing experience, being with people who were more interested in other people than in things. I had my first child when I was twenty-six, which was quite late for that time. All of my peer group had had children by then and although I did want children, I have an awful feeling that I had mine because everybody else was having them. For a year, I did nothing but be a mother with a young baby, which was the time I enjoyed most about having children. But by the end of that year, I realized I couldn't go on in that way without doing something else or having another child. I was quite clear, I didn't want one at that point.

Then I started to get involved with the part-time training of youth workers which was just becoming developed by the ILEA. It was all very casual and haphazard, but I began to get involved with the self-awareness movement, about fifteen years or so ago now. The ideas then were all very ill-formed and although I understood the potential for human development by becoming more self-aware, I didn't realize in any way its ultimate importance for me. It was this area which I developed most during my thirties and forties and was really due to the people I met when I was working.

The second biggest change occurred while I worked for the FPA, but I find it hard to define exactly what it is. I had started helping out at a clinic in a voluntary capacity, then saw in the house magazine a vacancy for a job as an information officer. I was looking for a part-time job which I could run from home and which was paid and interesting, so I could have begun working at anything else as it happens. What was significant about working with the FPA was meeting people in the Education Unit and their reliance and excitement at my ideas. I had developed by then a lot of thoughts about how it was possible to help people become more in control of their lives, which I see as the really powerful force, but they were largely untested ideas. I was given the opportunity to develop those ideas partly through courses I ran and partly through the atmosphere at the Education Unit which was conducive to exploration.

My interest in counselling was a gradually evolving one and was something which stayed around for about ten years or so in my mind until four years or so ago, when I realized that I could make something significant about it for me. For quite a long time, they were attractive theories but in my late thirties, I realized the biggest jump I could make would be to make the theories work for me, in lots of ways. I realized it was a way I could not only earn my living but it could help me become more powerful and more satisfied with myself.

Around my late thirties I went into a very depressive state. What I felt was if I'd had the opportunity to know what I knew then, I wouldn't have got married. For a while I felt myself to be in a fairly boring relationship in marriage in contrast to all the exciting and different people I was then meeting. One thing I was very clear about and am clear about now, is that I would not have had children. I've done a real full circle about my marital relationship and I think it is a good one for me: whether I've made it like that or it always was, I don't know. Cyril is consistent, very reliable and a caring person and when I have fantasies about the excitement of living with someone who's more mercurial and more dynamic, I know now that I couldn't really cope with that.

The question of children is more problematic and I haven't really worked that one out. I'm aware too that the grass is always greener. I wouldn't want to send back the children I've got because I'm very fond of them and I think they're valuable people, but I do feel burdened by the responsibilities they bring, especially during the last two years since my eldest has been edging towards independence. Sometimes, and I feel a bit ashamed to admit it, I feel bored by all of it. I fulfil the tasks of motherhood quite well and provide a reasonable base for them, but I often get bored with adolescent traumas and find it a real nuisance. I do feel shamefaced about admitting that and sometimes feel absolute panic when a lot of the work I do is about the effect of early conditioning in our lives. I do believe that whatever we do to our children, they will still have to fight their own battles which, in an odd sense, makes very little difference what the parents do, providing the basics are there.

My fantasy used to be that things got better as the children grew older. The shock lies in the recognition that they actually get more difficult. I have had to be consciously aware that I'm the most important person for me and if I don't look after me, nobody else will. I could sink into just looking after the children, but I need to make decisions all the time which allow me to develop the kind of life I want to live, alongside the one which provides the obvious needs of the children.

An area for me that is very important is my feelings about my mother, who is becoming one of my dependants and that's going to be a problem. It seems that for people of our age we have a lot of adult dependants: children struggling to get away and parents struggling to get closer and you are in the middle. My fantasy is that my children will leave and my mother will come and I will never be free of dependants. What I hope is, that I shall retain as much self-consciousness with my mother as I have with my children. Probably you have to work much harder to remain adult, as an adult with your parents, as you both grow older.

Coming back to the time I was depressed, I had a series of physical symptoms and I thought I was physically ill. What I know now is that they were classic depression symptoms – palpitations, panic, and so on. So I went to the doctor who told me I was depressed. I said rubbish. Until then I had no notion I was actually depressed. Perhaps one of the biggest good fortunes I had at that time was a very good doctor who suggested that I should go to a therapist, but I was so well conditioned I didn't do that for a long time. All along, Cyril dealt with the situation very well, constantly urging me to do a lot of things and not to feel my duty lay in the home. His attitude throughout was that he would help in whatever way possible to organize the house in order for me to do what I decided to do. I'm very aware because of this experience, that there are lots of women who don't have this kind of support.

In the end I went to the psychiatrist for a very, very short while and he told me I wasn't mad, which was all the therapy I needed. From that assurance, I could work on the rest myself.

Around the same time, I started a part-time counselling course at which all the teaching was about self-awareness; it wasn't purely didactic. I found myself in a group of people who were all interested in the process of looking at and explaining themselves to themselves and I was given permission for one day a week to do the same. A lot of things began to come together at that point and led me to think that I wanted to help people achieve the same thing because it was so valuable.

During this depressive period, I never felt I wanted to get away because I never felt restricted at home. I wasn't living with someone who restricted me in any way and I was in a job which allowed me to be away on long courses in the provinces, so my therapy was being back home. Cyril was constantly saying things like if you want to get away, do it, but I didn't need to. I think the feeling of wanting to get away can be produced as much by the feeling that you can't escape: my feeling was that I could go anywhere and in that sense, it was hard because the choice was so wide.

One thing that contributed to this feeling of depression was my age: it was suddenly very important when I was about thirty-nine. Before that I had always felt extraordinarily contemptuous of women who felt obsessed with age, but when I was forty, I bloody knew it and I didn't like it. It was highly significant for me that around that time, I and a group of other women I was working with, decided to start a counselling company of our own. It was my way of telling myself that we could alter something ourselves.

The idea of starting a company wasn't a lifelong ambition, but something which developed from a wish that I wanted to work with people I liked and whose work I respected, and in an area we all wanted to work in. Those ideas came together around the time I was working with the FPA. Then I was thinking about creating a structure within which we could do the sort of work we wanted to. I discussed this with people who wanted to do this with me over a long tentative period. Skills with People as a company was actually created when I was involved with exercises about what you really want to do and how you go about achieving that. I think now, after our first counselling course we initiated as a group, we have a successful future and something we could only do as a group.

Age does have certain obvious advantages in not having to care too much about what other people think of you. It has certain disadvantages like not being so fit, so quick physically, and I find I get tired around ten at night. I know too that there are certain things I'll never do now and I sometimes feel regretful about that. But it's no longer an issue like it once was. Yet I know that in about five years' time, I could go off on a jag and I'd actually have more money and more experience to enjoy it. I do get twinges of envy occasionally when I look at the girls and think about all the things opening up for them. I am conscious now of fewer first times opening up for me, like your first sexual experience, but equally well I feel sure there are still other firsts around.

By contrast, my main feeling when I was adolescent was that I would never be able to do anything. Nobody thought or recognized I was bright, neither teachers nor parents: they were too involved with scraping a living and the fact that I might be someone or do something didn't arise. Part of the pattern of my childhood was being a late developer. I never shone at school and I was never put in touch with any ideas involving further education. I didn't begin to do my learning until I got married in my twenties. Since then it's been a more or less continuous process, with great leaps of insight sandwiched by long years of foraging away. I went into youth work because it was there and it was more fulfilling than office work I had done up to then. I went into it not really understanding it could be a career or have some influence on me. I didn't order or control my life in any way.

Lack of confidence was the condition which influenced everything for me. It was tied up with how I thought people saw me and therefore with my image. Confidence began to be developed when I was married, from the point of view that someone obviously thought enough of me to marry me. Cyril was very concerned that I should become more confident, and it was from about twenty or so that I began to see myself as a valuable person. Looking back on when I was growing up, I was concerned with the fact I wasn't important, that's a better word than confidence. I was there, but that was all. It was something to do with my generation being concerned with surviving another day during the war. It wasn't until I reached my twenties that I realized I was important to others and therefore became important to myself.

At some point I must have heard somebody say, 'You're important', and gradually I must have understood that it's possible to learn that of oneself. For a while I was very cynical and sceptical about it but then I discovered it was true. When I was working at the FPA I discovered I was good at making complex theories available to people for whom they were not as accessible. The discovery that I was good at this and at teaching was immensely exciting, not only for me, but that it could be so significant for other people as well.

I feel very satisfied at the moment, having discovered this, but don't in any way feel I've come to a full stop. I feel as if I've reached a point and I'm taking off from it as well. I think the social climate now is more conducive than it's ever been before for women to make changes in their lives, but maybe that's to do with class and education as well. All of my close circle of friends are highly privileged and have time to spend on their own development. On the other hand, I meet numbers of women who feel so circumscribed by their working lives that they feel they have no freedom to make any changes.

I think the problem for men is they don't have time to change like women. The big advantage for women like you and me is when we have children, we discover we have time. Most men are totally concerned with earning their living, so when the hell do they get the time? I can see satisfaction in that, which women on the whole don't have. Maybe because of the working pattern of most men's lives, they don't have the same need to explore themselves like women.

Now I feel quite proud of what I've achieved. During my depressed time I felt very low about not having any qualifications or education even, and felt that lack to be the barrier to doing anything worthwhile. I don't feel that at all now and in fact have a real resistance to doing anything about it. I don't want to take a degree, though I expect I could if I wanted to. Part of it is that I want to be able to provide a model for people in my position: I think I've achieved an enormous amount for someone who left school at fifteen. The assumption often is that I have a degree and I like the effect it has on people when they learn that I haven't. Possibly I've been fortunate in historical terms as well, in that I've entered jobs which didn't need formal qualifications at the time.

Women friends have always played an enormously important part in my life and certainly at periods in my life, my relationships with women have been more fulfilling than those I have with men, especially at times when I've felt dissatisfied. Rather than look for another man to supply what was missing, I've got what I need from women. If ever I found myself without a stable relationship with a man, I would choose to live with a group of women rather than search for another man to set up a similar relationship to the one I'd lost. I've talked to other women who feel the same way, because living in a community of like-minded women could, in lots of ways, be more fulfilling than searching for a man. I really don't think I could manage without the women friends I have, because it's to them that I turn when I'm really despairing in a way that I don't turn to Cyril, because there are things I want to explore with women. I feel very comfortable with women, which I don't feel in the same way with men. When I did the counselling course I began to understand the importance of the community of women, because I suddenly met great numbers of like-minded women and it all became clear to me.

My experience in my contact with men is that they feel the need to be defended, and having an intimate relationship with a man which isn't sexual is very difficult. Sex is never irrelevant in a relationship with a man and it can be with a woman. These differences can be illustrated for me when I'm with a group of Jews. I'm a Jew but I'm very far removed from it. I feel it very hard to identify with it, but when I'm with Jews I do feel different. It's something to do with a common history and it's like that with women. There's a difference of quality.

Annette Wagner

I can't believe I'm the same person I was fifteen years ago. I know myself very well and I like myself at last, although it's taken twenty years. I have good relationships and I'm in love all the time! I can't live without it. Due to my work, the people I love are often not in London, so I'm a bit like a sailor, knowing there is someone in the country I visit. It's a very peculiar life in that way, which I like. I don't think I could live with someone any more, although I've been very close to it a couple of times. It's taken so long to learn to live with myself, I don't think it's possible any more to live with anyone else. To me, domesticity's a killer. It's out of the question. I used to be violently against marriage and thought it was the worst situation, but I think now it can work for some people although the majority of married people I know continue with it out of fear, insecurity and that sort of thing. I want a relationship which is all fire and great things like that; even if it's only for a day or two, that's fine. I'd rather that than have someone around all the time. I'm completely on my own and it's absolutely wonderful. I don't feel guilty about anyone. The children are grown up and that's another weight off my shoulders. I've bought a house in the Midi and made a lot of debts over it, but I thought why not? I shall move there in June and work from home in exactly the same way I do from London. I'm going there alone and I want to be alone. I imagine myself to be in the country with my work and the phone and basically I just feel very happy about it.

I was born in Paris in 1936. I was three when the war started and we are Jewish. My parents found a village near Toulouse where we stayed for the length of the war. My father wasn't caught, though we escaped by the skin of our teeth and he hid above a blacksmith's shop. It was quite a terrible time, my mother being left alone with two children – myself and my sister. An accident occurred in 1943 which resulted in another sister. We came back to Paris when I was eight.

I had a normal French childhood, basically marred by my father's personality. Both my parents were foreigners: my father was born in Istanbul and my mother was Austrian. My father kept his oriental mentality which, combined with his Jewishness, made the household one of tyranny. We suspected he was paranoic then; we know now that he was. He died yesterday, which makes all this rather interesting. As the eldest I suffered most. My mother was weak and afraid and we lived in a small, three-bedroomed flat, sometimes with a maid. By 1948, there were four children. My father started up a business on his own which was quite good and earned us all a living. But I was very, very unhappy at home. My father had an obsession about me. He was obsessed by my virginity, and needed to get me married off as soon as possible so that no one could touch me. I was never able to bring friends home and was bound by all sorts of restrictions. Until I was married, I couldn't go out at night and be back later than ten.

There was tyranny on the professional side also. I always wanted to be an interpreter, from the time I started learning languages. I started with German and was very good, they just appealed to me. My father always regretted I wasn't a boy and was something of a patriarch. He was obsessed with his business and worked all the time and was never at home to be a father. Because I was quite good at school and even though I wasn't a boy, my father wanted me to take over the business. He actively prevented me from doing anything other than this, so I had to fight this as well. I was basically very weak and my mother's attitude affected us all. We were all afraid, all the time. It was a very difficult time, in particular for me because I then thought he meant well.

We went on holiday to the South of France when I was eighteen. I met an Englishman there who looked like Jeff Chandler. He was everything my father wasn't: kind, quiet, older than me and Jewish as well which made him more acceptable. We met a few times. I had started at the Sorbonne then and won a Fulbright Scholarship to the States for a year. So I went to Massachusetts, to a girls' college which was very Protestant, blue-blooded and exclusive. It was a most peculiar year and not a very happy one because I couldn't get along in that kind of atmosphere. In France we were small middle-class people and at the Sorbonne it was entirely non-racial and I was plunged into all these prejudices. Out of thirteen hundred girls, only two were black and they were working their way through college by working in the kitchens. By affinity I was attracted to them, because I felt comfortable in their company but set aside from the social life of the college as a whole. I fell in love with one of their friends. He was my first love: a lieutenant in the US Air Force, twenty-three and unbelievably beautiful. It was a very terrible time for me because I knew with the family I had at home, there was no way I could continue with him. Meanwhile, I still wrote to the Englishman.

When I came home, my father refused to let me carry on studying and put me in the business. I had to start from scratch and I spent a year making up parcels of the toilet articles he manufactured, supposedly learning the business. It was hell on earth, the most unhappy year of my life. The only solution was to get married. It never occurred to me there might be other ways out because at the time, I couldn't envisage living on my own. At twenty, my father was already making me feel I was left on the shelf and was always presenting sons of competitors to make great business alliances between the families.

There was this Englishman I'd met for two weeks and didn't know at all, so I made myself fall in love with him because it would be great not to be in France. I took a boat in secret to

England and we decided to get married. For me, it was a matter of getting away from it all. We remained married for twelve years.

I was very inexperienced about going out with boys or with people in general. My husband was of limited intelligence and limited experience too. He wasn't really in love with me either at the time but he made a good deal. His parents were quite poor and he needed to make a good marriage and thought he was on to a good thing. From the wedding night itself, it was very apparent everything was not all right but in my inexperience, I thought marriage was like that.

My husband used to work for a firm who made linen and at first we lived in a small flat in Gants Hill. I was a city girl and not used to this kind of life and used to sleep all day. My father came over and convinced my husband to import his goods and set up a business himself. We were in debt throughout our marriage, me working all the time at secretarial and administrative duties. By that time we had an office in Oxford Street and I used to sit all day there alone, waiting for the phone to ring. I was so conditioned into thinking this way I really thought this was marriage – a vacuum type of life. I never read any more, we didn't go to the theatre, my only contact was with his friends. I'd given up everything, burned my bridges completely, to get away from home.

In the beginning, I adapted. Things seemed OK. I was a bit of a freak because I was different and I used to be the life and soul of the party as it was the only opportunity I had to break out. I was brought up in the knowledge I would have to have children even though, after a couple of months, I didn't love my husband. I had to go through the motions and I did. I had a son when I was twenty-three and the second three years later, though by that time I was miserably unhappy. I started realizing that life was dreadful but I was surrounded by people who convinced me there was no way I could leave my husband now I had two children.

Things became worse and worse and the business was terrible. My husband owed my father so much money, my parents wouldn't come to England. They abandoned me. I had to go to France to see them. I worked all the time and I had the children whom I loved very much. My relationship with my husband was terrible. Sexually, the relationship between us had never been any good at all. It was unbelievably bad and my husband did his duty at night, but had no idea how to be a loving husband.

It took me seven years to come to the point when I knew I had to do something because I was going under. When my husband came home in the evening, I seemed to get a paralysis of the jaw and couldn't speak to him. We slept in the same bed but he repulsed me so much I used to go to bed early so I'd be asleep by the time he got there. Yet I still felt I had to do my duty as a wife and force myself. I couldn't stand being in the same room as him, yet the stupid man thought everything would be all right. To him, marriage was like that and we were just having temporary difficulties. But I could tell I was having a nervous breakdown. I was thirty-three and the children were ten and seven.

One night I got up and made tea about four o'clock in the morning. I said to myself, not another day, I'm going under. The next day I didn't have the courage to say right out I was unhappy. I hid that by saying I'd been to a psychiatrist and was quite ill. He'd advised me to have a trial separation. It took three months for the fact to sink in. I felt sorry for my husband because he didn't understand. He pretended to look for a place, thinking I would change my mind. Eventually he went.

I found myself overnight with two children, this flat with the rent paid for the next quarter and no money as I hadn't planned anything. My husband refused to give me anything. The fact that he left the flat meant to everyone else that I'd thrown him out, and with him went most of our friends. I was judged to be a dreadful woman. When he went bust three months later, I was judged as being instrumental in that as well. When I went to tell my parents, they were furious although they knew it was a rotten marriage and refused to help. Victor took all the furniture which was all right by me and the day he left (although we weren't strictly religious, Victor insisted on not having certain foods in the flat) I went out and bought about a kilo of frozen prawns. I felt delirious. I went back and moved the dining-room into a horrid room at the back and my bedroom to the front and I started to live on my own, by myself. This is when life changed.

I didn't know what to do. I had no money. The children were at the French Lycée. I couldn't go back to France, so I thought I might as well stay put because they could see their father. I couldn't take a full-time job because I wouldn't earn enough to cover everything, so I decided to do what I'd always wanted and be a translator. I was bilingual after all.

Those first two years I knocked on doors and presented myself and must have made a million phone calls. I realized too that knowing a language doesn't mean you are a translator. I had to relearn both French and English. I took two years to get something out of my husband: five pounds a week in the end, and I starved during that time. My husband had a good job, a flat and he was doing fine but he felt he was a martyr. I can understand he felt wounded and it would have been easier for him if I'd left him for someone else. It was worse too for him because I'd begun to grow on him and he was in love with me. After two years, we were divorced and he became very aggressive under the influence of a shitty lawyer. I was always afraid he'd take away the children, though I realize now he couldn't cope with the responsibility. There was also the chance the owners might want to buy out the flat and he felt he mightn't get his share of the money. It was all horrible.

Meanwhile, I started working, bluffing my way through. There was no work in literary translation, I soon found that out, so I had to become a technical translator. An old man I met on a job with a firm who were laying pipe lines in Algeria lent me some money to buy special dictionaries, so that I could become proficient. I'll never forget that kindness. So I learnt on the job and I became good because I was motivated. I was working all the time, very solitary. There was no opportunity to build a life around me. At first I had to concentrate very hard, even working with music was a distraction, there was total silence. It was very depressing always working against deadlines and being freelance, always accepting more work than I could handle.

I don't know how I survived those two years. My sister Nicole helped financially. It was very lonely and I had the two children but very few friends. Yet I was incredibly happy because, for the first time, I was master of my own destiny. I had transferred from my father to my husband and I began to realize I could function well on my own. There was no one I knew in a similar situation who could help. It wasn't the done thing in those days. At thirty-three, I felt too old to be wanted by anybody, neither sexy nor desirable.

Then things began to jell, started to snowball and I was able to breathe a bit. I started to interpret as well, I made friends. I had problems certainly about finding out what it was like to be a single person. I was considered a threat. It showed that I was sexually frustrated and in bad shape. Inevitably I gave out signals to that effect and when I meet women now in this situation, I can recognize that in them. I had to relearn everything: I knew nothing about men, nothing about my own sexuality.

About six months after we'd separated, I met an American locum doctor who came to see one of my sons. It was one of those great encounters and we fell madly in love. It was total passion. He helped me a hell of a lot and for the first time, I met someone who made me feel great. He made me feel that age had nothing to do with it. He gave me a sense of continuity and a feeling I had fifty years ahead of me. It was terrible when he left and it took me a long time to get over. I started to feel better and less vulnerable although I was still complexed about my own body. I didn't know whether I was good in bed or not. It's only been since the last three or four years that I can look at myself and say, not bad, not bad at all and discover it's even an asset to have a big behind.

I had many problems in my private life because I didn't want my children to be disturbed by the comings and goings of men friends. It became more difficult when I could no longer send them to bed so early. After the American doctor, I was not very selective. I made lots of mistakes. I felt I had to satisfy a need, even though they were never satisfied in this way. I felt as if I was twenty-five again and ravenous to catch up on what I'd missed out. It was almost like being a virgin again in every way. I didn't know how to behave, just did what I felt was right, but I always showed my needs. To start with, there were lots of married men and I had no moral sense whatsoever, no principles at all. I only wanted someone who wanted me and the rest didn't matter. It too four or five years for me to ask questions of myself about principles and satisfaction and so realize it would be better to go without than sacrifice everything. As I discovered more about myself, I developed selectivity. Now I think I behaved very badly then for a few years, which is out of the question now. I don't think I liked myself very much during that period but it was one of the things I had to go through in order to find out about myself. I'm not proud of myself, and I could have hurt people but fortunately didn't.

In the last ten years I've learned everything and emotionally grown up. At first I wanted to find somebody else but as the years went by and I gained more confidence, I realized I wasn't going to. I didn't need it any more. I'm perfectly content by myself. I've one son at university and another who's doing A-levels. I feel far freer now than I did five or six years ago. You do pay a price for being alone, because you don't always want to be, when you are. If I should get ill, it might not be so funny either. There are great satisfactions being independent, I have many friends whom I shall keep for the rest of my life. I attach much more importance to friendship whether I sleep with him or not. My catching up has been done; it's over, how I caught up!

In my work, horizons started to open. I started travelling. I could afford an *au pair* girl although I didn't go away for long when the children were young. Professionally things are fantastic. I do simultaneous translations at international congresses and conferences and all that sort of thing. I have a marvellous time, travelling all over the place. I'm well known and get called when people like François Truffaut come over. I've earned a very good living for a single woman for the past five or six years, and I can't think of any other way I could have earned so much money. Five years ago, the allowance for the children was twenty-five pounds a week and I left it like that. I couldn't be bothered to fight my husband any more; besides, I'm not very good at confrontations. The boys have had a very stable life during the past ten years, possibly more so than if we'd remained married. Their father sees them every week, he's never failed them and he's always been good like that.

I used to like the company of women and trust them a lot, but I had a very bad disappointment with a woman in Paris who betrayed me and that's made me wary ever since. I'm just friendly with people, whether they're men or women. My sister is very good and she's also a friend and in her I can confide anything. Not many women like me, because I project an image of invulnerability because I don't want people to be sorry for me. I'm obsessed by the feeling of not wanting people to feel pity for me: it's a fault, a vanity, a pride, that I don't think will change. I present this image because it's my way of survival. I never talk about my troubles and have got into the habit of doing that. Possibly women get closer to one another when they are in trouble, but I've never had the opportunity to be surrounded by many women. Men friends may be ex-lovers, but I trust them more and feel more comfortable with men than women.

Professionally I may often be the only woman amongst twenty or thirty men and I'm one of the pals. It's such a male environment they often forget I'm a woman. Besides, interpreters are not exactly angels as a group and they're always in competition with one another. Perhaps because of the life I lead I've never discovered a women's community in this country. It's very cut to pieces, with two months here, three months there, there's no continuity. Women need that to be friends, I think. If I was married, it would be difficult to have men friends so I would more naturally turn to women. I've missed a great deal the type of friendship you have in France. It's more easygoing. I don't think there are many people who really listen and I can't bear speaking into a void so I don't bother to air my problems. I asked for a lot of advice before I left my husband and it was lousy. I was quite hysterical then because I didn't know what to do. I wasted years because of that – it was such disastrous advice. I had to sort things out for myself.

I found reserves in myself I didn't know I had because for the first few years it was plain survival. I never regretted any of it for one moment, except I should have done it before but I guess I wasn't ready. You can't become a different person before you've worked through who you are. In some ways, I feel I wasted twelve years but again, I had my sons; there was that result from them. I was such a wet rag when I married, it's taken me that long to develop. There was no way I could envisage making changes then. It would feel great being thirty now with all this freedom, it just wasn't around when I was sixteen or seventeen.

Life is wonderful now because I feel so confident. At forty I'm able to lead a normal life which would not have been possible thirty years ago. I've had to learn all sorts of things about relationships, like not needing to be beautiful to be desirable. If you live with someone who doesn't really desire you, it's very hard to get over that and it takes years to discover it's all in the mind anyway. It's taken me a long time to acknowledge I don't like my father. He did something terrible to me about five years ago. I cried a lot, then woke up next morning and realized I was free with no remorse or guilt. I was able to see clearly the type of man he was and why he'd done the things he had to me. I was thirty-nine then and it was both difficult and sad to come to terms with this. Parents affect your life much longer than you think, and coming to terms with my father was like the beginning of a new life for me. The moment I started doing well my father began to be proud of me, asking if I needed anything. I could have done with help during the first two years I was separated and this later hypocrisy sickened me.

My example has encouraged a lot of women. They look at me as a possibility because they can see I've survived. From the outside, what I've done looks like a good idea because I managed to succeed. But I couldn't let myself go and sink under because of the children and whatever happened, I'd always have to prepare my face in front of them. I think people get over anything, except maybe a death: you do in time. I've left my husband but I've never, ever lived alone. It's a wonderful feeling to think of being alone in the Midi. It's going to be the start of another new phase in my life.

1
Before and After

> The Middle years, caught between children and parents, free of neither: the past stretches back too densely, it is too thickly populated, the future has not yet thinned out. No wonder a pattern is slow to emerge from such a thick clutter of cross-references, from such trivia, from such serious but hidden connections.
> Margaret Drabble, *The Middle Ground*

When we consider change we tend to think about creating a different pattern of thought and deed, producing a before and an after. In order to understand the nature of the change itself we need to know something about the past. We expect the young to change because their age inevitably alters and brings about different patterns of behaviour in the process of growing up. Until relatively recently, however, adulthood has implied a form of consolidation, building on but not necessarily altering the foundations laid down in youth. In many ways society is only now beginning to recognize that constant technological developments will induce changes throughout most people's lives: the working day and working life may grow shorter, the skills and training which were appropriate in youth may become redundant in a few years and individuals may find the expectations they had when younger, constantly altering as they grow older. Life is much less fixed and permanent now than it was in the heyday of 'the rich man in his castle, the poor man at his gate', when everyone knew his place and change was a much slower and more gradual process.

For women particularly, the changes during this century have been enormous: their situation is in a greater state of flux than is true for most men, though of course changes in the female must also affect the male condition. The flux exists because of changing social expectations about the role of women in all aspects of life: in personal relationships, in the home, at work, in relation to men. Nothing about women is not being reappraised as the extent of their potential is gradually realized. Most exciting of any group of women alive now are those in their middle years: once expected to settle down with their greying hair and knitting and coast along to death, they appeared an indistinct and undistinguished category hovering somewhere between youth and old age. Women who did 'do' things in their middle age were the exception rather than the rule, but now more and more ordinary women are turning that preconception on its head and finding capital in the fragmented nature of their lives. Fragmented in the sense that having children, running a home and working in paid employment produce constant changes and the need for adaptability; one aspect of life spinning off against another provides the opportunity for growth and development of the whole person.

Anyone can fall into a rut and stay there; this is easiest of all for women at home all the time with small children. The reverse of this is the recognition of the changes which occur naturally within the domestic sphere, which can be applied to the woman herself outside it. The patterns of the past do not have to dictate the same pattern for the future. Change vibrates in the air – even if it veers towards economic decay at present; women are accustomed to adapt by virtue of their traditional role as wives and mothers, and more and more of them are using this skill outside the domestic sphere and – in the process – altering the very basis of female prescription.

We are all changing constantly – if only in terms of age. Some individuals are more consistently concerned with internal, personal development which does not necessarily manifest itself in any marked fashion. Lee talks about the way age has affected her personal reassessment:

I can't remember a time when there weren't agonizing reappraisals going on; every year is a year of reappraisal.

Recently my husband has had a sort of redundancy forced on him and because he is so important to me, there is much additional reappraisal of his particular situation as well. In any case, much of my thinking is concerned with political developments and they need constant reassessment. Besides, the older I get, the things I once thought I was clear about, I now realize the answers were far too simplistic – about everything.

Many of us probably share Sheila Dainow's way of developing: 'I didn't begin to do my learning until I got married in my twenties. Since then it's been a more or less continuous process with great leaps of insight sandwiched by long years of foraging away.' Others go through different stages which are marked by particular passages of more intense reappraisal than usual. The middle years (for reasons which are developed in the next section) are a time of great reckoning, especially among women. It appears to be a phenomenon of our times that women are increasingly less prepared to accept the humdrum repetition of domesticity and have an urge to alter the basis of their lives while there is still time and they still feel capable. The middle years are dominated by time; it becomes a much less vague concept, correspondingly more important to use than passively to allow to drift by. Mary Baker commented:

> Forty was definitely when I began this great change. If I'm coming up to something I always rehearse it. I'd read *Passages* and one or two other things like *How to Live 365 Days* when I was coming up to forty, then I started taking action all over the place, I left my job, took a lover, rented this room in a girl-friend's house and started a professional course. It makes me so sad that women feel they can't take action for themselves. Maybe it's part of our generation not acting for ourselves?

It seems possible, on the basis of talking with many different women, that for many of them an understanding of their full potential is not reached until their middle years. Many in fact never achieve this, but for others the process of maturing can seem to take longer than has hitherto been assumed. The middle years then become particularly exciting and challenging, perhaps because they are set against long periods of what can seem mere existence. Penny McGuire said:

> I suddenly feel rather powerful in a strange way. Not since the age of seventeen or eighteen have I lived on my own but for the first time I can see that I could just about support myself. It's rather exciting to discover you have nerves and senses you didn't know about, because there might be others. I feel obscurely there's some goal I'm working towards; although I don't know what it is, there is something there. I'd like to think I will achieve something but sometimes I feel I don't put in enough effort to reach a goal.
>
> Each thing I've done has been a challenge. It's all part of unconscious progression and constant assessment, which has become more analytical as I've got older and I'm thirty-nine now. There's no way I'd go back.

Another exciting and particularly rewarding realization during the middle years is an acceptance of what and who you are, which does not imply stasis but does mean individuals coming to terms with what they are rather than what other people would like them to be. This kind of change may well be unspectacular and possibly pass unnoticed by the rest of the world, but the relief of being yourself and not following plans and prescriptions which you feel are laid down for you, is enormous. On the face of it, it seems such a little thing to talk about being yourself, but how many individuals truly allow themselves to follow their own instincts about what is best for them, feeling compelled instead to fulfil parental and societal expectations and becoming increasingly constrained by them? Nancy Roberts took stock quite literally at thirty-five and came to terms with the fact that she was a fat lady, something which had dominated her entire life and was only now assuming a proper perspective. After twenty-seven years she started to enjoy food and stopped worrying.

Identity, or knowing who and what you are, according to Erik Erikson in *Childhood and Society* has overtaken sex as the all-consuming passion of our age. This is not an altogether surprising conclusion given the state of flux in which our society exists and – within that – the multiplicity of choice now available, particularly for women. There is no fixed mould which women have to follow, though many girls still seem to 'choose' a conventional, traditional and domestic alternative, the unsatisfactory nature of which often becomes obvious during the middle years. Girls tend to conform very much during their adolescence, but this early conditioning is often questioned later when the effect of following a restricted and limiting life-style becomes increasingly unbearable. Many women may be deeply convinced about the undesirability of their way of life yet be unable to do anything about it, hindered by an over-developed sense of the cause and effect of their actions on their families. Some reckon they pay too high a personal price for maintaining the *status quo* and set about changing it – thus encouraging others to do the same.

The one change which it has become entirely acceptable for the middle-aged woman to make, is to go back to work outside the home. Indeed, if we are talking about changes during the middle years, it is this aspect above any other which is assumed to be under discussion. What is also assumed is that a woman returning to work is doing so because her family no longer need her full-time and give her 'permission' to do something else instead. Work in this sense becomes a substitute for a woman's primary function as wife and mother and so is seen as secondary husband's work – not important in itself and easily relegated to second place. This is of course true in many cases, given the sort of 'typical' female employment which is sufficiently flexible to absorb the demands of child care – jobs like office and factory work and the other service industries such as teaching, nursing and social work.

One of the problems about experience of running a home is that this is seen as a non-transferable skill in terms of running a job outside it. Domesticity having no status and no real value on the scale of paid employment, women who return to work after long years of absence are penalized in more ways than one. But being mistresses in their homes, they can turn this skill into a positive asset when their abilities are used elsewhere. Women need to be able to capitalize on the assets they have, not necessarily and automatically discounting them in the desire to start afresh. There may not be time. June Barry, who went back to work after fifteen years at home, found difficulty in taking orders from younger people, but over a period of time used her maturity and experience to such good effect that she was made manageress and subsequently director within four years of joining the firm.

Work for some women during their middle years becomes of prime importance because for the first time they may have to support themselves and possibly children also. This entirely new perspective can fire them with a formidable determination to be as self-sufficient as they were once dependent. Eileen Curry describes how she reacted to her situation:

> I have changed a lot in the past five years, learnt to know myself which a lot of people never do. I had changes forced on me when my marriage broke up and I took the chance to use that constructively. But until that happened, I can honestly say I hadn't thought what I wanted to do. I did a lot of accepting what other people thought I should do.
>
> A job came up with a firm, I went after it, presenting myself well and got it and I've been with them for about ten months now. We have good training and I knew I could sell and I've done very well. After six months I was offered the Southern Region manager's job but I couldn't move to Kent; I was stuck with Simon doing his O-levels.
>
> It looks as though I'll get the Eastern Region manager's job but I'm biding time at the moment and I've got to be patient.

The road to female liberation in the middle years appears to be strewn with broken marriages. Possibly there is a parallel between this and the worldly success which comes to men later on, which can then inspire some to trade-off a first wife in favour of a fresh one. For women the situation is a little different in that it appears that when they begin to find their worldly feet, they are often unable to contain these new freedoms within marriage: sometimes because husbands do not wish to or cannot make changes as well, sometimes because the woman herself perceives marriage as a sort of strait-jacket which she is no longer prepared to wear. Annette Wagner abandoned marriage because she was losing what grip she had. With two children to bring up and no money, she nevertheless experienced elation at starting to live her own life and feels her subsequent success as a translator was due in no small part to a basic determination not to go under.

What a paradox children are: sometimes used as the means of cementing a decaying marriage together, sometimes the reason for breaking it up. The survival instinct of a parent for a child is so basic that a woman may feel impelled to destroy her marriage because of children, whereas without them she may accept and adapt. Getting out of a marriage when this appears to be the only solution for her children, although still feeling intense emotion for her husband, may trigger many changes as a result. Julia Mitchell's decision to leave an alcoholic at the age of thirty-three, with children of seven and five, was so traumatic as to have devastating results which ultimately led to her marriage to a man twenty-four years older who offered the emotional support she craved. Yet now she feels she *could* have coped on her own and that in seeking an emotional prop she gave up 'the real me'.

Divorce for some women may be unexpected because they have not been able to recognize the clash between personal independence and marriage; in that sense divorce is visited upon them. The shock of finding oneself alone may present either a defeat or a challenge – which is what Christine Merton eventually managed to rise to. Twenty-five years of marriage having ended, she nevertheless is now 'consciously happy' and feels she has found confidence as an individual human being.

Of course, love linked with marriage is a relatively new idea and the disappearance of one has only recently, in terms of the institution of marriage itself, heralded the dissolution of the other. Despite what Shakespeare did for Cleopatra (aged thirty-eight when she died) and all other middle-aged women, love continues to be associated not only with marriage but with the young also. Not by any means exclusively, but by and large. Also on the whole, and again until relatively recently, women have been less free to manoeuvre – for obvious reasons. We tend to be more aware of passionate women in literature, such as Colette's Léa de Lonval say, than in history. Female sexuality is only now perhaps beginning to be understood on its own rather than male terms. But turning cultural expectation on its head is still not easy, for although we may accept logically that there is no reason why love cannot exist between people of different ages and the same sex, custom has dictated a distrust and a dislike of the practice. Elizabeth Knight's fears and joys at falling in love with a man twenty-four years younger illustrates this clearly. If the inhabitants of her small village in Somerset can tolerate, if not accept, the unconventional, it does suggest that it is becoming increasingly possible to change the conventions. One of these is that love properly exists between members of the opposite sex. Coming to terms with the fact that one has been swimming along with the conventional tide and not following the dictates of one's emotions is bound to be a shock, especially in a society which is swift to castigate any variation from the norm. Helen Ness describes what recognition of her true sexuality meant when she was in her early thirties:

> I didn't realize that what I felt for Pam was not ordinary friendship, I actually fancied her. As a young girl I had had a similar friendship with a girl at school but the sexual side of it never hit me. Everyone knew that sex was with boys only. Now I didn't realize what coming to terms with how I felt about Pam was actually going to do to me. I saw her the next day and said there was physical attraction between us and she said she knew. I hadn't realized at all because of naïvety and repressing feelings like this.
>
> Until I come out with some kind of strength in other ways I'm not getting involved in a close relationship, but I'm learning how to be a parent without loss of identity. I'm pretty well celibate now, not exactly asexual but other aspects of my life are more important to me than that.

It is cheering to know that love continues to be a source of creative inspiration in middle age also. There is a possibility that custom and habit within marriage can dull the senses of both parties so that when intense emotion hits – in this instance – a woman, after she's almost forgotten what it was like, it re-awakens all manner of possibilities. Love can be the trigger which fires a new purpose, especially if it comes at a time when she had thought it was all over. Linda Thornber, who wrote a highly successful comedy series for television, talks about how she came to do this when she had never done anything like it before:

I was in love for the first time in my life and I was thirty-bloody-eight and divorced and he was married with three flaming kids. He got my phone number out of me because I was stoned and he just never stopped. It was murder! But it was a lovely feeling. All those things happened which should have happened when I was sixteen or seventeen and I was thirty-bloody-eight and I felt I was right over the bloody hump.

I looked at him and I thought I want him and that was it and that's the reason I write, just because of that moment. Knowing him has jolted me into doing what I should have done before.

A more prosaic instrument of change has existed in education – though not perhaps for quite as long. What is different now is that possibilities are open to women which were once the prerogative of men. There is also increasing recognition that because most women still tend to follow the traditional pursuit of marriage and motherhood, often taking unsatisfactory jobs beforehand, they need courses later on to supplement what they missed only too willingly at school but now recognize they lack. They need help also in finding out what possibilities exist beyond the 'typical' female jobs. In spite of gloomy prognostications about things not changing for women, on the basis that the vast majority do not envisage careers but see marriage as the central fact of life, the existence of NOW and Fresh Horizons courses does suggest that women are beginning to change direction in their middle years. The young do not make changes as such to alter course because they have not had time really to set one; it is those in the middle years for whom direction changes have real meaning, set as they are against all the general conformity of youth.

It is well documented that women tend to get the worst deal in education, and it is a tribute to their tenacity and sense of purpose that more and more of them wish to pursue it either for its own sake or with the idea of getting a better job later on. It is now possible to have second, third, fourth, as many chances as possible if you have missed out the first time around, and that is an enormous advance. Sometimes children growing up can provide the spur. Sometimes it is a matter of time which prods a woman to take up the threads of her unfinished education. For example, Kelly Anderson started with a TOPs course in office skills while her children were still at home and proceeded to take A-levels and then a Social Science degree.

How women sustain their interest over long years at home without much, if any, encouragement only shows their tenacity and indicates the continuing need to provide the opportunity for formal education throughout life. Age never has been a bar to learning but society has yet to make the leap from providing the facilities for continuing education to the possibilities of continuing employment, particularly for women. To raise expectations, only to leave them unfulfilled because age proves to be a barrier against employment, is not only a cruel waste but leaves part of the equation unfinished.

For many women, lacking formal education can mean lacking depth and meaning in life, which can have a further spin-off by making a woman feel inferior and less than adequate, both in relationship to her husband and the type of work for which she is qualified. Education is not only intrinsically interesting but in terms of expanding personal and professional horizons, it probably has as much to offer as love as a means of boosting the female ego. Although motivation in later life is probably a good deal higher than it was in the normal course of school days, the domestic complexities involved in pursuing it add to the sense of achievement and make the effort doubly gratifying. Two friends, Liz Ahrends and Jane Worthington, discuss why they pursued further and higher education:

JANE: I was thirty-four when I got a job teaching sculpture, feeling very superior I'd got a job at all without going through all the hassle of studying. I'd got A-levels but hadn't got a degree. I taught at a comprehensive school part-time for four years, then I had to leave because I wasn't qualified.

I decided to be an educational psychologist because I thought anything to do with education had school holidays but I had no idea what it involved. Eventually I got a job after qualifying and I've been incredibly lucky.

LIZ: I think Jane's picture was one of growing up and going into education later in life as a fairly mature person, but I look back on those early days as fairly barren ones.

At the age of thirty or so I came to the conclusion that education was what I was missing and I could have got a whole lot more out of everything else if I'd had some.

JANE: I think that's false. It's not education itself but what education meant to your view of yourself. I was feeling completely lacking in confidence because I'd opted out from my education and being at home with the children does sap your confidence in a most incredible way.

LIZ: I think the feeling to pursue more education was always there in me and growing stronger and stronger. A friend of mine was doing A-levels and it was really only because she was, that I thought that would be a starter for me too. Maybe I would just try.

After I finished at Middlesex, I took a job as a research assistant at South Bank Poly. I got experience of teaching, of research and got a research degree out of it for myself. I'd already started teaching for the WEA and since then all I've managed to do is to expand my teaching in adult education, doing lots of different part-time jobs.

There are some activities, however, which have certain time restraints placed on them: these are stronger even than the feeling that one is probably unemployable after the age of forty or so.

Arguments about male and female biological determinism have winged their way back and forth interminably, but the one inescapable fact amongst all the verbiage is that women cannot go on producing children *ad infinitum*. Women during the middle years may well have to decide whether they are going to have a child or not, before it is too late. Just to have that choice is a relatively recent development and the difficulty can be compounded by consideration of whether to have a child within or without marriage, alone or with a non-marital partner. One woman said she was profoundly glad she had never had to make the decision about whether or not to become pregnant because she was a Roman Catholic. Irma Kurtz, who had her first child at the age of thirty-eight, felt this was a natural development following a varied and adventurous life, whereas early motherhood might well have made her frustrated and resentful.

Having a baby is a catalyst to change at any stage in a woman's life: probably more profound in its consequences than any other event. Having one unplanned and unexpectedly in middle age may provide the opportunity to consolidate various strands which existed fairly aimlessly before. Pat Hull talks about the changes which happened to her:

> Having Emma late in life, unplanned, has made other big changes in my life. I see the changes which have resulted from this as ones I would have liked to make and having a daughter has turned out to make this possible. I'd taken it for granted for years that I wouldn't have children and around the age of thirty-five, I thought, 'It's not going to happen' and I decided to get on with other things. I've never lived anywhere longer than five years, so now I'm here like a leech. It's as though my travelling is over in all senses. I did a lot of jobs for short periods and I thought it was because I didn't like that kind of work, but a friend suggested to me that it was symptomatic of my life in general: for instance, my relationships with men and my moving around showed a similar lack of commitment. Having a child is of necessity such a long-term commitment, it allows me to be long-term in other ways. I still do worry about the long-term effects on Emma in her situation; I feel guilty about it but I suppose most parents do. I feel that to be circumscribed by having a child can be quite liberating, rather than the reverse.

All the changes so far – within oneself, in marriage, with work, in education and so on – are, initially at least, the pursuit of one aspect of life which may result in bringing about changes to the whole. Occasionally some women accomplish total changes in their life-styles which affect every area from the outset; they effect the change knowing this will be the case. Another reason why change during the middle years is so fascinating is that there is such a distinct 'before and after' flavour which no other stage of life can offer.

Few of us have the opportunity to give up fame and fortune; in an aggressive, competitive society many individuals are possibly striving desperately to achieve just that, as a tangible recognition of getting somewhere. As one of the symbols of the sixties, Jean Shrimpton became a household name, synonymous with the spirit of the so-called swinging decade. But she gave it all up because '... I didn't want to go on modelling. I'd done it all and it was getting boring.' Her contentment with her present life – husband, baby, running a hotel – she finds frightening.

The sixties were characterized by all kinds of alternative livers; one movement which gathered great strength was communal living, a reverse thrust to the highly individualistic notions prevalent at the time. Many dabbled with co-operatives and communes but few actually made a success of it. Judith Bicknell did and describes why she opted for this:

> Having a child was a major change because it meant I stopped work. With two children it seemed imperative to get out of London. We didn't feel very happy about bringing up children there and Renchi was very keen to work on the land. Many of the changes we made were his. I was interested in moving into a community but not so much a rural one necessarily, but for him that was most important. Things are changing all the time – the last couple of years have been particularly good for me. Maybe because I've a little more time for things not purely domestic, maybe because of therapy which has helped me a lot, or because the community's come together more and is more outward looking and creative, or because I've a greater sense of inner security. I don't know. I feel very creative, perhaps too full of projects ever to complete.

Enormous though the changes are in abandoning a public life for a more private one, choosing a communal rather than a nuclear existence, the change brought about by leaving a semi-closed institution and entering the world at large is possibly greater. At least when changes are made in the 'world at large' there is knowledge of the factors involved because you have been experiencing them, although from a different perspective. Being cut off from them to some extent, and subject to the rules of a convent, must inhibit some of this awareness and make the change all the more profound and drastic. Marion Burman, who left her convent after some thirty years, had had an exceptionally full professional life within the religious one, yet came increasingly to feel that she had entered for the wrong reasons and has now – after many initial difficulties – discovered a different kind of faith and contentment.

These women are a few of the vanguard who are helping to bring about change in society's expectations of women as a whole. For the first time in history ordinary women, not just those privileged by birth and circumstance, have altered the shape of their lives in ways unimaginable at the beginning of this century. This has not been possible before on any scale – nor probably is it possible for most men while they remain strait-jacketed as the main bread-winners and supporters of most women. Women are more fortunate in this sense and by recognizing this, they will help bring about changes in the roles of both sexes which will result in a more equitably balanced society, allowing more opportunity for everyone to realize their full potential. To do otherwise is simply wasteful.

2
Time

There is a tide in the affairs of men,
Which, taken at the flood, leads on to fortune,
Omitted, all the voyage of their life
Is bound in shallows and in miseries.
On such a full sea are we now afloat,
And we must take the current when it serves,
Or lose our venture.
        Shakespeare, *Julius Caesar*

There is a tide in the affairs of women,
Which, taken at the flood, leads – God knows where.
        Byron, *Don Juan*

There are few occasions as adults when we are not conscious of time – its passing, its lack, brevity and so on – perhaps only during moments of high passion can it be temporarily forgotten. Perceptions of time appear to vary with age: from the very young who want to know how long is half an hour and what *is* thirty minutes, to the very old who appear to have a greater sense of time past than time present.

  One of the advantages of being the middle generation which bridges youth and old age, is having had enough time to gather a personal history together but still, all things being equal, having time enough ahead to alter course. Just when is the right moment to act? A technically oriented society has little room for either instinct or intuition. Instinct is generally associated with dumb animals; intuition is traditionally supposed a female characteristic and therefore suspect as a viable human attribute. Most of us are unable to accept that there is a part of the human make-up which can respond instantly to a situation. Usually we rely on a lengthier process of intellectual analysis before reaching a conclusion because this is felt to be more reliable and trustworthy. The conclusions reached by intuition and by analysis may well be the same but few of us dare rely on intuition as an accurate reflection of what we think and feel. Intuition is seen to be unscientific and as we can readily see from advertising propaganda, science is the hallmark of acceptability.

Sadly too, instinct and intuition have come to have flower-power, 'laid back', ultra-cool associations; they smack of getting in touch with the cosmic rhythms and 'doing your own thing', and are therefore the more easily dismissed by establishment ways of operating. But the timing of a change of direction is not always a matter of *knowing* when, but the conjunction of thought, circumstance and an instinctive recognition of when to act. It is a matter of recognizing one's own individual pattern of life, not just in retrospect but as a whole. Bernice Rubens was particularly conscious of this and of the need to 'recognize when the time is ripe'. In her opinion survival is something 'women do superbly, men don't do it half as well'.

P.D. James also feels that the prerequisite to any creative change is judging the right moment to take off, but is unsure whether women generally feel this more keenly than men although 'it certainly happens in the writing of a novel'. In her opinion, '. . . there may well be, I'm sure there is, a time when it's right to make certain changes which we ought to be able to recognize. You can begin certain enterprises either too young or too old.' Despite living in uncertain times, she feels it can be a mistake to grab at life or experience – 'just ordinary living, experiencing and growing are very important processes. Maturity comes and you know when the time has come to take a definite step and really change the direction of your life.'

The crux of the problem lies in the balance of controlling hot-blooded impetuosity and excessive caution; the traditional hallmarks of youth and old age. Simply by having lived and lasted until the middle years would suggest this equation becomes more possible. Linda Thornber illustrates the argument further; having achieved almost overnight success with her comedy series for television, she is sure that this could not have happened to her earlier when 'I hadn't really lived through anything worth talking about or worth comparing with anything else.'

Achieving this balance may become a matter of sheer survival, being pushed and pulled until the moment comes when you either go under or change. Annette Wagner, for example, 'found reserves in myself I didn't know I had because for the first few years it was plain survival'.

Not all points of departure occur as on the road to Damascus, like great shafts of light. Other decisions to make changes almost seem to occur of themselves, perhaps because life is led more intuitively or because some individuals have a clearer sense of self earlier on. Irma Kurtz does not 'consciously remember any moment in my background when I had a moment of conscious decision. They seemed to make me in a way.' And Pat Hull said, 'It's like all my decisions – I never seem to take one but arrive at the state which I know is right for me.'

Presumably truisms become clichés because they state a universal truth; 'in the midst of life we are in death' being one of them. When death comes to the elderly, we half expect and are less surprised by it. We are no longer accustomed to the young dying and the blow is all the more shattering because we are not conditioned to it. Such an event may completely alter perspectives so the transience of life cannot be forgotten and is itself a basis for action. Kelly Anderson found that the death of a daughter's boy-friend gave the family 'a feeling of the impermanence of it all. I resolved then that I would grab whatever came along. . . We've tried to do this ever since.'

A further aspect of time, less final but to some no less drastic, is its relation to age, reputedly particularly harsh to women. Few can take comfort in the thought that 'age cannot wither' (in a literal sense anyway) because they know it damn well can and an enormous cosmetic industry exists lending credence to the fact. Women have had to rely so long on their looks; even the generation strongly influenced by and active in the Women's Movement cannot totally ignore the fact. Perhaps it is a particularly fraught question for the present generation of forty-year-olds, who were brought up with traditional ideas about womanly looks and beauty but then came under the influence of the Women's Movement which suggested an over-concern about appearance was not a 'good thing'. Possibly women in the future may choose to be concerned about their looks but entertain fewer intellectual and emotional hang-ups about it. In time, the issue may be thrashed out further and it will be possible to admit that human frailty is such that few of us, male or female, like to be reminded of our mortality: Jenny Kent admits to 'a feeling about not being attractive to anyone else for much longer. I don't really believe that in my head but I do, reluctantly, feel it on another level.'

Time can be seen as the means by which certain options close. It suggests too how ingrained is the notion that attractiveness = youth. Beauty may well be only skin-deep, but the way of the world is such that we are afraid there may not be time to discover the character within if the vision without is old and felt to be repellent.

Other, specifically female options are foreclosed by time. It is a moot point whether women would wish to go on producing babies all their lives or whether it is not a blessing in disguise that there is a foreseeable end to it. But the very finite quality of female reproduction does impose certain constraints, to which men are not directly heir. Time becomes particularly crucial for a woman who may have delayed having children in her twenties and early thirties, now has an established career and possibly marriage but whose options about bearing children grow narrower as the years go by.

'Time's wingéd chariot', which begins to gallop rather than stroll with advancing years, can force a hand in another productive fashion. Realization that time is not endless may cause projects which have been shelved to be taken out and embarked upon, in order to accomplish them at all. Many women talked about the importance of personal growth from a number of different aspects but all were concerned about the 'now or never' angle in particular. P.D. James, for example, in her late thirties 'realized that unless I made an effort and wrote my first novel, I would eventually be a grandmother and telling my grandchildren what I always wanted to be was a writer'. This was not so much a matter of time past but time future, which seems to be the general pattern of thought during the middle years. Able to look in both directions, orientation during this time is to a future not stretching endlessly but with a foreseeably finite end.

Looking to the future, the middle years is the time when work is either taken up after a long pause at home with children – the expected and usual change for women – or because it is the time for a job change. P.D. James found that 'after my husband died I did feel I wanted a change from hospital administration. I think this is the time of life possibly (I was then forty-eight) when women who work feel "Do I really want to go on doing this until I'm sixty?"'

At the other end of the working spectrum, time inhibits in another fashion – not enough of it, which perhaps explains in part why women embark on some careers late. Bernice Rubens, who wrote her first novel at thirty, feels that she started writing late because 'Two things are needed for writing: obsession and time. You can have the obsession, but it helps to have time, so I had to wait until the children were at school. . .' By this time she was 'emotionally rich' and had a variety of experiences to draw upon. Yet is is children rather than time which women can use as an excuse not to extend their lives beyond the home, and she also comments that 'Bringing up children can provide an excuse, almost become a cult which allows exhaustion to become a legitimate excuse for not doing anything else.'

Clearly there are certain stages along a life span when change becomes crucial; there appear also to be certain times of year when this is most likely. Undoubtedly this is connected with changing seasons, with a temperate climate and the various festivities which are concentrated at the end and the beginning of a year. 'It's a bad time, Christmas, it's bloody shitty' said Linda Thornber; a sentiment echoed in one way or another by many women. Supposedly focusing on togetherness, Christmas and the New Year also bring stress and pressure on the family unit which is unrelieved by work and normal daily activity. Men find they are husbands and fathers, women that they are wives and mothers for days on end instead of a few hours. The rifts in a marriage which it was possible to contain within the daily round, now seem to crack wide open, suggesting too that some marriages and by extension family life cannot bear the strain of change and departure from routine.

It is an awareness of chronological time, the gradual accumulation of days, months and years which becomes more acute as we grow older. The most forceful reminder of this comes with death, particularly of a parent or friend. Studies of adult developmental psychology suggest that one of the characteristics of the middle years is an awareness of mortality, bringing with it a heightened sense of personal isolation – possibly echoing an earlier, adolescent realization that each individual is, in some senses, an island. This too can act as a spur to change, a moment when metaphysics joins forces with practicalities. June Barry 'had this great urge to be me. Death seemed very close. I'd become more aware of it when my mother and father died within a month of one another.'

If time in terms of age implies maturity, it is generally assumed that being an adult is in itself tantamount to acquiring this. But given the fragmented nature of most women's lives, their development is often arrested, possibly side-tracked, by having children and becoming absorbed in the minutiae of domestic life with little space or time to think beyond the immediate. It can become a habit to act within one restricting plane and then proportionately more frightening and inhibiting to escape from it. On the other hand, when the trigger to explore beyond the domestic sphere is fired, the motivation to try to succeed is powerful and enormous, particularly because time is at a premium and therefore more precious.

Reappraisal during the middle years may not be so much a matter of reassessing adulthood as such, as picking up aspects of oneself which were not fully developed in adolescence. Developmentally girls tend to mature earlier than boys, then regress during adolescence: the yardstick for maturity tends to be a masculine one. Even allowing for idiosyncratic variations, many women appear to be so-called late developers as compared with men.

Irma Kurtz feels she was 'a late developer in everything', but Joy (NOW) supports the supposition that at some point an individual is mature – 'Probably around twenty-eight I thought I should be able to stand on my own two feet and it took a couple of years after that to grow into the role' – rather than assuming that a form of maturity may be achieved by virtue of motherhood for women, which may not extend beyond that one primary role. A form of domestic maturity may well be forced on some women who escape into marriage and motherhood when young, which is not to say they feel confident or responsible in any other role.

Development may well be arrested too for girls within the family, simply because they are girls. Parents envisage unspeakable horrors for their daughters and inhibit their development in the real world, restricting areas of exploration which, in the nature of things, need to be discovered later. Sheila (NOW) found that 'My parents could always interfere with my social life because I was a girl and not like my brother, hence their concern for me. I accepted that. At twenty-two I was very immature, I didn't really find out about myself until I left home and only found individuality then.'

Many women simply do not know what it is to be independent and alone. They do not experience being totally dependent on their own inner resources and acquiring a sense of individuality, and their personal development is hindered because of this. Too much time is spent by too many women organizing the comfortable surface of things for others; not enough is spent on the individual organizing woman within. June Barry 'took an awfully long time to mature', having been so cosseted at home that 'I'd never even washed a pair of nylons for myself or cooked a meal – though I knew how from school.' When she married, her husband took over, and she was 'pre-conditioned that wives run after husbands'.

Ripeness then, is all: when to judge the right moment to take off. It takes time to develop and experience to assess when to change direction. Time need ravage only the shell and women are no longer as bound by biology as they once were. The middle years can be a time full of exciting promise – after all, there is nothing to relish in an unripe apple.

3
Ageing

> The rigidity of age is not so much a matter of brain cells as of attitude.
>
> Alex Comfort

> I don't feel myself to be forty-five; I see myself as me. I've got more energy now than I had at twenty. The worst period in my life was between eighteen and thirty. I felt very old then. The best time for me's been since I was forty, yet when I thought I was going to be that age, I was devastated. To think in five years' time I'll be fifty. I don't believe it! I don't relish getting old and not being able to do what I want. Age is relative, I feel, and very much an attitude of mind.
>
> Elizabeth Knight

You are as old as you feel – corny, and true only up to a point. It is likely you will never feel as old again as you felt during adolescence with all the Mozart, life-and-death problems to sort out, and probably truer to suggest you are as old as social norms decide you should feel. Age is the most basic guideline to all social intercourse, for every time we meet someone we adapt and adjust our behaviour according to the age and sex of the other person. Theoretically at least, for instance, we reverence the old and parent the young; though more often than not in our society when confronted with both extremes of age, the years merge – perhaps on the basis of 'once the man and twice the child' – and we behave with restrained tolerance towards each.

But what does ageing involve and how does it affect changes during the middle years? Scientifically speaking, every multi-cellular organism undergoes a process of biological ageing; that is to say, there is gradual loss of ability to adapt and an increasing possibility of becoming diseased. This is not too encouraging, but we can take heart from the knowledge that the rate of decline is not fixed and varies with individuals. Interestingly, ageing appears not to cover the process of moving between birth and death. In spite of the fact that we obviously do age from birth, that is called growing up into adulthood; having reached an ill-defined point of maturity, we then undergo the process of ageing itself.

As far as mental abilities are concerned, every individual has a capacity for initial growth which then declines. We are said to reach maximum potential around the age of twenty-five to thirty, and from then on it is not so much a matter of downhill all the way but more of a steady jog. That being the case, why bother to fight something inexorably beyond individual control? It is also quite obvious that we do not all give up around thirty-five, otherwise those old saws about life beginning at forty would not be around either. There is manifestly some confusion between native ability and the ability to use and apply knowledge already acquired – in a word, experience. In effect, you can teach an old dog new tricks but not in the same way that you would teach a young one.

Undeniably physical strength does decline between thirty-five and seventy by as much as thirty per cent over the years. Then again, with advancing years you learn to harness your energies and be a little more circumspect about how you use them. Comfortingly the similarities in the process between the sexes far outweigh the differences, which makes one wonder anew why the state sees fit to classify women as old at sixty, leaving men another five years to go.

There are many theories about ageing, some dividing the life cycle into three phases, others into five or more. Many seem rather schematic and not much more helpful than any individual could suggest by using a form of concentrated common sense. It does not seem greatly productive, for instance, to postulate that the average age when options start foreclosing is forty-eight and a half years precisely. The studies are helpful in that they suggest *general* characteristics about particular stages in the life cycle. Christine Merton, in describing what the middle years mean to her, said: 'It's easy being over fifty because by that time so many troubles have fallen away: I'm physically more fit, the sex drive seems to go a bit and I've more energy more clearly directed.' She feels this is a time to explore one's identity and direction; discovering how to direct one's energies into activities regardless of whether or not these have status makes for a better person, which leads not only to an improved atmosphere all round but also to increased self-discipline and less resentment. It is also essential, in Christine's opinion, to 'recognize the importance of being aware of your limits because if you don't, that too can cause misery. During the middle years one must recognize that to overstep or over-drive oneself will undo your creativity in the end.'

In effect, the second half of life is said to be characterized by a switch from physically-based to mentally-based values in terms of how individuals define themselves. During these years there are probably more and greater ranges of relationships than ever before but against this, increasing marital inflexibility is likely. Marriage itself is often called into question, as Sheila Dainow felt when 'around my late thirties I went into a very depressive state. What I felt then was if I'd had the opportunity to know what I knew then, I wouldn't have got married.' For a time she felt her own marital relationship seemed dull in contrast to the lives of all the exciting and different people she was meeting, but concluded that 'I've done a real full circle about my marital relationship and I think it is a good one for me – whether I've made it like that or it always was, I don't know.'

Marriage is one of many aspects of life which are questioned, as a study of the middle-aged in Chicago suggests: 'middle age is a period of heightened sensitivity to one's position within a complex social environment; and that reassessment of the self is a prevailing theme'.[1]

Qualitatively different from the young by virtue of age and experience, the middle generation has a sense of proximity to and identification with the older generation. Between the old and the young, the middle-aged begin to exchange roles with their own parents and reassess the role they have with their children (a theme to be explored more fully later). Role swapping is said also to take place between the sexes during these years. As men grow older they become increasingly receptive and want to concentrate more on their relationships. Women on the other hand become more aggressive, less guilty, with more egocentric impulses: that urge to be 'me' at the centre of all the other roles which so many women have spoken of. Jenny Kent commented that 'What I had to overcome were my feelings of guilt, that I should be spending more time with the kids and cooking meals, doing family things and so on.'

However, all these aspects of ageing are probably not those which immediately spring to mind when this is under discussion. More often than not it is a matter of *how* you cope with it – which, given the emphasis on youth and beauty in our society, is not surprising. As *the* figurehead of youth and beauty in the sixties, Jean Shrimpton's feelings about ageing are perhaps particularly relevant:

> I'm aware now that I'm gradually becoming middle-aged and I'll never be a bright young thing any more. It's very important for me to grow old gracefully and not cling to my youth. I do think most women find it hard to accept the ageing process. In general I do think it's hard to reconcile oneself not to be a beautiful person if you once have been.

The vast majority of women, however, do not have the burden of beauty to cope with and ageing is more a matter of becoming reconciled to what you are and enjoying the assets you have rather than those you might have had! As Bernice Rubens says:

> Beautiful women have an additional factor to cope with as they grow older and lose their looks. Personally I don't have that burden, but as looks are lost for a beautiful woman, this is also the loss of her main weapon. I consider I'm getting more beautiful as I get older. I remember as a child being deeply jealous of beautiful girls and not liking myself because I was fat and dumpy and all those things you weren't supposed to be. You're only beautiful when you begin to like yourself.

On the whole ageing does not have a good press, because it tends to concentrate on the externals which inevitably do become a little battered with the years. Because of this, the point half-way or so along the 'three score years and ten' still tends to loom as a watershed, particularly for women. Traditionally women begin to see themselves becoming redundant around then; having done what they were put here to do, they feel they are finished. The number of women for whom that is untrue is only now becoming obvious in any quantity. Simone de Beauvoir was particularly damning about this time of life, which was consistent with her view of women as the 'Second Sex' but one which is becoming increasingly less relevant forty years later. She said, 'It is in the autumn and winter of life that woman is freed from her chains . . . she finds this freedom at the very time when she can make no use of it.'[2]

However, the view persists even among women whose lives are otherwise full and satisfying. Sheila Dainow, who had always felt contemptuous of women who were obsessed with age, discovered that, 'it was suddenly very important when I was about thirty-nine . . . when I was forty, I bloody knew it and I didn't like it'. For Pat Hull, this was a very traumatic time:

> I felt I was failing all round – as a mother, in my relationships, even at my tiny job and the sense of failure was made more acute by the fact that I was coming up to forty. I know thirty brought its reckoning but for me, reaching forty was crunch point. I was obsessed by it months in advance – dreaded it. It seemed to me that if I wasn't managing my life at forty, I never would. I decided to get some counselling.

Is this dread of what has been called the 'deadline decade' in part due to a self-fulfilling prophecy? Do we in fact feel what society has for so long suggested we should feel: that is, increasingly impotent with age rather than recognizing the time has come to change gear? It indicates too how potent is the conditioning which we receive in youth, and it is only by demonstrating alternatives that the myth can be destroyed. Change is not only possible but pertinent to the middle years: we know better who we are and what we are doing to alter the existing pattern.

The reverse side of the coin lies in the liberation which age can bring: the marvellous freedom of minding less what other people think of you, of being more in control of yourself so that you can *be* yourself. This is delightfully expressed by Mary Baker, who says 'I'm enjoying growing older. In every way I'm coming into my own. I don't want to get to eighty and still be fluttering like a bird inside. I know I look better than many of my friends and my plumpness doesn't matter to me any more.'

The middle years bring an ability to accept *what* you are, the more easily to pursue the lifelong quest of *who* you are, as Annette Wagner discovered;

> At forty I'm able to lead a normal life which wouldn't have been possible thirty years ago. I've had to learn all sorts of things about relationships, like not needing to be beautiful to be desirable. If you live with someone who doesn't really desire you, it's very hard to get over that and it takes years to discover it's all in the mind anyway.

What an individual is depends in part on gender, whether male or female. The developmental studies mentioned in relation to ageing have all been concerned with ageing in general – with mankind, the generalized sex meaning men but including women. Women do not generally speak on behalf of men and are therefore deemed the specified sex. There are developmental theories exclusively based on the female capacity for reproduction which, until relatively recently, has defined a woman's social status almost entirely – and still does in some parts of the world. Female theories of development fall into three basic stages: virginity, childbearing and loss of childbearing function. This hardly seems helpful either because it is so limiting and does not extend beyond the biological. Simone de Beauvoir certainly takes that line, but the argument does little beyond providing one conceptual framework. It is a partial and historical way of looking at a woman's place in society which has been displaced by technical advancement.

Given the availability of contraception in this country, however inadequate, no woman needs to be defined by her fertility, proven or not. Why in any case should one aspect of being a woman determine what it is to be a female person as a whole? It does seem a little unbalanced, to say the least, to consider a post-menopausal woman in terms of 'it', when no one talks about a pre-pubescent boy in the same neutered way. Both are non-reproductive beings, but that does not destroy their sexuality.

However, no discussion about women and ageing could justifiably avoid mention of that great medical euphemism, the menopause. Was it called 'pause' when it was first named to lessen the blow, since it actually means no more, cease, the end to reproductive life? Traditionally it was *the* feature of middle-aged women's lives, but interestingly enough, not one of the women who were interviewed either pre-, post- or during the menopause, mentioned it. This underlines the inadequacy of relying on exclusively biological theories as the basis of adult female development and suggests too that we are at last breaking through the myth that women's lives are one long battle with their wombs. In fact, the only characteristic symptom of the menopause is a disturbance in body temperature because of lack of oestrogen which arises from shrinking ovaries; most of the information about this is gathered from women attending gynaecological clinics – hardly a balanced sample.

Hitherto the menopause has been viewed in crisis terms but in the previously mentioned study of women in Chicago, Bernice Neugarten found it made no difference to personality measures. This period in life is primarily a matter of concern because of its traditional image; combined with old wives' tales and fears that it heralds the end of sexual activity, and in a society which values physical attributes above all, the menopause and its anticipation become something to be dreaded. At the same time, before adequate contraception was available, life beyond it did represent a glorious freedom – provided you were still fit enough to enjoy it. Many women said how much their health had improved as they grew older and it is apparent that women who lead satisfying, fulfilled lives often seem to enjoy better health – even to the extent that they are sometimes intolerant of those who do not!

Although the transitional nature of the menopause is now more widely recognized, leading to a generally more balanced view, it would be simplistic to suggest we have reached that stage of collective female awareness when every woman can cope with equal ease. Quite obviously this period of time can provoke a crisis for a woman who wishes to have children but has possibly left it too late. It seems a deep and irrevocable unfairness to have restrained one's fertility for many years, only to find oneself cheated by time out of the final chance. Given too that the menopause occurs somewhere between forty-eight and fifty-two on average, it is likely that it coincides with children leaving home, the 'empty nest' syndrome and the death of parents. There seem to be unavoidable shocks to the system at this stage which, if all energies are concentrated in the home and there are few other outlets, may be difficult to ride. Indeed it can seem that life has little else to offer. This no doubt accounts for the view that the middle years are a time of crisis for women. The argument suggests that by removing the object and purpose of a woman's existence – her children – she is left with nothing but a harsh realization that she has been somehow cheated. That realization constitutes the crisis.

Common sense suggests that if it was only reproduction women were good for, the menopause and death would coincide a little more closely instead of currently about two-thirds of the way along. *Homo sapiens* is the only species of animal whose females experience a menopause and nature, though profligate in many ways, must have evolved this for some good reason other than out of a delayed sense of population control. Moreover, it is not constructive to view women's reproductive capacities as the counterpart to male production in the world outside the family, because that division of labour is relatively recent. Surely it is only since women have been defined in terms of the home and removed from the 'real' world that there has been so much concentration on their reproductive systems, because that was the only shared attribute which defined them all of a piece. Now that there is more choice, however bleak and unfair in comparison with men, childbearing can be put in to a clearer perspective as a unique female function which nevertheless must take its place among others. Viewed thus, the removal of that capacity leaves more room to develop others – all things being equal, that is. There is still a long way to go in this respect, but we are moving along in the right direction.

Time was when age inspired respect. Goneril's comment to Lear, 'As you are old, and reverend, should be wise' echoed a common sentiment of the age: it was an achievement to have survived when it was customary for many to die in infancy. Nowadays that rarely happens from 'natural' causes, which further intensifies society's dislike of the ageing process. Ageing goes against the grain of the youthful feeling of immortality which dies hard, but more especially it is contrary to the notions which a technological society inspires. The accent is on the new, the young, the expendable; durability, age and the old are then redundant by implication. But the paradox remains that there is still room for a form of accumulated wisdom which can only come with age. P.D. James feels that the present-day emphasis on youth not only inhibits mature women from returning to what they see as the 'jungle' of the world outside the home, but is responsible for the short-sighted attitude of so many employers towards the middle-aged.

For women this age barrier is hurtful in other ways, as all the varied experience gathered during the time spent at home – both there and in the surrounding community – counts for nothing when they attempt to return to paid employment. Not only do they have to fight harder to get a job in the first place but having gained one, their pension and insurance rights are adversely affected by those years at home. There is work and work – like poverty it is relative – but the only work that counts in terms of benefits is that in the 'real' world outside the home. Irma Kurtz suggested that one approach to overcome this when 'doing things late rather than in due course', would be 'to tackle them in a slightly eccentric and original way'. All of which demands courage and support, especially in a social climate which induces a feeling of uselessness with the advancing years. It is rather a vicious circle: be young and therefore employable, and if you are no longer that at least *look* young, which keeps the cosmetic industry afloat and reinforces the necessity for a woman to keep her looks as an employable asset. Even if age and looks are no barrier in themselves, there is a clash between an older colleague who has experience but is no longer a whizz-kid and a bright young thing who is abreast of latest developments. Women do have to be extraordinary to cope with the slings and arrows of the working world, but only in comparison with what was traditionally expected of them: it is not extraordinary to women themselves.

Only by demonstrating their ability to break through the 'protector myth' and show they have more to offer than reproductive skills, can women begin to break down barriers of age and sex in society and so create new possibilities for themselves. It is indicative of the waste which exists everywhere that although training and education is more prolonged (admittedly for the more privileged) and lives can be extended with better health care, useful contributions are often prematurely cut short.

We have become conditioned to expect certain behaviour from certain age-groups: a form of social control as insidious as it is powerful. For example, how many women feel ashamed when they become pregnant by accident over the age of forty? They feel shame because it is demonstrably obvious that they are still sexually active and creative, whereas 'the norm' is for the young to have babies. And by what yardstick do we judge the sheep dressed up as lamb? Clearly demarcated along the biological curve of life are social definitions suitable to each particular age and stage. It is customary to marry, to train, to lay the foundations in youth and to capitalize on these later in life. Responsibility, for instance, is generally assumed to be acquired with age, as Joy (NOW) discovered:

> I came up against a bar in my job when I was seventeen. I was running this department and my boss told me because I was seventeen, a girl, and too young to run the department, he would have to put a man in over my head. So I trained him and was his second.

Social expectations vary between different socio-economic groups. When combined with expectations which differ according to sex, the outlook can be even more grim for women. Those who have been thwarted in their youth from taking advantage of their natural abilities either lose that determination – often having been side-tracked into conventional jobs and marriage – or the sense of purpose builds up a more powerful head of steam later on. Vivianne (NOW) feels:

> It's a grim determination to do something other than office work. I haven't really got this lack of confidence because I've had part-time jobs since I've had children. The thought of

being hemmed in an office for the next twenty years is awful. I like being my own boss at home, it's preferable to being answerable to someone else.

The problem lies in keeping up the struggle without becoming either defeated – which changes nothing – or aggressive, which is basically unconstructive and ultimately unprogressive, helping neither the individual concerned nor others who will be affected. Social expectations about women *are* changing, but presently exist in an uneasy cohabitation between traditional prescriptions and current alternatives. Why else would many women feel ashamed at admitting they are 'only housewives and mothers', yet suffer endless guilt and anxiety when they combine domesticity with paid employment? Men do not: they expect to combine both, but less often take the helm at home.

The Women's Movement has made great inroads into the traditional ideas of what a woman should be. But most women of forty plus were conditioned by one way of thinking and only later came under the influence of a radical alternative. The effect of a woman breaking out during her middle years and defying her age expectations is both disconcerting and uncomfortable, but demonstrates above all that age sanctions which were once appropriate are so no longer. It will become the rule that women use their potential to the full because it is becoming increasingly unacceptable to them to live a symbolic existence – in the shadow of man rather than alongside him. Annette Wagner doubtless speaks for many in saying, 'I would feel great being thirty now with all this freedom; it just wasn't around when I was sixteen or seventeen.'

However, we have not yet reached a point when women can cease to feel they constitute a special and different case because individuals, regardless of sexual differences, are making the most of their abilities. A technological society, alas, does create the need for drones, it binds as much as it liberates, but there is no reason except custom for the majority of the drones to be female. It is the roots of ageist custom which need to be undermined and new patterns of normality and expectation generated. The present generation of middle-aged women are leading the way, but the problem remains in the difficulty of reconciling the promise which a youth oriented culture inculcates with the reality of age still being unacceptable. It is lonely and isolating being out front and despite the support which women as a whole can offer it is as individuals that new patterns are created. Liz Ahrends illustrated the two sides of this particular coin when she said, 'It's a lovely time of life really. . .' but also, 'I guess I just don't want to be a pioneer. I wish all the work had been done already by other people for me but how many other role models are there for me?'

Who wants to be a pioneer? Why is, 'I don't' the reflex answer? Why does age inhibit action, and how is it that we cannot retain a sense of individual uniqueness as well as recognizing our sameness? Lee suggests a further link between age and our society:

> I think adolescents often feel they're amazing and capable of doing great things if only people realized it. I think that's a very precious and marvellous feeling that people should keep, because people are amazing and are capable of doing great things. But as they grow older they discover they are no more special than other people and such is the destructive power of this competitive society, that this realization seems to devalue their own capabilities.

'What is the point of it all?' becomes a more poignant question in the middle years, because past action has demonstrated how an individual has coped with that basic existentialist problem. Finding answers later in life becomes increasingly more turbulent because the middle generation has responsibilities and dependants either side of the age group, to a far greater extent than earlier. There do seem to be parallels between adolescence as such and what may well be a second 'adolescence', particularly for women during their middle years. The first half of a woman's life is often fragmented, the second allows more consolidation but experimentation too. Mary Wollstonecraft in *The Rights of Woman* considered women of thirty had reached 'the most perfect state' when vivacity had given way to reason. Allowing for that sad reflection of the times and for differences in life expectancies, we could suggest that that 'perfection' is now attained a decade or two later.

Notes

1. Bernice L. Neugarten (ed.), *Middle Age and Ageing*, University of Chicago Press, 1968 (p. 93)
2. Simone de Beauvoir, *The Second Sex*, Penguin, 1977 (p. 595)

4
Society

I think the social climate now is more conducive than it's ever been before for women to make changes in their lives but maybe that's to do with class and education as well. All of my close circle of friends are highly privileged and have time to spend on their own development. On the other hand I meet numbers of women who feel so circumscribed by their working lives that they feel they have no freedom to make any changes.

Sheila Dainow

What is significant about the second half of the twentieth century which makes it different from any other period in history and a time when it is increasingly possible for women to bring about change in their lives? Women over twenty-one have had the vote since 1928 and in theory have attained equal citizenship. Until recently that achievement has possibly been more symbolic than real in terms of widespread opportunity and progress, but as the twentieth century has advanced women have gained increasingly more control over their fertility and there is now no necessity for them to be defined in terms of their wombs. By extension it follows that they do not have to be dependent on a man for either status or economic support – *though most women are.* Women can receive more education than they once did, more are working in a wider variety of jobs than ever before, and technology has reduced the drudgery of housework a great deal. Against that, it has imposed higher standards of housework and domestic fetishism and reduced many job opportunities outside the home. However, none of these factors in themselves accounts for the social climate now making it more possible for the middle-aged to take advantage of the opportunity to alter the pattern of their lives.

To appreciate just what social changes have occurred in relation to women, we need to make a lightning tour of their 'place', to see why that 'place' has rested in the home and not outside and why that state of affairs is in the main no longer acceptable. Female horizons are no longer bounded by the kitchen sink and the double bed. Why not?

Back in the hunting/gathering period of man's evolution, the social consequences of biological determinism first made themselves felt. In other words, because of the reproductive differences between the sexes, it became necessary for one to hunt unimpeded by offspring and the other to gather with one eye on the cradle. It seemed logical then that the individual who had produced the child should be the one to look after it. There was after all no question as to maternity but paternity was rather different; no man was going to hunt on behalf of a family unless he was entirely sure it was his. So some system had to be organized whereby women could be looked after while they were temporarily but repeatedly handicapped by pregnancy and childbirth. At the same time that system could also ensure the paternity of particular children.

One way of establishing both a social and a conceptual order was to organize distinct categories within the group and to make sure that a recognizable distance was kept between them. For instance, men could have sexual relationships with any woman other than their mothers and sisters. Kinship, or how x is related to y, is one way of representing the biological facts of sexuality, and is also a logical manner of coping with the universal facts of reproduction. The family in our society is therefore linked historically with the notion of paternity, and one is bound to assume that this has come about because no woman could be trusted to tell the truth about 'who the father was'. Women became valuable exchange objects by virtue of their reproductive abilities, and men needed a formal relationship with them, not only to be certain about the children they had fathered but also to ensure continuity of line. In time, women became dependent on men for their status and security.

Thus patriarchy in a nutshell is a system of order which arose out of the natural biological differences between men and women. Being natural, that was equated with being good – something of the same principle that wholemeal bread is better than refined white. As it was the natural function of women to procreate, that was seen to be their prime function in life, to the general exclusion of most other options. This natural ability has been considerably undermined of late by technical developments in contraception, and further displaced by the state, which has taken over many of the traditional tasks of women in terms of health, education and welfare.

Most forms of birth control are geared to women. Most women reduce the number of children they could have as their standards of living improve. All women spend proportionately less time looking after their children than they once did. In theory at least, women need no longer be as dependent on men by virtue of their rampant fertility; they can now choose whether or not to take up the maternal option, within or without marriage, with a man or with AID. Such choice is relatively recent, however. The effect of generations of women having been controlled by their biological functions cannot so easily be removed by the presence of a pill or a piece of intra-uterine plastic. That is made only too clear by experience with family planning schemes in India, which were doomed to failure as they did not co-exist with other welfare, legal, political and social changes. Some of these changes have taken place in this country, but not yet sufficiently to rectify the balance. More particularly, all the legislation in the world will not necessarily bring about changes in attitude and behaviour. While women in our society are no longer the second sex, they are not yet considered to be on a par with the first one!

Why has patriarchy such a stranglehold on social organization that it can continue to pass itself off as the 'natural' state of things? It has lasted for such a very long time that it has become possible to establish custom as the seal of approval. It is also very widespread, and both factors constitute strong psychological weapons. Until relatively recently, culture – 'the intellectual side of civilization' (Shorter Oxford Dictionary) – has been dominated, organized and oriented by men. Since standards, judgments and norms have been determined by men, but to include women, these must inevitably be one-sided. In some instances they may well exist to the obvious detriment of women because they do not necessarily take into account the different modes of being as between the sexes. For instance, in modern medicine many women may be categorized as mentally ill in terms of male norms and standards, whereas viewed from a female perspective that 'illness' may assume a very different dimension. It is not unlike talking about strength: the same word covers a multitude of different meanings for both sexes. A viewpoint which is largely that of one sex must inevitably produce a distorted view of mankind as a whole, which contains at least two sexes. The balance is beginning to be rectified; it is becoming possible to develop a psychology for women that is not male oriented, but there has not yet been sufficient time to reach a totally new perspective. Women are only now beginning to realize the full extent of their potential, the exploration of which has given rise to a state of flux and uncertainty in society as a whole.

Up to now, a male oriented society has worked on the assumption that men are active and are defined by the work they do. At the same time it has been assumed that women are passive, procreative and dependent. If women are no longer defined by their reproductive abilities, the norms for society as a whole can change, but the process threatens the existing *status quo*. The present generation of middle-aged women is uniquely qualified to lead the direction of that change and alter female norms and expectations for all time. Born and raised within the traditional female mould, they later became active in or influenced by the Women's Movement, which itself was the outcome of a number of social changes. Jenny Kent's experience was probably fairly typical:

> In the fifties I didn't dream there were choices because I still went along with the idea, however cynically and even though traditions were breaking down, that marriage was what I was going to do. I never clearly imagined a career or the hard reality of absolutely having to do a job after leaving college

which I don't think is true of women in that position now. I thought there were things I might do but I was incredibly naïve in a way, thinking that life was there to be experienced but really in a sort of pre-hippy middle-class way. The key to my change was involvement in the Women's Movement.

One woman has called this present middle generation of women a 'guinea pig' generation because they are the first group of ordinary women who have been in the position to *choose* either a traditional role or a more radical alternative. Unlike younger women, they have the personal experience of having lived through a gradually changing social climate, which has moved from constraint to relative freedom. They are less likely to reject everything which smacks of the past or to swallow wholesale the philosophies of the present. The freedoms which do now exist for all women, will have been achieved by the middle generation in the light of their dependencies. Choice, as one grows older, becomes increasingly relative.

Traditional roles and current alternatives were mentioned previously but not examined beyond the stage of the early nuclear mother occupied in gathering. The woman's place in the home became thoroughly entrenched when industrial technology forced job specialization. As the nineteenth century progressed, it became a sign of status for a man to have a non-working wife whom the later Victorians dubbed 'The Angel in the House'. It was then that the true separation between working-class women and their bourgeois sisters grew up, one existing on the backs of many others. Parallel with the non-employed wife and mother developed a separate culture for children, who until then were merely regarded as miniature adults. Domestically centred women in the nineteenth century, unlike their mediaeval forebears, rarely had an entire community to control and organize in the absence of their husbands. They concentrated instead on developing a new cottage industry which centred on children.

Towards the end of the nineteenth century, women who could not bear to contemplate a life of total domesticity and who wished instead to enter the professions, were only able to do so in the main by abandoning one for the other. Nowadays women are generally unprepared to give up sexual fulfilment and motherhood for the sake of a career, but may still meet the same kind of opposition in its pursuit as they did a hundred years ago, as Rosy (NOW) found:

> I rebelled into domesticity and got married and was then shattered to find that I wasn't taken seriously. People said you can't think much of your career if you get married. I had a lot of trouble getting research posts and I didn't get the one I wanted because I was married.

The suffragettes exposed the sexual antagonism beneath the Edwardian veneer but were unable to visualize the overthrow of the existing patriarchal order. They did not question the very basis of oppression for so many women, that of marriage and motherhood, because this remained the only viable means of economic survival for a respectable woman without financial resources of her own.

The period immediately following the First World War saw enormous numbers of single women – without hope of marriage – being thrown onto the job market and having to fend for themselves. This coincided with a greater availability of secretarial and administrative work. Contraceptive advice was becoming more generally available through the efforts of Marie Stopes. Clothes were indicative of new freedoms as corsets were temporarily abandoned. Life was beginning to be less circumscribed than it had been before the war.

The Second World War established a clearer working pattern for women. More were employed in the war effort than ever before, but when hostilities ceased it became obvious that they were considered expendable: only a reserve army in effect, useful when there were not enough men to go round, but, in peacetime presenting a competitive threat to men on the job market. However, for the first time on any scale, women had experienced being in charge of their families and gainfully working as well, more often than not in the absence of their men. They had also had the benefit of some welfare provision for their children while they were employed with the war effort, which had the effect of disguising real progress in peacetime.

The net effect of war in terms of its social repercussions on women was to reinforce the sexual conventions and polarize male and female roles, in an attempt to return to 'how things were'. The ideal was postulated that men should work outside the home, leaving women contentedly within it. Privileged women who did pursue careers were then able to employ help with their homes and children as a matter of course. However, in an atmosphere that did everything to encourage a woman to stay at home, those who did not do so were made to feel their children were suffering from maternal deprivation. The 'pull together' ethos of wartime validated the absence of fathers, yet it was never suggested that children suffered from paternal deprivation in the same way. Because it was felt women did not *have* to work for economic reasons if they had a man to support them, those who did work were made to feel they were deviating from the expected norm. Many women who had subscribed to the '*kirche, kinder, küche*' ideology no longer found it quite so satisfactory. The war and subsequent social upheaval made it impossible for them to find either status or identity within total domesticity. Having acquired both during the war and discovered they were essential beyond the purely domestic, they were now expected to resume a back seat and become dependent once more on their husbands.

Peace gave everyone more time to consider the male and female condition. Women saw themselves caught in a double bind. There was less of an onus on parenting then, more on mothering as this was still considered the primary task of most women. Public and private sources of child minding gradually diminished, so the women who did go out to work found it harder to cope with a job plus family commitments. It is a moot point whether there was a male conspiracy to keep women at home by means of intense consumerism, immediately post-war. If there was, it was doomed to partial failure at least, because women themselves reached satiation point.

The sixties saw the second great watershed for Western women, and also brought concurrent protest movements to the fore: those concerning women, Black Power, students and so on, all with an emphasis on subjectivity and politics. More higher education produced greater awareness of the contradictions between the idea of freedom and how that freedom related to economic reality. How 'free' was a woman if all she could do was spend her husband's money? Those years also saw the gradual abandonment of marriage as the only valid pursuit of middle- and upper-class women. It was seen to be possible to pursue other avenues instead without having a sense of failure. 'Doing your own thing' was the flavour of the moment. At long last, too, reproduction was separated from sex with the widespread use of 'the pill', which in turn created a relaxation of sexual *mores*. Sex was now openly permissible outside marriage, 'trials' of which became a thing of the past. Women were finally freer to be sexual rather than reproductive beings, but how real that freedom was beyond sex was still debatable. Permissiveness and the consumer boom effectively hid any real progress – except those freedoms associated with the young. It was all very heady and euphoric – not unlike the Restoration following the austere years of the Commonwealth.

The concern with individual destiny brought together numbers of different women with varying areas of interest, with the common theme of rectifying systematic social injustice towards all women. The phrase 'Women's Movement' tends to suggest there is one united group, when in fact it developed as a collective and co-operative umbrella for numerous and assorted gatherings beneath. Although there had always been a community of women who were supportive of one another, it had existed as a substratum beneath the dominant male network and was not identifiable as a group sharing equal weight and prominence with those of men. What was remarkable about the early days of the Women's Movement was that it attracted women from widely different backgrounds and interests who not only shared a common anxiety about the female condition but actually said so publicly.

This public concern with things female, both an ideology and a concern with specifically female problems, was to bring out into the open new ways of thinking and acting. From time immemorial, women had been relegated to second place by virtue of their sex; now the validity of those existing modes was being questioned – in marriage, in relation to children, work, education and so on. Men and women who did and do not see themselves necessarily as feminists, were nevertheless influenced by a new awareness for and about women – sometimes, it was felt, *ad nauseam*. The spin-off effect was to encourage women to see themselves as valid individuals in their own right who were capable of making a contribution to society independently of men. Jenny Kent, for example, found herself

> . . . in a classic situation amongst those of us who went into the Women's Movement in the late sixties, from a middle-class educated background, moving from my father's to my husband's home. There was a kind of excitement around then that you could engage in new ideas, knock on doors and feel that life was by no means over. A whole generation of women were wide-eyed, feeling they could do anything.

However, many individuals, both male and female, were only aware of the bra-burning, hysterical actions of the more strident sections of the 'movement'. The underlying message became thoroughly distorted by the media, and many women would probably agree with Julia Mitchell that undue publicity given to the more extremist aspects has obscured much of the real work being done and diverted attention from the basic issues.

For women who are now middle-aged there are no new role models, no precedents to follow other than the traditional or exceptional. As the opportunity to make personal changes was not available to the same extent when they were younger, they may resent the freedoms which their younger sisters can now enjoy. Emancipation can be rather a bitter pill for the older woman; for example, the single parent of a generation ago suffered both social stigma and severe economic hardship. The single parent today, at least in the metropolis, can escape much of that censure and there is very much more understanding of what is involved. Current economic realities are such that some women may well be in the vanguard in encouraging others to fall back into their traditional role. Economically independent women are a threat to husbands' jobs, and while men continue to gain their sense of validity and identity through their work, working women may well undermine the *status quo* in more ways than one.

Can the technological, legal, political and social advances, which together are gradually liberating women, be strong enough to continue to make inroads on a male dominated society in a recession? Jenny Kent comments:

I think it's going to be very interesting to see what happens in the eighties to our generation and to the one behind us. I think the 'psychic' differences between our generation and previous ones are quite profound, based on a series of cracks within society, cracks that are so great they're not going to be pulled together. But the economic situation is so bad that the material reality is going to put great constraints on it. The idea that women can make changes, do different things with their lives and have a basic right to search for a way of living that fulfils them, is going to come under tremendous strain. There's going to be a huge attempt to re-accommodate feminism within traditional structures and a hell of a lot will depend on what women can actually do within and against these constraints.

She feels that the next ten years will be a real testing time in terms of the conflict, between 'material reality and women's expectations of the possibility of being able to fulfil themselves', in addition to the necessity for 'us older feminists to keep our commitment going'. However, she distrusts the 'terrific focus on individual development, especially for women' in the States, commenting that, 'The idea that individuals can make their own solutions can only have a partial reality in an upswing in society when the economy is at an optimum level.'

Is a more balanced view of society beginning to emerge? Inevitably, after having remained unheard and unsung for so long, there is now an enormous backlash by women. There appears to be an imbalance of concern about things female in all aspects of life – but only in relation to the paucity of material and interest available previously. Middle-aged women can contribute a great deal towards creating a more rational perspective of humankind. The changes they make, because these are now more possible to achieve, cannot be swept aside as youthful aberrations. As seasoned individuals they are more likely to alter the pattern of their lives with a concern for the effect this will have on others. Change in the middle years is not just an individualistic enterprise but must reflect concern about the human condition as a whole. That is where age and experience are an advantage, where being in the middle is a positive asset: the changing life-style of a middle-aged woman will have a direct effect on the generations either side, and as more and more women of the middle generation discover their latent potential and bring about a change in the social expectations of all women, their influence will be increasingly important.

In the past, women were always suspected of twisting the rules to get what they wanted because they were not in a position to change them in a more orthodox way. It was all rather underhand and devious – of necessity to a great extent because of women's subordinate role. Now all that is changing and women are getting into situations where they can alter the rules openly and in public. We know that in proportion to men there are very few women in positions of power in government, trade unions, management and so on, but it does take time to undo generations of conditioning. We have not yet gone beyond the stage of attracting publicity for the first woman bus-driver, mechanic, electrical engineer and so on. When that is no longer newsworthy, women will know they have got somewhere.

It is a positive duty for the middle-aged woman, both to herself and to future generations, to establish new patterns of a more fulfilled existence which will eventually lead to the abolition of all notions like ageism and sexism. The young have not accumulated the experience to try and the old may feel there is not enough time or energy to make an attempt. It is all up to that once despised and neglected generation, the middle-aged.

5
Individuals

> It is not easy . . . to change the patterns of the past: to forego the reassuring pleasures of servitude, to face the unknown.
>
> Fay Weldon, *Remember Me*

Time, age and the social climate: each contributes something towards making the moment conducive to bringing about change, but all are as nothing unless the individual herself can organize the components and make them work for her. In a general sense these are external factors, largely beyond individual control, but the final contribution is made by the sum of all the aspects – the personal one: each unique but at the same time reflecting the condition of many other women.

'You're never satisfied!' is often said in a tone of abuse, as if the person at whom the criticism is aimed has no right or justification in feeling like that. This is an existentialist variation on the Oliver Twist theme. Sometimes the comment comes from someone who resents the creative dissatisfaction which fires others to experiment, to take risks and to try something new. It is a form of 'if only' which Bernice Rubens has spoken of, often tinged with regret and envy which is a major contribution to uncreative living. Sheila Dainow feels strongly that dissatisfaction is a powerful motivation for making change, but this must be channelled positively into a conviction that change is possible.

This attitude is a philosophy of life and a way of living common to many individuals, not just women, and is not a question of being unsatisfied with what you have but rather the root of a constant search to improve. Above all, it implies there is never an end to development, never a point when you can say, 'I've got there, I'm finished', but it provides a pattern of living which is at the same time a resolution and a point of taking off.

More specifically, many women feel a nagging lack of fulfilment which gains focus during their middle years, a conviction that there are areas within themselves that are going to waste and not being used. Admittedly this also can be a condition shared by many men but not by virtue of their primary role as wives and mothers. Generally speaking, men are not defined primarily by their relationships with others, that is 'being', but in terms of 'doing' within their work. The Boston Women's Health Book Collective describe what this feeling meant to them:

> Most of us feel that contrary to what we were promised in childhood, we were not totally fulfilled by marriage (a man), and/or motherhood (a child) and/or a (typically female) job. This is not to say we have not grown a lot within marriages and with our children and in our work. We needed space to discover who we were separate from those primary relationships so that we could become autonomous adult people as well as have important relationships with others. (*Our Bodies Ourselves*, p. 17)

The Boston Collective came together to produce a book which was not only relevant to themselves but to other women also because they shared a common feeling at the time (1970s), that their traditional role was wanting and they needed to do something about it. They found the artificial world they lived in as wives and mothers inadequate and frustrating as a total way of life, because it was separate from the 'real' world outside it and whatever activities went on within domesticity, these were held to be less rewarding and of less value than those concerned with paid employment. The Ancient Greeks after all had a very clear idea about the value of certain areas of human activity and employed slaves to carry out those which were less savoury.

Almost inevitably, there is an inherent danger that women who are at home all the time will be taken for granted and become an indistinguishable part of the background. Sheer habit and repetition leads to a loss of individual identity within the corporate one of the family, as on the factory floor. That is, until one day when a trigger sets that woman thinking, 'Is this all? Is this what life's all about?' June Barry's experience was probably typical – a feeling as she stood at the sink with the children rushing through that 'I could have been anyone standing there'. Having arranged her life around her husband and family for so long, 'I found myself thinking I must find a space for me to be me. I had this great urge to be me.'

How much more can this feeling of being used extend into grandmotherhood when children – now parents themselves – assume as they once assumed of their mothers that this is the right and proper function of grannies which they will perform with joy and gladness. This is made the more galling when 'grannies' themselves may have realized the opportunity to do their own thing later on in life and are not therefore at the beck and call of their offspring. Kelly Anderson, for instance, 'didn't want to be a perpetual babysitter to my grandchildren. There's more to life than that.'

Occasionally an opportunity can occur within marriage that gives a glimpse of independence which marriage and motherhood have quashed, habit and repetition having established ways of dependence that are constantly reinforced by looking after small children. When Helen Ness's husband got a job which initially involved his staying away during the week, she discovered that:

> I got into the way of looking after the children by myself and began to enjoy it. I realized I had got so much into the way of being a dependant, I had forgotten what it was like to be on my own. When it came to the crunch I had to ask myself whether I wanted to go to Bournemouth, and it was this single event which proved to be the crisis point for me.

Breaking through the 'protector myth' encourages new perspectives on the rest of life which may then confirm either the desirability of being part of a couple or the impossibility of ever being truly independent within marriage.

Because many women feel taken for granted by their families, the lure of a job then appears to promise greater freedoms which of course it does in the sense of providing another dimension to life but not necessarily in terms of providing fulfilling work, given the nature of many women's employment. How many women have to sit back, their worth unacknowledged, while their bosses take all the kudos and most of the cash? And how many women take jobs which are often no more than extensions of the type of work they do as a matter of course at home? Mary Baker felt that 'Always percolating through my whole life was this thing that I was cleverer than the job I was in and the people I was with and I wasn't fulfilling my potential.'

Many women accept the fact that they are being used at work because they are disproportionately grateful for getting jobs at all or finding employers who accept the constraints that mothers of children will bring. As well as being reproductive cattle, many women are factory cows as well. Few are in a position of being used on a grand scale, such as are film stars and models, most have their sensibilities and capabilities worn away by the lack of challenge and enterprise in their work. This situation is by no means exclusive to women, but it is still true that on the whole women assume the bulk of domestic responsibilities as well, which leaves less time to manoeuvre. Jean Shrimpton's experience as a model doubtless highlights in a more dramatic way what many women feel on a more prosaic level.

Choice of work depends of course on options, being aware of them and then being in a position to pursue them. Many women are not even given the opportunity to train for work they would like because – like Vivianne (NOW) – they are assumed to be a bad investment:

> I was furious because I'd been told I had talent but couldn't put it to any use because I would get married and have babies and therefore wasn't worth training. Even if I'd gone to art college and got qualifications, very few people at that time managed to make a living. I wanted to be an illustrator but it was just brick walls all the time because I was female.

Following this type of experience, they then turn to work which can be acceptably fragmented and either give up the fight for alternatives or wait until such time as they are freer of domestic commitments to try something else. Often the availability of choice has been quashed long before careers as such are even considered. This is probably less so now, but twenty years ago Sheila (NOW) found that, 'In the environment I was in, it was almost if you decided to have a career, you decided to be a nun.'

This is an attitude which those of us who live 'south of the Wash' tend to forget still persists and flourishes to the north of it. It is easy for women to moan about the lack of current opportunity, forgetting how much things have improved and are still improving. There are still countless girls in the same position as Kelly Anderson, who talks about the way her school shaped or did not shape her future; but nowadays if a girl misses out on the education stakes the first time around, there are numerous opportunities to catch up later on, probably with a good deal more motivation. The problem about formal education is its identification with the young rather than viewing it as a continuous life process.

While education may hinder development of potential early on, it is also the traditional way of finding alternatives later. Initially many women take up further and higher education to gain qualifications, but the spin-off in terms of opening up wider personal horizons may well be more profound in the long run. Education might well be the ultimate goal for entirely practical reasons, but the spur can sometimes arise through a feeling of inadequacy and being second rate in comparison with a partner. Many wives sublimate their competitiveness within a marriage to preserve the peace and the *status quo*; but if a marriage cracks apart all the accumulated resentment can focus into a competitive need to succeed as well as – if not better than – the ex-partner. Eileen Curry's experience is a perfect example:

> I started to explore myself while I was working at the college and thought I'd try O-levels to see if I was any good; so I did and got A grades. What I realize now is I was competing with him, proving I was just as good. I did A-levels, then thought, right, I'll show him, I'll do a degree.

Penny McGuire also said, 'I was absolutely determined to show my ex-husband that I could succeed in academia and to go to the best university.' Even a generation ago, most women would not have considered competing with a man for these reasons, nor would the opportunities have existed for them to try to the same extent.

The natural corollary of feeling unfulfilled is to ask why – which can be a risky business, especially for those women who have opted for the security of marriage and for whom this has remained unquestioned for years. Having asked why and embarked on some form of self-analysis, the underlying determination to answer the question may well spark off a fresh starting point around 'who?' Mary Baker found that, 'I started thinking about all the bullshit women are fed and I decided I'd had enough game playing. I've grown from that point on.'

Highlighting the desire for veracity at the centre of one's being is the story of a woman who lost her faith and felt she was living a lie, so left a convent after thirty years. Marion Burman's story provides a radically different dimension from the domestic one but she also shares similar experiences with many other women who reach a point during their middle years when the existing centre no longer holds and the need to be true to themselves becomes of paramount importance. A number of things led her increasingly to question her faith, to feel that the convent hierarchy was unreal and that the degree of submission required to make 'a good nun' was incompatible with the capacity of each person to develop as an individual. Paradoxically, her successful professional life with the order, which she felt 'had prevented me from realizing how out of harmony I was with the spiritual side of things', subsequently gave her the necessary objectivity to make her decision.

The basis for most people's lives though is the institution of marriage, providing either a launching pad or a prison for the partners. There does seem to be a pattern in the middle years which suggests that the road to female independence is strewn with broken marriages. Sometimes marriage has become the alternative to growth, particularly for women with children, and there comes a point when getting out of it is a matter of sheer survival. For Annette Wagner, who had married to get away from home, there was increasing disillusionment with the relationship, but 'It took me seven years to come to the point when I knew I had to do something because I was going under.' The first two years on her own were 'very lonely' but 'I was incredibly happy because, for the first time, I was master of my own destiny.'

Sometimes the break-up of a marriage precipitates a completely new way of thinking, the obviousness of which had not occurred previously because of a combination of conditioning and lack of real alternatives before marriage. Eileen Curry commented that, 'It wasn't until I was on my own that I realized I'd either got to do something or look for another man and go into the same old routine – and that's basically not me.'

Marriage being such a core aspect of many women's lives, it sometimes requires a hard objective look in order to see it for what it is and come to terms with the fact that a woman may be colluding with herself and her partner to maintain what is no more than a hollow shell. Having the guts to abandon it for the lonely unknown is often more than any woman can face. Elizabeth Knight had tolerated her husband's many affairs over the years feeling that 'It's a big thing and very traumatic to suddenly break up a marriage and be completely independent. Sometimes it's better to have somebody than nobody.' Although the marriage becomes increasingly rocky over a period of time, she feels that, 'Possibly we'd still be rubbing along if James hadn't happened.'

Husbands are obviously instrumental, either directly or indirectly, in the break-up of a marriage. Within it, as the main bread-winners they may often unwittingly precipitate changes for their wives if they are forced to change their jobs or places of work; moves with which wives are naturally expected to concur. If this happens at the same time as a wife begins to feel redundant at home and the pressure of time and age are being experienced, the combination of factors is ripe for a woman either to launch off on her own (with or without her family) or to find relief and forgetfulness in valium. When June Barry's husband was promoted and this necessitated a family move to a new area, she was surprised to experience difficulty in settling down and it took her a little while to realize that with her husband absorbed in a new job and the children in new schools, she 'desperately needed someone to relate to, someone who could see me as me and who could sympathize without being emotionally involved'. It was at this point that she 'saw this part-time job advertised, applied and got it'.

The elasticity of a marriage may well be put to the test when a woman finds independence outside it. Sometimes both parties are able to find a new form of accommodation within the partnership which allows greater space for each; sometimes the outward form is retained, often to protect the children, while to all intents and purposes the partners exist side by side but not together. Often this is the time when a woman feels most cheated by marriage and a stultifying way of life; she wants no more of it in any shape or form and is determined to find a solitary solution to life, love and the pursuit of happiness. Some women become so embittered after the break-up of their marriage that they foist all their hatred of one man on to the entire sex and adopt a policy of using men as they once felt used by them.

Of course, one of the associated problems is the link between love and marriage, an association which has become rather entrenched. The upper echelons of society did not necessarily always subscribe to it and the link is now beginning to be queried lower down the social scale. So it is hardly surprising, if love becomes a little jaundiced within marriage over the years, that it should be abandoned altogether outside it. Indeed, one of the rationales for an extra-marital affair has always been that it keeps the marriage together. Romantic love is still generally seen to be the prerogative of the young (said to be wasted on them by others) but that is also becoming outdated. Annette Wagner stated that she was in love all the time and could not live without it, and Mary Baker said: 'Romantic love in middle age is like spring cleaning inside as the menopause approaches, so that you're not depending on externals any more. It's such tremendous fun having a lover.'

That causal link between love and marriage needs to be extended to include sex for many people as well – another area in life which is taken for granted because it is natural and therefore one does not expect to think about it. Most people are conditioned into thinking that 'sex' is something to do with the opposite sex, not one's own. Recognition that this may not be true may well surface during the middle years, when individuals are less inclined to accept what *was* so as being conditional on what *will be* so. Helen Ness describes what happened to her:

I met Pam for the first time when she was setting up the group. I felt very drawn towards her, I couldn't understand the situation but I knew she was someone who cropped up in my dreams and who came before my eyes. I had three small boys all under school age, a husband coming up for his fourth job change in three years and weird things seemed to be happening in my emotional life, which I sat on very hard for about three months. I couldn't let it come out at all. I actually fancied her.

It does take time to question conditioning, which is one of the reasons why the middle generation is the one to make changes. Many women have been helped by the Women's Movement, which has suggested alternatives to the stereotype. A great many of them have picked up the medium in terms of language – words like 'sexist', 'male chauvinist' and so on – but there are still relatively few who live by its message. However, we are still in the early days. Several women mentioned books like *The Feminine Mystique* which were of significant influence, starting a whole new train of thought and leading to a realization that there were others who felt the same way. Some women do base the changes which have come about in their lives on the Women's Movement, like Jenny Kent:

When I was pregnant with my second child I went along to a women's meeting, more out of curiosity than necessity. I was then twenty-nine or thirty. It was amazing, like one of those instant 'clicks' you get. I date whatever self-conscious changes or struggles I experienced from that point, so that even though things didn't change dramatically in my life, the seeds of whatever changes I felt I was going to have to make were there.

Another form of stimulus, but no less profound, can be provided by moving to another country which gives a different perspective on living. Most women within conventional marriages would not view this as possible, and our insularity has not markedly decreased on entering the Common Market, so for most of us other countries are experienced only on holiday. For Jean Shrimpton, the situation was rather different; at the age of twenty-five when at the height of her modelling career, 'The first period of reappraisal came when I went to New York . . . A new place and a different culture helped me to clarify things about myself and I began to realize there were lots of things I was doing in my work which I didn't really like very much.'

Having asked why women bring about changes in their lives, it is merely human to rationalize after the event, if only because it is hard to admit failure. Yet we accept the principle that it is better to have loved and lost than never to have loved at all, so on that basis many women have found it better to grow through change than to stagnate through custom. Jane Worthington sums it up by commenting, 'If anyone's embarking on anything involving personal growth, it's a hell of a lot better to do it than not because I honestly think it's far worse to have regrets about things you've never even attempted to do, than to have failed at something you tried.'

Risk and experiment are two of the keys to change; the alternative is to settle for the inadequate, which is basically destructive not only to oneself but to all the other relationships in which each individual is involved. Elizabeth Knight emphasizes her conclusions: 'I would say to anybody to do what they want to do. The only person you can please all the time is yourself, with regard to other people and their fears.'

There are no easy formulas which can be learned in order to bring about change and, as we have seen, the variations upon the theme are wide. It helps that women are 'allowed' to show their weaknesses and their fears; this is a form of strength which need not inhibit progress and is a tremendous advantage which men have denied themselves – emotion having come to be associated with things female. To launch off on your own is fearful and frightening, like abandoning your standard monthly payment for the uncertainties of becoming a stall-holder in a market. Why some women have mid-life crises and others set off on quests is not just a matter of privilege, nor of being better equipped – neither is it an accident. Possibly it is a conjunction of factors which are coming together for more women more frequently, and in time their activities during the middle years will no longer be remarkable.

6
Why Change Can Be Inhibited

The fault . . . lies not in our stars
But in ourselves, that we are underlings.
                              Shakespeare, *Julius Caesar*

It's a pity women feel they have to make an identity for themselves outside the home and cannot do so, in most cases, within it. We should be liberated enough to feel free whatever we do. But how can you be free if you stay at home? Sometimes women pay too much perhaps for being independent and doing their own thing. Maybe things have to swing to the extreme as they are doing now before reaching a balance.
                                            Christine Merton

It must be rather cosy to be able to blame the stars, or religion or being a woman for not succeeding as you might have done. So if the times are particularly conducive to women bringing about changes during their middle years, why are we not more aware of cohorts of them taking off in all directions? It seems only fair to rectify the balance by suggesting factors which inhibit some women from making changes, yet which others manage to overcome. We are here considering women in general, the mythical 'average', although it is individual women who illustrate particular aspects which are doubtless representative of many others. For in the final analysis, whatever the external influences which help shape female destiny as a whole, it is the individual herself who is ultimately responsible for the pattern of her life. Women are not the 'underlings' they once were, so why haven't more of them come out from under?

The fact that until relatively recently, most women have been defined in terms of their relationships with men, means that many are – and do feel – unequal to them. Many women are conditioned from very early on in their lives to take a rather utilitarian stance about everyday living, on the principle that it is better for everyone to maintain the *status quo* for the sake of a bit of peace and quiet. Women are generally the mediators between different members of the family in aiming to achieve this. However, when they begin to question its wisdom – the basis not only of their own existence but also that of their partners – this not only flies in the face of centuries-old conditioning but it can also rock the familial and societal boat. Bernice Rubens feels that there is enormous frustration for women who become more aware of themselves yet cannot put that awareness to any use. 'Women understand cause and effect,' she says, while 'men can do things and not envisage the results. But some women, just because they are aware of the consequences of their taking off, refrain from doing so. What gives some women the strength to make boat-rocking changes, I don't know.'

Recognizing the pros and cons of bringing about changes, many women are nevertheless inhibited from making them – the responsibility is too great and too frightening, especially as they may never have experienced total responsibility for themselves – or others. The conflict which change inevitably produces also has destructive associations; these are often confused with aggression but nevertheless remain linked – words such as war, violence and so on. More constructively, conflict can imply growth, but that in turn cannot be generated from a state of dependency. Women have to begin to move out from under and risk venturing into the unknown, or at least into the less easily calculable situations. Many women, unfortunately, are not in the position of having any support to encourage them to such an enterprise, so they feel even less able to try.

Playing safe is said not only to be a characteristic of ageing but more particularly of women regardless of age, because they fear displeasing others. If, as is still largely the case for the majority, a woman's place is in the home making life livable for the main bread-winner and his children, then the risk of upsetting the apple-cart and becoming displaced from that traditional role is formidable. The alternative may well be unimaginable isolation, which most individuals cannot cope with, made all the worse when it is set against the previous companionship of family life. Women may not only fear this for themselves, but also be inhibited from taking action because they fear it for their husbands too, suspecting they may cope less well. This echoes Bernice Rubens's comments about cause and effect: women do not always act in their own best interests for altruistic reasons, because they cannot justify to themselves the possible destruction of someone else's life which may result from their taking off. It may also be the case that women suspect this to be true of their husbands and use the knowledge as an excuse for cowardice. Against this, a woman who sets about creating change can in the process produce a more equitable balance in her marriage, one that does not rest on male-dominated power.

Fear of taking risks also depends on a lack of personal assurance, an uncertainty about who you are which demands not only constant self-questioning but inhibits the ability to get on with the job and forget yourself. That too is something learned early on and has a cumulative effect. In Lee's opinion,

> Self-esteem is terribly important in learning and I didn't have a lot. Having self-esteem means you don't have to keep questioning yourself but can be more interested in the subject itself. It's a blockage in learning if you keep asking yourself, could I do it? I did have that blockage. I'm loath to say it's too late now because I wouldn't let anyone else say that about themselves. But I do know that the bad habits I acquired in learning make it, if not too late, very difficult.

This point in turn reflects back on lack of confidence, a factor mentioned by almost every woman who was interviewed, which above all appears to be the major reason why growth, change and development are hindered and delayed in so many women. Lack of confidence imparts a feeling of inadequacy which in turn results in a form of impotence and stagnation. The waste of potential is appalling. Many women who do not doubt their competence in the home, in the community and with their children are nevertheless unable to transfer that ability into working situations beyond the domestic: possibly because domestic experience is neither valued nor considered valuable as a form of employment.

For many women, lack of confidence is equated with unimportance. Some spoke about their lack of importance as girls in the family in relation to their brothers, because it was assumed that girls leave their father's house to move into their husband's – therefore contact with society outside the family was, psychologically if not actually, restricted from early on. If you are treated like a pawn virtually from birth and always subject to other people's plans for you, it does not encourage much self-motivation. To Sheila Dainow,

> lack of confidence was *the* condition which influenced everything for me. It was tied up with how I thought people saw me and therefore with my image. Confidence began to be developed when I was married, from the point of view that someone obviously thought enough of me to marry me. Looking back on when I was growing up, I was concerned with the fact that I wasn't important, that's a better word than confidence. I was there but that was all: it was something to do with my generation being concerned with surviving another day during the war. It wasn't until I reached my twenties that I realized I was important to others and therefore became important to myself.

Because lack of confidence is almost endemic among women, it has been suggested the cause may not be merely cultural. Irma Kurtz, for example, is still 'terrified of the blank page and terrified of getting a commission'. She feels this is something with which only women have to contend and she is 'not sure . . . it's not hormonal or physiological'.

A frequent suggestion is that marriage is the root cause; that living in a state of dependency, women lose their sense of individuality and are only persons in their own right at home. Some women said they hid behind their husbands or their children because they could not face social situations alone: the cumulative effect of having no other outlet apart from the home being a form of social castration. As Sheila (NOW) says, 'gradually you don't expect so much out of life and you begin to accept what you've got'.

However, the effect of a woman's inability to stand on her own two feet is not confined to herself; living through her husband and family, in effect vicariously existing, places an intolerable burden on others. It denies responsibility for oneself but perpetuates the existing imbalance between a couple, both partners sharing a different but distorted view of the world which contributes to a societal distortion. Jane Worthington puts it strongly:

> This business of a woman being deprived of her confidence in marriage and living through her husband, what a bloody burden to her husband! If you're living through someone else, you can then say poor little me, I don't have a life of my own, I'm so oppressed. I've only learnt since living on my own how little responsibility I had. I was party to every decision we made, but I was actually irresponsible.

A woman's view of herself can become even more distorted when she enters a male-dominated profession, like management; nineteenth-century professional women must have felt much the same way. Nowadays women are not prepared to sacrifice marriage and motherhood in order to enter professions, but they do resent the necessity of becoming quasi-men if they are to retain credibility as working women. Julia Mitchell, whose 'confidence still needs constant regeneration', feels very strongly about the fact that when she is the only woman at a business meeting, 'I have to say what I need to in a way that men find acceptable, in their language with their values, almost playing the role of a man. It's disgusting having to do that . . .'

June Barry is convinced that training courses to help women overcome their lack of confidence are necessary 'because they help you stand up for yourself and your rights and think things through and have more faith in yourself'. That there are courses for women as women who lack confidence, suggests there is now more formal recognition of the fact that they need help in order to overcome a real disability. The opportunity to share these feelings of inadequacy also reduces the isolation which many women experience. As Kelly Anderson said about a course on women's assertiveness, 'It was fantastic. I found out how lacking in confidence even the most confident people are, which absolutely amazed me. I'd recommend the course for anybody.'

Many women have remarked on the joys of having enough confidence to be themselves and 'sod everyone else'. Life is wonderful once that handicap is overcome. But how to overcome it? How do women achieve the real freedom of being themselves, not just someone's wife and someone's mother? Because it is doubtful whether domestic confinement will ever bring about the birth of a fully-fledged female – nor indeed should that be the be-all and end-all of anyone's existence.

We have explored some of the changes which women make during their middle years: from going back to work, to taking up further formal education, to a much broader assessment of where they now are, as individuals. We have also considered why the middle years are particularly conducive to altering the direction of one's life: how time, age and social conditions each contribute something towards making this possible. It seems likely that most women assess their lives during middle age, but many may be unable to go beyond thought. It is all too easy to contemplate change in the abstract, but turning that idea into practice is a very different thing. Just how the pattern may be altered in order to get the very best out of the second half of life is the subject of later chapters.

7
Marriage

> Her old lust for living, her serendipity, had been sapped by marriage . . . she had lost all her instincts, it seemed.
>
> Elizabeth Troop, *Slipping Away*

> Marriage . . . it had a kind of admirable cracked solidity, a warm peacefulness, like an old plate. Why throw it away, when it still served? Why change for change's sake? . . . There was something comforting about the cracks: something sweet, familiar, sanctified by use.
>
> Margaret Drabble, *The Middle Ground*

Nearly everyone has something to say about marriage, whether or not they have experienced this relationship. It has an enduring fascination. Like many other aspects of life during the middle years, marriage comes under scrutiny, sheer duration bringing a necessity for review. For women who are now middle-aged it is a particularly interesting time in this respect: many were probably confirmed in the idea that it was the main option open to them in their youth but time and social change have now presented alternatives. How this change comes about depends to a great extent on how marriage was seen in the first place.

Basically, marriage is no more nor less than a contract between two individuals, but over time it has acquired other characteristics. From the earliest days it was seen as an economic contract, in which it was assumed that the husband would be bread-winner with a dependent wife and children – the 'horse and carriage' of popular song. Except that the song says that it is love and marriage which go together like a horse and carriage, suggesting that to have one without the other is unthinkable in our society – so the original economic contract has come to assume considerable emotional investment, particularly for women. The traditional marriage has come to be one in which the wife's role is passive and dependent while the husband is the outward looking, strong protector – both wedded in a situation of some inequality. Until relatively recently, this was by and large true for many individuals, given that marriage was the only means open to women to achieve economic and social security.

Before the widespread use of birth control, marriage also meant motherhood and therefore sex. As P.D. James expresses it, 'If you wanted to have a sexual life, you married. It was the same for me when I was a girl. In this sense, the Victorians may have had life a little easier than we have in regard to choice because there was none.'

Because of the increasing use of contraception it has been possible in the last twenty years or so to disentangle the eternal triangle of sex, love and marriage and see them as separate issues. It was not until around the sixties that girls began to abandon the idea of marriage as the primary goal and were able to consider variations on the theme. Some contemporary marriages are now based on a more equal relationship between the couple, which has the effect of making the institution both stronger and more fragile: stronger in the sense that the power base is more equally shared (though the intensification of the nuclear family tends to increase internal pressure on it), fragile because the situation is relatively new and there are fewer models to follow. Obviously, marriage can be viewed as either a blessing or a burden, depending on the degree of reciprocity within the partnership. Its continuing popularity would suggest that the vast majority still see it as a form of mutual support against the increasing hostilities of the outside world. That expectations of it continue to remain high is reflected in the number of marriages and remarriages. And if longer life is any proof of success, the married win hands down over the unattached.

Just why is marriage so popular and how does it fit into the female pattern of things? As indicated, until recently it provided the main focus of female destiny. P.D. James thinks that

> . . . quite a number of women do still see marriage and children as the ultimate fulfilment and of course, in one very important way, it undoubtedly is. I feel with many women, the drive towards marriage and children is probably a biological urge and it's very important if the race is going to go on at all.

Not only was marriage the ultimate fulfilment for most women, but most were (and are) conditioned towards achieving this goal in a way which is not true for men. Presumably, given the number of married women, there must be an equivalent number of married men but marriage for them is not generally seen as a primary goal to the exclusion of most other options; it takes its place as *part* of the whole, which puts it on a completely different footing for each sex from the start.

Seeing marriage as an alternative to a career, combined with the low standards of self-worth which many women experience, not only devalues marriage but makes it, in effect, a non-option. Many women simply do not see themselves as having a choice about whether or not to marry – they follow the 'natural' course of things. Eileen Curry 'adjusted quite well to being at home with a small child, but I began to think I was incapable of doing anything else besides being a wife and mother'.

Choice apart, the universality and longevity of marriage as an institution suggest it has something positive to offer at a certain time during the life cycle. Bernice Rubens concludes that 'there is a time when you identify yourself with it'. She believes in marriage, and sees it as 'a beautiful and wonderful experience' which yet has 'its own time and place', and should not be continued out of habit unless mutual affection remains.

Marriage can be seen as a good way of ordering one's personal life, which is how Linda Thornber regards it while at the same time she herself 'wasn't very good at the management . . . I was a bad wife.'

The married state can also supply a firm emotional base which affects every other aspect of life. For women particularly, because it still holds considerable status, it can bring confidence and a form of maturity which may previously have been lacking. Sheila Dainow, for example, experienced this in a very positive way, finding that 'the age-old maxim that in discovering someone loves you, you can then begin to love yourself, was true for me'.

Our society is based on the couple unit, and recent variations on the marital theme have made few inroads on the couple orientation. As Bernice Rubens says, 'People think in couples; it's convenient but what kind of people are we that we're reduced to thinking of man, woman, man . . . around a dinner table? It's all very unliberating.'

So conditioned are we to thinking in these ark-type terms, that few individuals can contemplate any alternative – initially at any rate. This, coupled with the strong urge for conformity in youth, is almost enough to ensure the continuity of marriage. In P.D. James's opinion, 'women are so conditioned to see themselves as one of a pair, the prospect of being alone is something they never face or train themselves for, either psychologically, physically or economically'.

We are still a long way from disengaging parenthood from marriage – by design rather than accident, that is. Women in particular, because they may choose to direct all their energies towards the family, can find the achievement of the initial goal eventually less fulfilling than first anticipated, in which case the way is open for them (as the children get older) to discover other forms of personal fulfilment. P.D. James is emphatic, however, that whether fulfilment is found within marriage and motherhood or within a career, 'We ought to have a choice, that we would know ourselves what kind of life we want and what things are important to us. It's not for society or other people to dictate what form that should be.'

Whatever may happen within the relationship later, marriage can be seen as a form of freedom. Unlike most men, some women may have the choice of giving up boring work to opt for marriage and motherhood. Becoming a wife may also seem to offer more freedom than remaining a daughter at home – Annette Wagner, for example, married when she did because it seemed '. . . the only solution. It never occurred to me there might be other ways out, because at the time I couldn't envisage living on my own.'

Many wives find this initial freedom tends to evaporate once children appear; marriage and motherhood then become more like a prison. Being tied down and unable to escape is perhaps one reason why some couples years ago opted for 'trial' marriages rather than the 'real' thing: you could have your cake and eat it and be doing exactly the same as everyone else with rather *outré* overtones. By the sixties or so, this marital pretence had been abandoned in favour of more straightforward living together, which was hard for many parents to become accustomed to and accept. Possibly parental expectations, particularly of daughters, continue to be one reason why a couple living together decide to regularize the situation, and this was Helen Ness's experience:

The main change which happened was that I got married, as that wasn't my ambition or part of my schema of things. There's no doubt it wasn't what I longed for as a child. When I was in the Sixth Form I thought very highly of myself and I did not see myself as the Mother or the Wife, my ideas were incredibly ambitious. In fact my parents were disappointed when we got married; I was twenty-one and it was three weeks after finals, but John and I had been living together for a year and were going to move to London, living right under their noses. It looked to me then as if I had a choice between getting married or getting out of the relationship altogether.

However, all these reasons are merely contributory to the main factor, which is that even today many women feel a form of personal and social failure if they have not at least experienced marriage. There is still a feeling that lurking beneath a 'Ms' is really a 'Miss', which signifies that you have not quite made it to 'Mrs'. Things are changing though, and the mere existence of this clumsy alternative does indicate that women want to be seen as themselves, not as appendages to men or failures because they are not so. Bernice Rubens reminds us of the progress which has been made: 'At the time when I was of marriage age, if one didn't get married that was something to be deeply ashamed of, so I went to university as a kind of standby just in case I didn't fall off the shelf.'

The cracks in this lifelong ambition were beginning to become apparent when the present generation of middle-aged women were younger. The social climate was not such that you could afford to eschew marriage altogether, but personal expectations of it were sufficiently high that if it did not match up to them you could at least get out without fear of appearing a failure. Jenny Kent describes the prevailing attitude when she married:

> I belonged to a rather cynical bunch of college girls in the late fifties/early sixties who didn't think marriage would be the be-all of their lives. By the time I got married at twenty-two I had friends who'd already been divorced. At the same time we all assumed we would get married. It wasn't as if I didn't want to, because I pushed it so that we would; I didn't have this idea it would last for ever and ever but I wanted to give it a try.

Having achieved the goal, what happens in marriage? Why is it that many women later question the goal itself? Myopia must have something to do with it, for like parenthood and childbirth the first time around, neither partner actually has experience of what is involved – it has to be learned at first hand and cannot really be taught. Through the examples of parents and friends, each partner may think he or she shares implicit assumptions about marriage which only time can prove to be erroneous or otherwise. This alone is sufficient reason to reappraise after a few years, as Jane Worthington found: 'We never actually worked out and thought things through and I thought we shared implicit assumptions about it, that because of the way we were brought up we didn't talk about. As I developed I realized we didn't share the same view.'

Immaturity may aggravate the situation further, which was Julia Mitchell's experience. Her five-year courtship commenced when she left school and during those years she lived with strict parents; she found that, 'When we did get married, we began to learn things about each other which were not pulling us together but very definitely pushing us apart.'

Fear that all is not well may inhibit discussion about a marriage in case it should fall apart completely under investigation. Things may jog along all right until some outside trigger forces scrutiny, as Helen Ness found:

Before we went out together we used to argue fiercely and often end up on opposite sides. When we started going out, the liveliness disappeared as if we couldn't afford to argue any more. John talked about marriage as if we were consolidating a position which we needn't talk about once we were married. I never challenged that at the time but I now realize if you don't question a relationship, it goes away.

One of the least pleasing aspects of marriage is that which maintains wives to be no more than legally kept women, not simply by virtue of their sexual but also their domestic services. Women with children who concerned themselves only with things domestic, which did not rate as worthwhile in terms of paid employment, tended to consider their efforts within the home were without value.

JANE WORTHINGTON: It absolutely amazed me years ago when you were talking about what a wife contributes because I'd always thought a wife was being looked after, as she wasn't earning.
LIZ AHRENDS: We did think like that in those days and it followed we should be duly grateful.
JANE WORTHINGTON: But you pointed out that we were contributing by servicing; that had never occurred to me.

This feeling of lack of importance is enhanced by the continuing tradition of man being the most important individual in the household by virtue of his role as bread-winner. Eileen Curry's comment illustrates this and throws an interesting sidelight on possible regional differences in attitude:

I was very keen on my husband getting on and was there to support him: that's very much a North Eastern way of life, to put men first, give them the lion's share of whatever's going. I accepted that. Jim was the centre of my life and everything else wasn't to be taken too seriously.

It is not too difficult to see that if a woman identifies herself entirely with one man, she excludes the possibility of identifying with the world at large. By living vicariously through her husband a wife places a huge burden on him, often hiding behind him and their children because she cannot face social situations alone, being in effect a person of no worth in her own right. In concentrating all her energies in the domestic sphere, a woman can effectively lose a sense of identity outside the marital and familial one; ultimately she is in danger of becoming an 'object', in her own eyes and those of others, as Dianne (NOW) found: 'I knew who I was before I got married and I was all right until I had children and stayed at home all the time and became a skivvy.'

This form of self-negation may increase if a husband has other girl-friends. Because many women do not see themselves as equals within a marriage, and in numerous respects feel they are lesser beings than their husbands, they have a tendency to question their own inadequacies and blame themselves for what goes wrong, rather than seeking a shared reason. Elizabeth Knight's collusion over her husband's girl-friends is a perfect example of this.

Choice is one of the major areas of controversy about marriage today – within and without it. Most of the arguments tend to focus on women, which is understandable because it is the first time in history that they have been in a position to 'take it or leave it'. But what about men? Julia Mitchell comments on their behalf:

> To a great extent, many men get a raw deal out of marriage: condemned to some sort of drudgery in jobs which they often hate, for people who belittle them, with no choice to get out. I deplore the attitude which so many women adopt that the man should be the stable provider. I think it's rather immoral and I expect there to be more changes in that attitude. When they can make arrangements for their children, women do have the choice to work.

Nevertheless, few wives with jobs would disagree with Rosie's (NOW) rejoinder that 'They do have us to back them up at home very often. Whereas we come home after a nine to five job and are expected to cope with the home as well.'

So is independence within marriage possible or is it a myth both sexes share? Is it a paradox which only begins to emerge after a marriage has existed for a few years, needing resolution during mid-life? Because of the social focus on marriage, some women do see it as an alternative to developing themselves in other directions. However, this is a point of view which can change with time, and Bernice Rubens suggests it might be a good idea 'If women held board meetings with themselves from time to time . . . all it requires is an initial bout of dissatisfaction when you look up from the ironing board and wonder whether this is all there is to life.' Her own conclusion is, 'The logic of it is to live alone, to find one's own instincts and feelings. This kind of independence I have found as a woman, is not possible within a marriage.' Although few would dispute the value of reappraisal, many might feel that what Bernice calls 'one's own space' – into which she considers 'man's perception of self intrudes' – can co-exist with that of one's marriage partner without having 'to fit around it, but on the periphery'.

Many women consider they can justify having space in the home only by 'doing' all the time – and doing things for the family, not for themselves. Kelly Anderson found this even extended to reading, when her husband would talk to her about *his* book and she would 'listen to him and think I'll read what I have tomorrow'. This only confirms Molière's comment that, 'Reading goes ill with the married state.'

The double bind which many women have to cope with in relation to work both outside and inside the home, is still not true for most men though the situation is changing. Englishmen apparently do more housework a day than their European counterparts but this may not include the 'psychic' time which women spend in organizing their households. Jane Worthington expresses the conflict between motherhood and a career: 'I think the danger is if you get married young and have your babies young, it's fine in one way but if you're going to do the growing up, your marriage is at risk. The alternative is to grow up with your husband before you have the babies, which then puts your career at risk.'

However much parenting is shared within the home, wives are still at a disadvantage in paid employment, because so many employers assume a married woman will have children and therefore that her work will be jeopardized. Thinking like that reduces training opportunities for many women even before marriage, as Sheila and Rosie (NOW) discuss.

> SHEILA: I found in my mid to late twenties they were pushing me too damn hard because I was a girl and single and I'd look good on their statistics – that women can make it. But the minute I got married and there was a possibility I could get pregnant, the situation changed.
> ROSIE: That's what I mean about not being taken seriously when I got married. I went after this research post but the professor said as I'd got married, I wouldn't take the job seriously. If that had occurred to me I wouldn't have got married but stayed living together. I was told I'd be too preoccupied with cooking and housekeeping.

So far, the exploration of why women get married and what happens during the early years has shown numerous pointers towards mid-life assessment being a logical outcome of the situation. Many women who have concentrated their energies in the home and whose biological functions in terms of motherhood are largely over, may well question what else life holds. It is this particular stage of marital life which has often been deemed a crisis, as P.D. James emphasizes: 'It may only be when this biological urge has been fulfilled that women look, even at a happy marriage, and say, "Is this everything? Is this all I intend to do?" For many women, I think they would say, "Yes, it is." '

Conversely, many others who have concentrated on their careers to the exclusion of marriage and children, may consider both during the middle years while there is still time. Again, this is an option which remains open to women and not, apart from parenthood, open to men. P.D. James reflects that 'perhaps women who fall very deeply and very romantically in love . . . never have to make the decision whether to marry or not, these decisions are more or less made'. But those who have postponed marriage and had lovers, she feels, 'seldom fall in love in the way I'm describing and they do look at relationships with a more dispassionate eye. Obviously they are not needing to marry for sexual fulfilment.'

Time and habit may obscure awareness of the married state because it is difficult to remember a time when one was single. Sheila Dainow's reappraisal during the middle years began with a feeling that she was involved in 'a fairly boring relationship in marriage', but now 'I've done a real full circle about my marital relationship and I think it is a good one for me – whether I've made it like that or it always was, I don't know.'

Ripples in a marriage are bound to be caused when a woman launches out later in life, and she may provide the catalyst towards reaching a new and better accommodation within the relationship. Liz Ahrends found that becoming a mature student had far-reaching effects:

> I think that [a] crisis had to occur and I think maybe if you've been married for twenty-five years, it's not so bad to have one. A lot of stuff had to come out and be talked about – all the implicit assumptions which can be quite harmful. What I learned from that experience was good, finally. I hadn't realized to what a tremendous extent my security was based in the marriage; everything I had done in the outside world relied very much on that security. It came as a complete surprise to me that marriage could change like this.

On the other hand, the middle years can bring a recognition that the marriage one is part of is, to all intents and purposes, a non-event. To Elizabeth Knight this had been increasingly apparent for some time, but 'It took twenty years of married life for me to realize there was nothing beneath the surface.' Her experiences, however, do show how easy it is to continue jogging along a familiar path, however unsatisfactory; as she said, 'I never imagined I would become divorced until I met James.'

If the continuity of a marriage depends on each partner fulfilling specific functions within it and not stepping over certain agreed or implicit boundaries, it may not be elastic enough to cope when one partner runs out of alignment. Bernice Rubens is convinced that when she began to break away from the supportive role, '. . . there's no question that that contributed to the break-up of my marriage. I began to question my place.'

Having passed through the 'school' of marriage and experienced one version of it, some women become determined never to have anything more to do with the marital state. The middle years can be the first time in a woman's life when she lives alone, and she may find the freedom rather heady. Once she has become used to not being part of a couple, marriage may not seem to offer anything that cannot be obtained outside this partnership and that is certainly a freedom which is not only new to women but also liberating for men. No wonder middle-aged women can feel unexpectedly powerful when – contrary to how they expected to feel about a broken marriage – they conclude in time that the change is a boon and a blessing.

This does underline the importance of reviewing a marriage as circumstances within it change; staying together for the sake of the children, for instance, has become increasingly a non-argument since more and more single parents prove it can be done. But one aspect of human frailty is to think the grass is always greener on the other side, and P.D. James feels that assessments about marriage during the middle years may obscure its initial desirability years previously, especially for those who married young and now 'possibly overlook the strength of the need they had for marriage and the family. Had they stayed in their office jobs . . . and missed the husband and marriage, they would possibly be feeling much more frustrated.'

A severely blinkered view of what life holds in the round for both sexes, is bound to lead to distortion within marriage as well. If men see their role both as head of household and main wage-earner, and women see theirs as servicing the worker and his children, there is very little chance of meeting on common ground or of reciprocity. P.D. James comments that a wife who takes a job later in marriage presents a threat to her husband not only in terms of being no longer economically dependent but also because 'the woman who is meeting people outside the home is in a world which the man cannot share, any more than she can share his working life'.

We have seen the middle years as times of reckoning, from many points of view. Harsh and painful though the process is bound to be, ultimately it can be a fruitful and positive experience because self-exploration brings greater knowledge and truth to light. In relation to marriage, for instance, some women may find it possible to admit during this stage in their lives that they have made a mistake. Knowing themselves, they may also accept the situation and recognize that they will continue to live with the error because they cannot face the alternative. This may well be a form of compromise, but it is one made in the light of experience, not as a cop-out. Mary Baker, who married when she was twenty-four, now feels:

> . . . it was probably a mistake because Tim's a father figure really – he's nine years older than me. I was never what I'd call a crashing success with men and Tim was good-looking and a catch and I got enormous kudos from this. I nearly broke it off once because I felt it was somehow wrong, but I feel now I would probably have done the same thing given similar circumstances.

What is later seen to be a mistake in marrying a certain man, is bound to be compounded if one of the partners grows and develops away from the other, as happened to Elizabeth Knight and her husband. A woman who has taken off during the middle years will have become a different person in many respects, and she may feel she has endangered her marriage as an unintended consequence. The personal conflict which ensues can be a mixture of fear and elation, for a sense of achievement can be whittled away by fears that personal growth has also undermined the basic security of the marriage by upsetting the *status quo*. A wife may be confident of accommodating her new sense of self within the old marriage but afraid that her husband cannot do so. Perhaps, too, many women perceive themselves as being the cause of marital unrest and are reluctant to accept the responsibility for that. Kelly Anderson, whose husband thought she might 'blossom out into an intellectual woman and leave him behind' when she took a degree course, was still looking for the right career opportunity when interviewed:

> I think I'm really a bit afraid of my marriage going by the board. Before we were married my husband used to come back on leave every two weeks or and so and I was very happy to see him but I think I got a false impression of what he was like and what life would be and how I felt about him. Perhaps I was not wholeheartedly committed to him at first though I made myself be. It was probably not what I really wanted to do.

Now that her horizons have expanded, 'We don't know how

to get into a new pattern', she still feels 'very constrained by family commitments' though 'this is my own attitude, not theirs'.

It still seems the case that many wives accept playing a secondary role in their marriage and baulk at the responsibility of reversing or equalizing the situation. But how many women consider there is a real alternative to marriage? There is still a belief abroad that marriages are made in heaven, which is highly debatable: however the unions may come about they function here on earth. Many continue to do so out of sheer habit, for despite deep rifts there is a shared pattern of existence which can be very hard to break, as Linda Thornber found when she 'waited so long to be free of the marriage because you just go on and there was nowhere else to go and it isn't something which just happens to you'.

Jenny Kent describes how frightening the alternative to marriage can seem '... the fear that independence could be a disaster. I might be a pathetic creature in a bed-sit and in achieving this, I might be sacrificing something which is solid and good...'

Many women find the support of their female friends of enormous benefit to their marriages, removing some of the pressure from the intensity of the couple. Lee found that, 'One thing which cushioned life for me was sharing the house. There were always so many friends around, neither of us depended solely on one person for support or for company.'

Some wives weigh up the pros and cons of individual freedom within marriage and wonder which price is the highest:

SHEILA: If it involves something which can rock your husband's boat, you think is it really worth it? Women are very much the ones to look for a peaceful life.

ROSIE: You also think, is it going to make life unbearably complicated? I've got to this course because I can't spend the rest of my life in the situation I'm now in. Working out how you're going to do it is the problem.

Nevertheless, it is one thing to have experienced marriage and to have had the choice whether or not to reject it; it may still represent a desirable way of life late in the middle years because there has been no opportunity to consider it earlier. Marion

Burman was quite clear that she wanted to get married a few years after she had left her convent, but previous generations of middle-aged women would have found this hard to achieve long after the accustomed time for marriage. The existence of agencies today emphasizes not only the profound couple orientation of society but underlines the difficulties isolated individuals experience in achieving that goal. Marion was lucky in that her first agency introduction was Harry, to whom she is now married.

A small minority of women now in their middle years – though there are possibly far more among subsequent generations – rejected the idea of marriage from the start. The security which marriage offers for many can also represent a form of imprisonment for others. Irma Kurtz, for example, says that 'From the age of eighteen, there were certain things I knew – I knew I wasn't going to get married. I feel like I was born knowing that. Frankly, I've not liked the look of it and I can't stand the feeling of being trapped in any position.'

So can there be an ideal solution to marriage? Perhaps we should stop thinking about it as a lifelong commitment and start considering variations within or without this relationship which suit different times of life. It is impossible to present a solution to something which has yet to be experienced and is held to be highly desirable, and no one person can adequately inform another about what is involved in marriage. Until there are a great many other legal and social changes, marriage will probably remain a goal for many people, but perhaps what is really important for members of the middle generation is to realize just how much choice they really have. Two very different women came up with the same solution, which combines independence and marriage. Bernice Rubens comments, 'Of course, the ideal solution for me would have been to marry the boy next door and for him to stay next door.' Eileen Curry has the same feeling: 'What'd be ideal would be someone to stay in his house and I'd keep mine and we could meet two or three times a week. That'd be perfect!'

So what price the image of the clinging vine? Middle-aged women are helping to bring about changes in the whole concept of marriage, so that both partners can be more free not only to be themselves but also to share a flexible base for the rest of life's activities. Perhaps if more men and women could think of marriage as a 'school', as Bernice Rubens suggests, they would be better able to view it as an experience they may in time pass through and grow beyond. To see it as a possible phase of life rather than an ultimate goal for all time would remove none of its desirability or joy, but would perhaps place it in a much more balanced perspective for both sexes.

8
The Family Game

> The restraint (or masochism) of my generation sometimes amazes me . . . Criticized by our parents, attacked by our children, we hold fire, seldom fight back as we could do. It has something to do with the pace of change. Our parents were disciplined into believing that you did what you had to, not what you wanted, that the future was worth waiting for, that you respected your parents and worked hard for your children. We have some of that discipline, though the strain is watered down, weaker, and in most of our children it has disappeared altogether. Trying to provide a frail bridge between the old and the young, protect the one from the other, we accept absurd handicaps in the family game.
>
> Nina Bawden, *Walking Naked*

It is not at all original to suggest that families are like the Mafia: they are synonymous with blood relationships – in every sense of the word. But in one odd respect they can exclude partners because these are chosen and not acquired, though it goes without saying that they are essential to the continuity of the family. Nevertheless we tend to ask questions like, 'Have you any family?' which effectively means, 'Have you any children?' Or if that is not appropriate, it applies to your inherited family or the one you have acquired with marriage. The existence of a partner is often assumed or even taken for granted, but he occupies a separate and distinct place within the family in relation to a woman's role as wife, mother and daughter. A husband or partner does play a very specific part in the life of a woman contemplating or bringing about change, and because of that, a separate chapter is devoted to exploring all the ramifications (Chapter 14). This chapter, therefore, will explore what the older and younger generations mean to those in the middle years, for nowhere is the state of being 'in the middle' more clearly focused than in relation to the family.

It is a very paradoxical time, being in the middle generation; there is nothing more odd and disconcerting than being both adult, parent and child, spanning past, present and future generations. A middle-aged adult may still feel like a child in the presence of his parents while at the same time actually assuming some responsibility for them. Because of the early years of inequality existing between parent and child, there is often a residue of that feeling of safety and security with parents, even though the adult is now also a parent. Yet for the middle-aged there is also the increasing possibility of a parent's death, which not only emphasizes a personal sense of mortality but marks the final severance of links with childhood.

If we are not all 'bound upon a wheel of fire' (which may be a more accurate description of family relationships than we often care to admit), the cyclical nature of family life is most clearly illustrated during the middle years. As our children grow up, leave home and seek independence, at the same time our parents are growing older and becoming more dependent. Middle age thus brings greater dependencies from both generations, not fewer, as Sheila Dainow feels:

> It seems that for people of our age we have a lot of adult dependants – children struggling to get away and parents struggling to get closer and you are in the middle. My fantasy is that my children will leave and my mother will come and I will never be free of dependants. Probably you have to work much harder to remain adult as an adult with your parents as you both grow older.

In theory, at least, the maturing child is moving towards a situation of equality with his parents, but it seems doubtful whether this can ever be attained in an absolute sense because of the memories of inequality on each side. Many of the present generation of middle-aged people consciously rejected parental influence when they achieved adulthood around the early sixties, opting for the support and guidance of contemporaries and non-relations instead. Nancy Roberts suggests that although you can do your utmost to sever the links, parental influence remains a powerful force throughout life, to the extent that 'If you imagine a pint measuring jug, it's full up when you're a child, pour out half an ounce and that's what's left when you die. My brother's favourite quote, I think it's Woody Allen's, is "To not become one's parent requires eternal vigilance." '

Is parental influence particularly enduring for daughters because of the traditional inward/familial orientation of most women's lives? Perhaps it is harder for them to achieve a sense of autonomy because for so long women have not only acquired the main nurturant role in their own families but at the same time been felt (by some men) to require more looking after themselves.

The possibility of a daughter becoming the unwitting instrument of her mother's unfulfilled ambition increases with the rapidity of social change, which has created for the daughter opportunities which were not available when her mother was young. Sons have always been potential victims of their mothers, but it is a relatively recent phenomenon for mothers to be able to focus on a career as an alternative to a 'good' marriage for their daughters. Rosie (NOW) explains her situation:

> For me it was very much what my mother said: 'Don't do what I did, this is what you've got to do.' It was my father who said it was important to get my qualifications first, get my MA, then take a year off. It was pressure to get qualifications regardless of whether they suited me for what I really wanted to do.

Refusal to go along with her mother's plans for her career created such bitterness for Marion Burman that she persisted with becoming a nun despite strong maternal opposition.

Mothers also tend to imprint on their children the necessity for 'getting on', not only for their own good but to escape the treadmill the parents had no opportunity of avoiding. Linda

Thornber's mother 'was one hell of a lady . . . her sole object in life was we weren't to go to the Mill. She used to go into the chip shop and ask them for the crosswords off the newspaper and she'd do the *Times* crossword with no bother.'

Conversely, because the traditional goal for daughters has always been marriage and motherhood, some parents have felt it more acceptable to sacrifice future career opportunities for their daughters for the sake of supplementing current family income. The effect of having career ambitions thwarted early on for a woman now middle-aged may make her all the more determined to achieve goals later. Vivianne (NOW) recalls: 'There was this parental pressure on me not to take extra qualifications when I left school. I wanted to go to art school but there was this mute pressure to go out and earn some money because we weren't well off.'

We tend to assume nowadays that sons and daughters occupy equal, though possibly different, status in the family. Although there have been periods when small boys were dressed like small girls until the time came for them to leap overnight into manhood, if parents felt disappointed about the sex of a child it was more likely to be because that child was female. Coming to terms with that deep, incomprehensible unfairness may take years and cause immeasurable guilt in the process. Annette Wagner's father 'always regretted I wasn't a boy . . . because I was quite good at school and even though I wasn't a boy, he wanted me to take over the business. He actively prevented me from doing anything other than this, so I had to fight this as well.'

In many ways, sexism within the family is harder and more damaging to cope with than that outside, because it conditions and sets a pattern which is more difficult to break. Nancy Roberts is certain that this is the real stuff of feminism:

> My early life is what feminism is about because there's no denying that a terrible wastage of human potential was allowed to exist just because I was a woman. My parents lived through my brother's success and his career, even to this day they're deprecating about me and my success.

Recently there has been a great deal of literature about the mother/daughter relationship: one which Christine Merton feels can become firmer and more truly equal when the daughter has children of her own. 'During the middle years a mother and daughter may come together again more closely. When the daughter herself becomes a mother she can open a new understanding between them.'

Most of the women who were interviewed commented about the role their mothers played in their lives. Given the pattern of life for the parents of the present middle generation, on the whole mothers were more likely than fathers to be a continuing and unbroken presence while their children were growing up. Many women spoke about the loving support and encouragement they were given by their mothers, especially during times of crisis.

A negative relationship with a father, on the other hand, can be a reason for a daughter to marry someone who is his complete opposite, escaping from the influence of inherited family relationships into one which appears to hold some degree of choice. Failure to come to terms with the paternal relationship – although seeming to resolve it by escaping into marriage with an 'opposite' type – does suggest that the unresolved conflicts which existed with a father in childhood and youth, become more complex with age in relation to a husband. Eileen Curry remembers:

> My father was very impractical and I fought with him in my teens a lot. He couldn't cope with me growing up overnight as I did. We used to go months without talking, me totally ignoring him which never got me down though it obviously had effects on my development later.
>
> When we got married, I was twenty; my father took the attitude I was no longer his responsibility and although I still feel very bitter towards him, our relationship did improve. Looking back I suppose I was searching for a man who was the complete opposite of my father.

Assuming the influence of parents becomes increasingly internalized and less direct as we grow older, it does so partly because it is pushed further away by the presence of the family we choose to create for ourselves – the chosen as opposed to the inherited family. When we talk about 'the family' in this country today, we tend to mean the unit comprising two generations – parents and children. It is interesting to note that under Roman law, *familia* meant the total number of slaves in a particular household.

The family as we know it today became established around the fourteenth century as a legal hereditary line. Traditionally, relationships within the family were organized on a vertical basis. Husband/Father was at its head but Wife/Mother was the lynch-pin retaining a total if restricted power within the household. The Welfare State continues to assume that the best place for a child to develop is within a parent/child unit and organizes its health, education and welfare services accordingly. However, with Child Benefits being paid directly to mothers, it does acknowledge on the one hand that it is women who are largely involved in child care and on the other, that they might be doing so without the support of their children's fathers. Custom and convenience has established the family as a neat solution for the nurturance of its members. However grim individual experience of an inherited family may be, most of us blithely assume at the outset that the family we choose to create will be different and therefore better and the syndrome is perpetuated.

As a total entity, the family may well thrust roles on its individual members which have long-lasting effects and take years to escape. For Julia Mitchell it now seems that the emphasis on music in her family probably obscured many other possibilities – 'I've only begun to see this clearly over the past few years and I'm forty. I've got to start now defining my real self which seems incredible.'

Conversely, by refusing to accept the role thrust upon her, an individual member may find herself rejected by the family, which will impinge in a different but no less effective fashion. Jean Shrimpton, who felt rejected when her sister was born, feels this coloured her entire life, and may also account for her success because 'to fail was another form of rejection'. Perhaps it is indicative of her experiences within her family, that she later says it is important to her to create a home: that is, the creation of a space rather than the relationships within it.

Regardless of the family we inherit, the choice is still open to women to escape from that into their own form of domesticity, an option available to few men. Having done so, the pattern of smaller numbers of children leads to greater intensity within the family unit, each member requiring more exclusive concentration. This fact leads some women to echo Annette Wagner's comment that 'domesticity's a killer' and to feel that the structured dependencies within it are constraining, as expressed by Jenny Kent:

> Personally I find family life incredibly oppressive, although for me this has little to do with day-to-day household slog. I cook once a week, do hardly any housekeeping and live with a person who in no way expects me to fill some stereotype role of housewife, wife and mother. Yet I feel the whole notion of a group called a family, immensely stifling. I see women who feel so trapped by it because of the way they and the outside world see themselves. If you're operating within a family situation . . . life is structured by other people's dependencies on you and by yours on them. I'm interested in exploring just how dependent I am on my husband and children because decisions that are made are always done so with regard to other people.

Though Jenny describes her personal reaction to a fairly typical family situation, it is not necessarily exclusive. More communal living arrangements with other families will reduce the pressure to some extent, although these still may not rectify the imbalance of parenting which tends to exist in more orthodox households, as Lee comments:

> I had (my husband's) encouragement which was very important and valuable to me, but when I could have done with his help in terms of domestic commitments, he wasn't there. When our children were young, they didn't see much of Colin because apart from his work, he thought the best way of doing things for his family was doing things to change the world through political work. I felt at the time he was getting things out of proportion and missing a lot and said so. He realizes that now and regrets it, though too late to have any real effect on the family. It was partly my fault that I didn't fight for another arrangement, that I wasn't more clear about the unbalanced existence he led. All the same, I think I had a

better deal with my lack of freedoms than he did with his comparative freedom.

Lee's description illustrates how both parents can lose out by polarizing their roles within the family. But there's another problem lying at the centre of family life which is particularly crucial for women generally and especially for those trying to establish new patterns of living. Christine Merton recalls that when she was married she did not at first want 'to do my own thing'; she loved her children and liked being a housewife:

> Although I struggled once having got to college, with the efforts of discipline and adjustment, it seems now that I was still cushioned by the feeling of security inside the family. I remained primarily in the position of being a mother and a partner to a man and did not emancipate myself into a fully fledged individual person or artist. That was still easily the secondary role especially for someone of my times.

Many women spoke of the difficulty of maintaining some sense of individuality apart from these basic roles, but their conditioning has generally been so effective that they often feel guilty when they are not occupied with domestic tasks. Kelly Anderson, whose feelings regarding family commitments were mentioned earlier endorses this:

> I never felt the children were my property but I was looking after them and helping them grow up. I don't feel their world would fall apart if I wasn't there but I just feel I should be around in case they need me – that's my way. I feel very guilty when I do something for myself. Am I always going to feel like that? I bet I am.

Families are never neutral entities so it is hardly surprising they are the focus of all types of social, political and personal struggle, particularly in relation to women. How to achieve independence without destroying the benefits of familial existence is the basis of concern to all individuals who are trying to live rich and full lives, not at the expense of one half of the population – whichever it may be.

At the centre of the controversy lie children. A couple becomes a family only when it produces offspring which consolidates the position for the present and ensures continuity in the future. Children form the greatest divide between those who have them and those who do not; as Christine Merton expresses it:

> Women who haven't had children don't know what sacrifice is. It's such a total thing having to be there with them. It's such a vital experience and such a demand. To become a mother is a change made for ever. In order to put up with the sacrifices, the constant pulling and tugging and having to be there for 'them', it is vital to develop one's own personality alongside as best one can, so as to have this thread in hand when the children leave later.

Until the arrival of children, male and female domestic roles can remain blessedly blurred and vague. Their appearance on the scene, however, demands clarification of the domestic situation and heralds a more specific division of labour in the household – who does what and why because 'they're your children as much as mine'. Perhaps it is this previous sense of co-operative and more spontaneous living which many women with small children are desperately struggling to get back to: the type of freedom which did exist before children arrived, as compared with the more circumscribed freedoms of parenthood.

The shock of motherhood may be all the more profound for some women because they discover they do not 'naturally' enjoy it, which is contrary both to their upbringing and to what they think they *should* feel. That the guilt syndrome associated with motherhood can set in very early is exemplified by Jenny Kent:

> I think having kids in my late twenties was my first real shock in life; it was a truly shocking event for me because I'd always been told by other people what a wonderful mother I'd be and had always enjoyed being with children. In fact I was really quite miserable about it; suffered from post-natal depression and went off sex completely after my first child.

Because women bear and generally take the greater hand in

looking after their offspring, custom and habit have generally elevated the moral superiority of those who fulfil their 'natural' function over those who do not or cannot do so. It follows in this respect that women who do not enjoy the whole process are bound to feel ashamed of their 'un-natural' feelings. Sheila Dainow is in two minds about this – loving and valuing the children she has but feeling 'burdened by the responsibilities they bring, especially during the last two years since my eldest has been edging towards independence. Sometimes, and I feel a bit ashamed to admit it, I feel bored by all of it.'

To give up a child for what a mother perceives to be its own best interests is therefore seen to be not only flying against the face of nature but against all the instincts our society has fostered in regard to motherhood. Linda Thornber, who had to make that decision during her middle years following divorce, says, 'One of the worst things that happened in the last few months was losing John. I couldn't have coped a few years ago, giving up a child, but I knew it was better for him to be with his father and I made up my mind and came to terms with it.'

Women now in their middle years can be faced with a variation on that kind of decision, whether or not to have children at all. By the late seventies, eighty per cent of adults were parents, which confirms another social norm but is one to which women can now delay subscribing because of more efficient contraception. P.D. James wonders whether the 'interesting phenomenon of career women, now deciding rather late in life that they will have children . . . may represent some disillusionment with their jobs and professional life'. She feels this is something both sexes may experience, but only women have 'a way out'. That a successful career woman may change direction in this way because of a feeling that something is missing, in her opinion is 'governed by biological laws and is a decision that can't be put off beyond a certain point. It is an immense freedom which has brought with it immense problems and its own tensions and anxieties.'

Maron Burman emphasizes the point in relation to her decision to leave the convent: 'There was a period in my early forties when I very nearly did leave because it was the last chance if I was going to have children.'

Irma Kurtz did decide to have a child in her late thirties and feels that it 'wasn't a decision, just going with the flow of things'. Having had an interesting and varied life until that point, and possessing great confidence in her ability to mother, she describes it as having 'come to the end naturally and then it was natural to have a child'.

Most women still react to the biological impulse earlier on in life, many for no very clear reason except that others are doing it at the time, which has repercussions later on when that 'decision' is reviewed. Another effect of motherhood, which again will not be reaped until a woman grows older and her children grow away from her, is amplified by Julia Mitchell:

> Traditionally men have made it their business to acquaint themselves with the business of wider issues. Once women have children they often seem to forget the whole of the outside world except other mothers . . . if they do this for a few years, they aren't able to cope in the world outside the home.

The middle years prompt many reviews and appraisals, one of which may well be of the satisfaction which motherhood brings. Many women find themselves swept into it without actually planning to be; later this may turn out to be an event precluding other forms of activity which were not fully appreciated at the time. Possibly many women in mid-life would admit to finding motherhood unsatisfactory as a total way of life – an attitude shared by all except those who feel that they are in some way called upon to fulfil a sacred mission. Single-track living must inevitably be found wanting and Liz Ahrends's feelings about pram-pushing – 'I felt so weird, it wasn't me' – will be echoed by countless others who, like her, 'always felt there was a bit of me that was being suspended somehow for the time being'.

It has been suggested already that many women achieve maturity considerably later than usually expected, partly because their personal development is arrested in the round by producing and caring for children. Against that, early motherhood can bring a type of maturity, possibly of the hot-house variety, in response to children's needs. This, however, does not necessarily imply maturity of the whole person, rather the forced development of certain skills out of necessity, like Penny

McGuire who 'had a baby when I was nineteen. I couldn't even boil an egg. I had to grow up and be responsible.'

A lurking suspicion that one is not a 'whole' person just by being a mother, may well cause many women to turn to work as a solution. They then find that the joys of motherhood as an occupation are often a good deal less alienating and more creative than many traditional female jobs outside the home – more often than not, these are only extensions of the home domestic role. The state has undoubtedly whittled away at many of the functions of motherhood in terms of health, education and welfare, leaving the role at home considerably curtailed. Nevertheless, women who lack a sense of occupational identity elsewhere may feel a real sense of power within the home; this is limited power, which does not stand up to much scrutiny but is real enough for the woman whose parameters are primarily domestic.

Being in the home for most of the time with small children, must create consequences for a woman which accrue with time. Children inevitably bring about a change of self-concept in mothers, as Jane Worthington explains: 'I was feeling completely lacking in confidence because I'd opted out from my education and being at home with the children does sap your confidence in a most incredible way. It wasn't the time for using my mind, I just slogged along.'

Cumulatively, a woman's self-esteem is gradually whittled away as her identity as 'so and so's mum' is enforced to the exclusion of any other. A woman agonizes about this, goes out to work to rectify the balance and then feels guilty about what she is doing to her children. Sheila Dainow takes a longer perspective about children in thinking that 'whatever we do to our children, they will still have to fight their own battles – which, in an odd sense, makes very little difference what the parents do, providing the basics are there'.

Other women may view the period of their lives which is predominantly occupied with children as one during which their own personal options are temporarily foregone. They may regard the time after the children have left home as a form of delayed gratification, like Julia Mitchell who has set herself a target 'to work as long as it takes to put the children through the educational process . . . Then I'll say, now's the time to do some of the things I want to do.'

Children really are unwitting agents of change in adult lives, especially for women; they may well be the reason for a couple getting married at all, and it is then more likely that they come to be more important than the marriage itself. As Helen Ness says: 'I think John found it difficult to cope with fatherhood so early and in a real sense, it's the children who've kept us together. Being married doesn't actually play much of a part in my life really, what to do about the children is more important.' Children are often used as the 'presenting' reason for continuing with an unsatisfactory marriage, as Mary Baker describes:

> I feel more trapped by my marriage than by my children and I certainly won't marry again. My children are the reason I won't up stakes. My daughter's a smashing kid, very vulnerable and yet so solid. I feel I just can't rock the boat. I made a bad bond with my eldest and I wonder if I could manage my adolescent son on my own.

Conversely, Julia Mitchell found that her decision to break up her marriage to an alcoholic husband was motivated by consideration of the effect on the children: 'If it had been just me I would have probably have kept the *status quo*.'

The break-up of a marriage and the subsequent process of divorce may turn out to be so traumatic that some women dare not risk a repetition, in case a future stepfather is not amenable to someone else's children. On the other hand, *ad hoc* arrangements which arise after a separation may be so complex that the mother regularizes the situation to ease the social repercussions for her children; this is what later happened to Julia Mitchell, whose plans originally did not take remarriage into account.

Variations on the theme in relation to children and marriage are infinite and increasingly wider. The discovery that alternatives to the orthodox couple exist may not arise until the middle years, when more conventional set-ups have been tried and found wanting. What does seem to be true for many women whose marriages break apart is the very real life-line which their children represent. Children become the main reason for survival, for starting a new life and for turning what may at the time seem to be a predominantly negative experience into a positive one. Annette Wagner is emphatic about the part her children played in her life when she separated from her husband: 'But I couldn't let myself go and sink under because of the children and whatever happened, I'd always have to prepare my face in front of them.'

However, it must be hard, while recognizing the sustaining nature of one's children, to carry on any sort of private life which excludes them. Single parenthood illustrates particularly clearly the double-edged nature of parenthood generally, so perhaps it is not surprising that a relationship which causes such passion will also be the cause of so much guilt. This is probably typified by Jenny Kent's feelings:

> There's one thing I've still not resolved and it's probably not resolvable and that's my relationship with my children. I don't enjoy living day to day with them. I'm intensely involved with their lives and want the best for them but I find the daily contact with them impossible. I don't feel guilty about that for myself but I do feel it puts something on them which they shouldn't have to cope with. We talk a lot about our feelings but they do make me feel unhappy. I thank God they get tremendous consistent love and appreciation from their father. What I had to learn to overcome were my feelings of guilt, that I should be spending more time with the kids and cooking meals, doing family things and so on.

Single parents probably feel more guilty about depriving their children of the statutory two, but that is a comparative focus set against the norm. A woman who has children later in life may find a focus of a different kind, as Pat Hull describes:

> It's as though my travelling is over in all senses. I did a lot of jobs for short periods and I thought it was because I didn't like that kind of work, but a friend suggested to me that it was symptomatic of my life in general – for instance, my relationships with men and my moving around showed a similar lack of commitment. Having a child is of necessity such a long-term commitment, it allows me to be long-term in other ways. I still do worry about the effects on Emma about her situation; I feel guilty about it, but I suppose most parents do. I feel that

to be circumscribed by having a child can be quite liberating rather than the reverse.

The crisis which only one parent is meant to go through during the middle years is associated with the loss of childbearing function and with the departure of existing children. Christine Merton's description sums up the painful and often totally unexpected feelings which so many mothers experience at this time:

> You may think you have your career or have developed an interest but all the same it threw me when the children left, especially so as it coincided with an early menopause. Life seemed to derail then because all the liveliness the children brought with their friends and the sense of being in a complete family disappeared. This can be a very crucial time for many women even if they've been developing as people and have been thinking wisely about careers, still much is lost. It has something to do with being a female and making a nest; men go to women for that. It hurts when the children go. When this being all together gets dispersed, it leaves a big emptiness. It helps to have a career built up but it's still a factor – there is more understanding of that now, life is more accommodating.

Men as fathers are not traditionally associated with 'empty nest' syndromes, presumably because they spend less time actively parenting. But it does seem hard that it has become an exclusively female prerogative, especially as many fathers now play a more active role with their children. Admittedly, children cause more change in women's lives than in those of men – on the whole – and what may seem to be an easy option for motherhood in youth may have consequences in middle age and later that cannot be foreseen earlier. As life expectancy increases, so the active post-parental phase lengthens and there are few precedents for this. As marriage adapts to and influences social norms, patterns of parenting also need to become more flexible and adaptable to accommodate other areas in both parents' lives.

This is the first time in history that women as a sex have had the choice as to whether or not to become parents and to choose when they take up the option. This extension of choice needs constant reaffirmation, especially by the middle generation of women who can demonstrate that other options do not automatically foreclose with children and can also be explored before their arrival. We should rejoice in the fluidity of choice now available and not succumb to the creeping but pervasive fantasy engendered by white weddings and blinkered motherhood. No one would deny that it is an enormous struggle to be a parent, a worker, a creature of leisure and possibly a wife. We have explored the experiences of women who felt handicapped by their families but who did something about it; others can learn from them the importance of adapting to each successive phase as it emerges in the pattern, rather than chasing the ephemeral freedom they had before parenthood. Undoubtedly, the middle years bridge the gap between older and younger generations, as this is also the time to come to terms with one's own youth and prospective old age. As such, these years are the richest time in life. There are so many reasons within the family alone to see the middle years as a 'prime time', as another beginning rather than the beginning of the end.

9
Work: Women's Two Roles

> The power of earning is essential to the dignity of woman, if she has not independent property.
>
> The superintendence of a household, even when in not other respects laborious, is extremely onerous to the thoughts; it requires incessant vigilance, an eye which no detail escapes, and presents questions for consideration and solution, forseen and unforseen, at every hour of the day, from which the person responsible for them can hardly ever shake herself free.
>
> John Stuart Mill, *The Subjection of Women*

Often when changes in the middle years are discussed, it is assumed that this refers to women going back into paid employment. It has become quite an accepted thing for women to take up where they left off in order to have children, to go to work for the first time or radically to change direction in this respect. The underlying assumption is that this work is in exchange for money and is therefore likely to be an activity which is carried on outside the home. But that is looking through a glass darkly. The term 'working mother' is quite simply tautologous; all mothers are 'working' by definition – except for the privileged few. Work as a word appears to have an inbuilt sex bias in the sense that convention has established it to mean the type of activity which men do in the outside world as paid employees. A working mother has come to mean a woman who works for money.

But . . . most women still carry the burden of responsibility for domestic arrangements in addition to working in paid employment, as most men still tend to be the major breadwinners. In this sense women have two working roles, which is likely to demand more balancing between the demands of a career or job and those of a domestic variety. Although family life is seen as an integral part of the state's system of social control and welfare provision, it works on the assumption that parenthood is in reality 'motherhood'. Most employers are unwilling to organize their work on a system of either job sharing, part- or flexi-time, to allow both men and women to be parents and employees. The situation becomes further aggravated by the lack of child-care facilities both public and private. If two parents are fortunate enough to be able to share both domestic arrangements and the burden of bread-winning without employing outside help, they are likely to do so at the cost of career expectations. Especially during a recession, this cost may be too high to risk, so the solution is more often than not for one parent to work full-time, the other when and how he or she may fit in with the children. Ninety-eight per cent of the latter are women, who will bear the additional cost in terms of job and career, knowing that work experience in the home and community counts as naught with future employers.

The pattern of women's work in paid employment appears to fall into three fairly distinct phases. The first is work after school or college and before children; the second is when children are young and mostly at home and the third when they have become less dependent and women feel freer to alter the pattern of their own lives. It is the last phase we are most concerned with, but to appreciate why (for example) an apparently home-loving 'Mum' decides to lauch out into a career in her forties, we need to consider working life during the earlier periods.

Patterning a woman's working life in this way appears to place a great deal of emphasis on children, which is true – but not entirely so. Women today still suffer from a curious hangover from the nineteenth century: they can be asked *whether* they work rather than *what* kind of work they do. Lee's experience develops this point:

I took pride in being able to work, look after the children, co-operate in running our nursery school, run a home and entertain and so on. That was a sort of vanity really to think that was what you ought to be doing in order to be able to go out to work. And that was affected by Colin's attitude as main bread-winner. He supported me about going to work but his attitude assumed that while he had no choice but to work, I could stop if I wanted to.

This is a form of female privilege which is not only double-edged but really should not exist at all nowadays. However, it is a well and truly ingrained idea that men are the bread-winners and a great deal of the masculine image is tied up with the notion of productive labour. All of which the state endorses by assuming that women are an economic burden and granting a tax allowance to husbands – as a form of compensation perhaps? The net effect is for a man's tax situation to improve on marriage while a woman's deteriorates.

However, we first need to explore the situation for women before children appear. Obviously, the type of work a woman does is dependent partly on her education and partly on expectations she perceives society holds for women generally and for herself in particular. Women do have one clear-cut role which is not generally taken to be a 'working' one – though it can be seen as an alternative to it – and that is motherhood. So entrenched is this idea that to some women there seems to be a choice between being a 'brain' and therefore by implication masculine, or being non-productive and female; everything a 'brain' is not. Viewing one's role as eventually domestic, work before the event then appears as something of a stop-gap and not terribly important, so whether or not it is satisfying does not seem to matter very much.

Like Gadarene swine (or sows) many girls are steered towards office work, as Carole (NOW) recalls: 'I did office work and didn't like it: I think that's often a direction girls are pointed to, or did then.'

Joy (NOW) describes office work as 'a way of earning a crust': it fulfilled no other criteria in terms of job satisfaction or promotion prospects. Of course, the reverse side of the coin can be true as well; precisely because mighty hordes of females go into office work and an occasional few become the bosses of international corporations, this is incentive enough to avoid it. In Nancy Roberts's words: 'I always had the fierce conviction I didn't want to be a secretary, though my mother urged me to be, pointing out all the successful women who'd started out that way. I just couldn't do it.'

The secretarial image was also the reason for Sheila Dainow going into the youth service, '. . . because it was there and it was more fulfilling than office work I had done up to then. I went into it not really understanding it could be a career or have some influence on me.'

Whether or not we wish to accept it, office work – the image and the reality – has quite a crucial role to play in working women's lives: both as an obvious way of earning a living and as providing a positive incentive to avoid.

Nursing, teaching and the other service industries are also typically female jobs, often taken up because there is no very clear guidance or awareness of alternatives. Mary Baker is a case in point:

> I took up nursing next, really because a very gathered-together friend was. I nursed in a country hospital and at a London teaching hospital, then I went on to a recovery unit and became sloppy. Matron felt I had slipped so for the next eighteen months I just slurped along because I knew I had blotted my copy book.

Nowadays, despite not-so-hidden forces promoting the idea of marriage/motherhood as a career, it does compete against a service provided in schools and colleges which did not exist to the same extent for women who are now in their middle years. Many women did not perceive work as a part of their lives at all clearly and stumbled from one job to another with no very clear direction, as happened to Jenny Kent:

> I've always been open to suggestion but what I've actually done is stumble about until an opportunity presents itself within my political perspective and I've been lucky to move from interesting part-time work to even more interesting full-time work. I wish I could say I set certain goals and plans,

but it wasn't like that for me. I think younger women tend to make plans more, both because their view of their place in the world is different and their options are closing down.

Others who fell by the wayside in school and were classified as failures, were conditioned to think of themselves like that for some time to come. A routine job was the answer: if you could not earn your living by doing what you wanted, you had to make space to do it outside your work like Julia Mitchell, who sang in the Bach Choir and took guitar lessons while working in a solicitor's office.

Partly because of the lure of having money rather than pursuing further academic qualifications when young, and partly because work assumed a secondary importance as compared with marriage, many girls went into jobs which had inbuilt limitations in terms of career, as Pat Hull describes:

For about six years or so I had wanted to change my work, because I felt it to be limiting and although I learnt something about a number of different fields, because I had no training in anything else it basically stayed the same job. This new job seemed to promise the possibility of edging into a different kind of work. I was working for a social scientist in the work field and got a glimmering into how surveys were conducted . . . Now although my employer was quite open to the idea of my participating at some level in research, I didn't have the training and I couldn't be very useful. Apart from which, there was an awful lot of work for which I *was* trained.

Many women felt they could ignore the necessity to acquire formal qualifications which were essential to career advancement, because they were confirmed in the way of thinking that this was not really important. An existing or future husband's work was what *was* important, which appeared to offer women the choice of being intellectually lazy and kept permanently in subordinate positions.

For individuals who have a strong sense of vocation, in some ways the choice is rather easier, as Marion Burman found when she entered the religious life and subsequently enjoyed a very successful and fulfilling professional career within it, which nevertheless 'in a way prevented me from realizing how out of harmony I was with the spiritual side of things – though again I was quite caught up in it'.

In matters of choice it is interesting that until recently girls did not perceive they had any choice about leaving home unless it was in terms of marriage and/or a job. Rosie (NOW) recalls, 'When I look back on it, marriage and taking a job I wasn't really keen on was a desperate way of not going back home.'

All this tends to assume that most women do not take work very seriously or have no specific idea about what they would like to do, because what they really want is to make a nest and have babies. Obviously there are women who do plan their careers and have a very clear idea about where they are going – more and more of them as they perceive it is increasingly possible to live outside legal wedlock. What is being suggested is that, unlike men, producing babies is a major factor to be considered by most women at some time during their working lives. Undoubtedly this may colour their thinking and initially distort more long-term perspectives about life as a whole.

Phase two of women's work in paid employment commences when girls become 'mummies', as my son categorized all women when he was small. There is probably relatively little domestic conflict nowadays between a working wife and a working husband for the simple reason that no children equals less mess. The real crunch comes with the children, which is what the division of domestic labour is all about. Does full-time motherhood equal full-time paid employment and if so, who does the washing up?

While children are young, the conflict may be resolved by a woman becoming a full-time mother and domestic employee of her family. For some, motherhood is a glorious escape from otherwise ghastly jobs and the freedom which domesticity appears to offer far outweighs all other considerations. This was how Penny McGuire felt:

> Suddenly I was this academic wife because my husband was teaching philosophy at Leicester University. It was like acquiring a new overcoat, acquiring this new status. I felt incredible relief in many ways because every job I'd done I was hopeless at. I detested work and it was an enormous relief

not having to get up and go to an office. I was very pleased to be married and have a baby.

Often lacking other means of achieving status, women develop a confidence in the home almost as part of a self-fulfilling prophecy, which more often than not proves to be illusory. For example, P.D. James has observed that men seldom talk of domestic matters in terms of 'we' but refer to 'my home', 'my car' and so on.

This is at least consistent with the concept of a woman being totally dependent on her husband, both economically and emotionally, and having no status beyond that which he confers. We have already referred to the essentially servicing role fulfilled by women at home, and the greater esteem in which *productive* roles are held by the outside world, so that although a woman may earn an enormous amount emotionally by servicing at home, time spent there will not count on the occupational ladder outside it.

One of the problems about being at home all the time is the very real possibility of being at everyone's beck and call and never perceiving that one should have time to oneself. Some women in this situation not only fulfil Parkinson's predictions about filling all available time with work but also use it as an excuse; however, Bernice Rubens is convinced that, 'There's no such thing as not enough time: if you want to do something you will do it.'

In time, it follows that many women who are exclusively at home gradually lose all sense of their own identity and of any purpose beyond the purely domestic – which is probaby how a good many OAPs feel, relegated to senior citizens' homes. When domesticity is seen in this light, it is almost understandable why some more extreme factions wish completely to abolish the family and all that goes with it. However, there is an alternative. If they are not driven to obtain employment by virtue of economic necessity, women can seek work to do from home while children are small and dependent. Julia Mitchell, for instance, ran a folk club for modest payment, but opportunities in the part-time sector are limited and as she says, 'How many jobs can you do like this?'

Many women would argue that it is essential to have some

work outside the home, however minimal, because it is vital to their sense of self-esteem. That this is probably out of all proportion to the financial reward received can cause other areas of conflict with partners. Liz Ahrends's comments about her situation illustrate both the satisfaction and the problems:

> Before I went to the Poly I did lots of part-time secretarial jobs, did agency work handing round champagne at ten bob an hour – when it was typing envelopes, they were a halfpenny each. Even doing that when the children were little, gave me a feeling of independence because it was a commitment I had made which was entirely my own. I always had some little thing going which fitted in with the children. None of the jobs were very serious in their way but it was important to me to have that two-hour commitment, to do something and get paid for it. It was a short period when I was more than just a mum. The sort of conversation which used to crop up again and again was that it's not worthwhile you earning this money because I'm taxed on it. I used to go to enormous lengths to try and explain it was my money and I had earned it. That was what was important, not the amount or the contribution to the family income. All you're saying when you say it's my money is that you have some say in the decision about how the money is spent. The person who brings in the most money has the most power, it's always like that. But it took a long time before my husband finally understood that need.

Others argue that unless they are employed outside the home, there is a danger of their sinking into a kind of maternal apathy. At the very least, that cannot be good for their children who were the object of their staying at home in the first place. However, the trouble with work which women can fit in with the demands of children is its similarity to the role they play at home. Sheila and Rosie (NOW) feel that, 'An awful lot of women's work is like being an extension of a machine', (Sheila), and 'The other options open to women are almost as dismal. They are often an extension of the women's role like teaching or nursing. That's stultifying for me. Or you've got to become substitute men, as in management for example.' (Rosie)

The activities involved in paid employment may not only be

very similar to those carried on in the home but also provide very little emotional relief. Mary Baker, who took up social work, found that, 'I was seeing women in a similar state to myself and it was quite searing. As a social worker I allowed myself to be sucked in, empathizing with their problems and constantly looking into myself. My worst moment came when I had a client who was like a mirror image.'

To keep going with a satisfying and fulfilling job as well as looking after children may also mean that a woman sets her career sights deliberately low because of them. Lee feels that:

> The children did stop me in a way because I never considered having an ambitious career as such; my work was enjoyable but it could never interfere with the time I had to give to the children. I was proud of the ingenuity with which I organized my life. As far as my career was concerned, I suppose I didn't fulfil my potential – but then I didn't think I had very much.

A combination of good luck and good management can make it possible to find work which fits in with domestic arrangements *and* is stimulating. Serendipity certainly worked for Sheila Dainow when she progressed from voluntary work with the FPA to an interesting part-time job 'which I could run from home'.

Finding oneself alone with small children to support may provide the final impetus for a woman to do work she has always wanted to undertake. When Annette Wagner's marriage broke up and her husband left, she 'decided to do what I always wanted and be a translator. I was bilingual after all.'

Whatever work they do in combination with domestic responsibilities, most women suffer to a greater or lesser extent from guilt. If they stay at home all the time, provided they can afford to do so, the domestic daily round may well reduce them to screaming pitch. If they work outside home, according to the prevailing ethos of the time they may be made to feel guilty by current experts on child psychology. Whatever they do, they will find other women who manage to combine various threads with apparent ease and competence and thus be made to feel inadequate. Until they can reach a point of knowing and feeling what is best for them as individuals, their self-image can be adversely affected even to the point of mental and physical illness.

Being at home all the time may bring a lurking suspicion that the grass is greener out in the world. As P.D. James says: '. . . much office work is by its nature, boring', but offers '. . . change of companionship, another world, other people and the economic independence of feeling this is money I have earned'. Women who have been at the beck and call of bosses before the beck and call of babies probably have a clearer perspective on this; as Vivianne (NOW) suggests, 'I like being my own boss at home. It's preferable to being answerable to someone else. I wouldn't mind running my own business if I knew what sort of thing I could do.'

Perspectives may well alter quite radically when the reality of motherhood has been experienced over a period of time; this is not unlike marriage in demanding a good objective scrutiny after a while, except that you cannot alter the fact of motherhood in quite the same way. It seems more than likely that a welter of conflicting demands around work, career, family and personal commitments may start to crystallize when some experience has been gained with age. Neither motherhood nor work may eventually turn out to be the supreme and exclusive answer to a woman's ambition, but it is more likely that some sort of balance can be achieved when priorities become clearer. Women who had no definite sense of direction before they had children, may subsequently find horizons have been altered because of them and the future is shaped more clearly. It is at this point that the third phase in the pattern of work begins.

However, a desire to return to work may come at precisely the point when it is traditionally most difficult for women to find employment. P.D. James believes the mature woman in this situation is doubly at a disadvantage in not only feeling hesitant about re-entering 'an unfamiliar world' but also encountering prejudice from employers because of her age.

Suspecting all this, why then do women forge ahead? Some will have anticipated a wish to return to work after being at home full-time, will have set out to obtain further and higher education and now feel poised and capable in a way they have not experienced for years. Perhaps one of the problems about discovering potential which has lain dormant, combined with long-term servicing of a family, arises when this potential can find no particular direction. Kelly Anderson has gained enormous confidence from her degree course – and a short course on women's assertiveness which 'was fantastic' – and 'Now I feel I can go anywhere and do anything . . .'

Other women become motivated to go out to work because their families have begun to take them for granted. At the very least, a job will bolster a crushed ego, and this was what drove June Barry to apply for and obtain a part-time job. Like many others she 'had become used to being needed and assumed I'd always be but the children were no longer of an age when they could be channelled into the direction I wanted them to take'.

Women who have worked more or less continuously at the same job, may well decide in their middle years that they have had enough of it and need a change. Mary Baker changed direction in this respect because:

> I veer to the positive side of things and I kept seeing people I'd visited years ago with no change in their lives and I'd had enough of their problems. It was all so uncreative and boring . . . It had got to the point when I could sit back because I'd heard it all before. I reached the point when I wanted to help myself more than I wanted to help others.

In much the same way that some individuals recognize the time has come to retire from full-time active working life and take up something different on a part-time basis, or pursue a hobby, others recognize the length of working life ahead and debate whether they wish to continue treading the same path. Sometimes it has not been possible to change earlier because of personal circumstances, but time and age provide the impetus as they did for P.D. James. While her husband was alive she had felt it necessary to stick to 'jobs I knew I could tackle and had experience in. But after he died I did feel I wanted a change from hospital administration. This [the Civil Service] would be something new.' Age is a contributory factor to change at this time, she thinks, '. . . when women who work feel, "Do I really want to go on doing this until I'm sixty?" Those last twenty years of working life stretch ahead.'

Women who have been working basically from home, may find they long for a change in middle age and want to work outside it. The job which has dovetailed with the school calendar and the constant 'in and out' activities of children; which avoided agonizing decisions over whether or not to stay away from work if a child does not seem quite well enough to go to school, is seen in a different light once they are older or have left home.

One factor which became increasingly clear about many women, particularly those whose marriages broke up during the middle years, was the discovery that they were capable of supporting themselves instead of being a dependant. Eileen Curry feels strongly about this:

> I want my own security. I don't want to depend on anybody for an income, nor ever be emotionally dependent on a man either. I've had the best and worst of marriage and I've got nothing to prove. I can concentrate on the next twenty years and I do what I want which is something of a challenge . . . I don't worry about not being super-woman or super-mum any more. I've come to terms with it and my priorities are no longer centred around home and family as they once were.

Marital break-up presents three stark alternatives for most women: either remarriage; work, because their lives and possibly those of their children depend upon it; or going under. After Christine Merton's divorce, she 'took up studies in ceramics and sculpture, and grew from that. Once I got going I had a searching time sorting myself out and found confidence in myself as a human being. I never thought at the time I could ever make the grade professionally.'

A previous chapter explored time as a crucial factor in relation to bringing about change. With regard to work, the middle years bring recognition that if a project is not started soon, it may never happen. When P.D. James began her first novel in her late thirties, 'I realized that unless I made an effort . . . I would eventually be a grandmother and telling my grandchildren what I always wanted to be was a writer.' In a similar way, a feeling of quiet desperation may creep in during the middle years, a conviction that too much time has been spent on too many jobs that are boring. This was what happened to Irma Kurtz in her early thirties when she had 'terrible jobs, really terrible, writing ad copy. Not only was I not a good copywriter but it bored the hell out of me.' She submitted a previously rejected article to a new magazine called *Nova* and 'They bought the piece, and gave me a job on the magazine.'

Sometimes the change can be so total that no area of life remains untouched, as Marion Burman discovered when she left the convent. At first she stayed on as headmistress at the school where she had been working, 'but I could never be anything there but a "sister" '. So she left, moved away and, deciding 'to go and do something completely different . . . went on a TOPs course in business and secretarial studies'.

To make a change when a woman is feeling full of untapped potential, at a time when society has come to expect her to settle down and accept her lot, obviously demands fierce determination. As we have seen, a number of factors come together to make this possible. Part of the possibility may be a recognition that there is a pattern to life which previously appeared to lack shape and coherence. During her middle life, a woman may better understand that the take-offs and plateaux which have repeated themselves over the years, do in fact point in a single direction, though this may be recognizable only to her. Nancy Roberts found that coming to terms with being fat sparked off a new way of thinking about herself, 'after twenty-seven years of misery'. Her association with Spare Tyre Theatre Company has proved 'a rebirth on so many levels'.

One of the things which many women discovered once they launched out during the middle years was the impossibility of turning back. Having set out, they became even more strongly motivated to succeed; perhaps because they felt they had a lot of catching up to do, they wanted to surge ahead. Acquiring a sense of purpose may well be something which many women do not discover about themselves until they have reached middle age: this was true of Linda Thornber, who says that at thirty she had no staying power. Sometimes the discovery is triggered off by a particular event, in her case 'falling in love at thirty-eight', but she feels that 'it would have happened anyway . . . You haven't got it when you're young: ability's one thing but acquiring purpose is another.'

Coupled with a sense of purpose must be an ability to take risks in order to find true independence: a capacity which many writers about women have suggested they are slow or hesitant to develop. But in many ways it is the hallmark of change: a necessary prerequisite – if only on the basis of ''tis better to have loved and lost, than never loved at all'. Wishing to change but never quite daring may lead to future regret and resentment for a lost opportunity. Linda Thornber, now a freelance writer, says of her previous work, 'The thing about teaching . . . you do get paid', but she has no doubts: 'This way is unsure, insecure and very exciting and I wouldn't give it up for the world.'

No one has suggested that it is easy to launch out late. Age, as we have seen, can be a barrier but is not insuperable. Grim determination can go a long way but when it comes to taking up work again, possibly after a pause, many women lack the necessary confidence. As Penny McGuire puts it:

> Maybe women who start on careers late find it difficult to project an image of themselves? When forced into formal interviews, they have to suddenly compete and maybe they're not aggressive enough. I still think I'm terribly timid. I'm cursed with it and still haven't resolved how to cope with it.

Being your own boss at home may have its limitations but you do not have to take orders from anyone. When June Barry returned to work, she found this aspect both a problem and a motive to forge ahead. Her way of coping with 'difficulty in taking orders from younger people' was to aim at progressing beyond them, unconsciously at first but with increasing success.

Women who have not worked at all or who have taken part-time jobs to fit in with the children, have had a frame of reference dictated by their demands. In many ways, any planning which exists is out of a woman's hands. Returning to work, with a career in mind, demands more long-term thinking as Nancy Roberts discovered: 'This planning ahead, I've never done this up to now and it's difficult and exciting to do it now. It's a way of thinking I've not done before, maybe because I'm a woman. Men have to think that way all the time.'

The price women of all ages can pay for becoming career orientated as things stand at the moment, is that they may no longer be 'one of the girls' but it is unlikely they will become 'one of the boys' either. However, many women would argue that economic independence is fundamental to physical as well as emotional freedom, as expressed by Liz Ahrends:

I put a lot of emphasis on economic independence. I think that's probably the most fundamental independence one needs. If you're economically dependent on someone else, that puts a certain light on that relationship whatever ideology you have about sharing. Ultimately the important decisions are the ones determined by the main bread-winner.

What happens less frequently, as yet, is role reversal in terms of bread-winning which we hear of occasionally when children are young though not as often when they are less involved. This assumes too that men have the type of work they can do on a part-time basis or else operate from home; the factors which militate against women doing this are possibly greater for men, as it has been tried less often. Julia Mitchell's experience of role reversal has been that 'By becoming the bread-winner, I've become the decision-maker. It's a great pressure sometimes and therefore increasingly I view Charles differently.' Her situation is slightly more complex in that the children's stepfather is twenty-four years older than she is, therefore for him 'the mothering role . . . is difficult because of the age gap', but it seems likely that such a change has lasting effects on any relationship.

While there are members of both sexes who think that women have an option to stay at home full-time, so that the idea of motherhood rather than parenthood persists, conflict seems inevitable for the 'working' mother. There is certainly choice available for the women in this respect, but what real substance does it have on examination? Many women need to work as men need to work – not just for essential hard cash but for their ultimate good health. In many ways, the structure of working life in the future may well make this more possible. Julia Mitchell, for example, suggests that the whole idea of careers is now antiquated and sees a future where 'Pursuing the whole idea of careers will have nothing to do with it. A person will have an ability, talent or skill which will be used part-time with other developed skills.'

The key to many people's working lives in the future may well lie in diversification. As things are at the moment, the vast majority of men and women cannot fully enjoy being working parents because of enormous constraints on the two roles, but an entirely different structure of working life would change this situation. With more individuals able to be workers *and* parents, without polarizing the roles on one or the other, it is more likely that the idea of men being 'instrumental' and women 'expressive' could be abandoned. Neither are necessarily innate characteristics but have become identified with each sex because of the structure of our society, to the detriment of both.

Much work within the house is positively 'unisex' by virtue of machinery, as is a great deal of it outside the home. Combined with fewer pregnancies, longer life expectancy and so on, this points to more and more women coming to think of work as an inherent rather than a subsidiary part of their lives. However, it is still the case that very many women do not discover their capabilities until the middle years. Having made the discovery, they find the courage and determination to thrust ahead, finding that the experience which comes with age and with having lived a little, can be a truly positive asset.

10
Education

> Miss Buss and Miss Beale
> Cupid's darts do not feel.
> How different from us
> Miss Beale and Miss Buss.
> > *Of the headmistress of the North London Collegiate School and the principal of the Ladies' College, Cheltenham.*
> > Nineteenth century, Anon.

There are few areas in life where sex plays no part, and society has evolved laws and conventions to make sure this does not get out of hand. Nowhere is this more obvious than in our education system, which makes few concessions to adolescent sexuality, probably the most potent force in young people's lives. If they cannot actually do anything about it, their thoughts and emotions are likely to be consumed by its fascination. But what do randy teenagers have to do with middle-aged women and education? The link is not as tenuous as it may at first seem and warrants exploration in order to appreciate more fully just why formal education in later years is so important.

In an earlier chapter we saw that for the vast majority of women marriage was and is still the primary goal. Education can come a very poor second, as expressed by Bernice Rubens: 'At the time when I was of marriageable age, if one didn't get married that was something to be deeply ashamed of, so I went to university as a kind of standby just in case I didn't fall off the shelf.'

Education as a means of earning a better, more enjoyable living does not carry much weight for most girls if success is measured in terms of getting married. In addition, the intrinsic value of education carries little weight when its attractions are obscured by the headier excitements of sex. So long as marriage continues to be accepted as a standard of achievement, girls will acquire more instant status in this way rather than deferring their gratification for some more nebulous and distant goal. This is especially so nowadays when qualifications at all levels are no guarantee of obtaining employment.

The way in which our education system has evolved has led to high numbers of female drop-outs, not necessarily in the accepted sense but passively through marriage and motherhood. We have developed a system which provides a continuous course of statutory education on the assumption that this is best acquired in childhood and youth, rather than recognizing that its benefits may be better understood if part of that course is deferred. After all, it is not uncommon for many girls to want a baby quite passionately in their early teens and to feel they are highly potent beings. For many this desire can become obsessional and quite obscure any value in the formal education they are meant to be receiving.

Later, when marital euphoria has perhaps worn a little thin, many women discover in the early middle years that it was all 'a bit of a con' and there is more to life than unending domesticity and possibly a fairly mechanical job. Education then takes on new meaning and its intrinsic value becomes more understandable. But what is it in our educational system which helps to create such unevenness in the development of male and female potential and which makes provision for further and higher education crucial later on?

There has been far more conscious effort of late to remove obvious gender differentiation in schools: in other words boys can, say, do home economics and girls play football. However, social and historical conditioning is still such that boys tend to make choices within their school careers which are outward-looking in relation to jobs, which in turn brings the reward of the most attractive females. Girls tend to 'choose' subjects that conform to their socially ascribed roles of wives and mothers, so that sex rather than intellect becomes the key to power. As a microcosm of the outside world, mixed schools tend to have highly charged atmospheres partly due to the pervasiveness of sex. Studies have shown that girls tend to perform better academically in single-sex schools up to O-levels at least, while the reverse is true for boys. In a school which is not particularly good, girls are even less likely to succeed if only on the basis that they require more encouragement to keep going. Eileen Curry is probably a good example of this: 'I'd not done very well at school, having failed the 11+, though I was always top in the secondary mod. Then I went on to secretarial college. I didn't think I was up to much because the system taught me I wasn't.'

If, traditionally speaking, educational attainment is not seen as important for females because they will get married, the assumption follows that it is wasted on them. What has been seen to be true for past generations of mothers may be handed on to the next, as Kelly Anderson found: 'I'd started evening classes twelve years ago, studying Russian which shocked my mother. "What does a housewife want with Russian?" she'd said.' Families may endorse society's view in one of two obvious ways. Either they apply pressure on a daughter to go out and earn money, or they concentrate their efforts on the sons in the family, whose needs appear to them greater. Families and schools may quite deliberately ignore the intrinsic value of education for daughters, so long as education continues to be viewed as a means of earning a living and women are assumed to earn theirs by getting married. When Sheila Dainow was adolescent, for example, she felt she would 'never be able to do anything. Nobody thought or recognized I was bright, neither teachers nor parents.' As a late developer who 'was never put in touch with any ideas involving further education' marriage gave her confidence, since when her learning 'has been a more or less continuous process'.

Apart from sex being a block to intellectual development, many girls in their adolescence begin to suffer from lack of confidence in themselves, especially when they are educated alongside boys or, like Lee, have a brilliant sibling constantly held up as an example. She recalls that:

As a child, I used to think other people might think I was intelligent but then if I had to prove I was, I would probably disappoint them. So it was better not to try, not to compete. Possibly it was also vanity, I didn't want to fail, but it didn't seem like that at the time. It seemed then more like a lack of confidence and ability to study. I think now that everybody has much more potential than they realize which means that I hope I did too.

Given all the distractions there are during adolescence, many girls (and boys) may simply lack motivation to learn; Pat Hull, for example, describes how 'Neither of my parents had been to university and encouraged me to go, but all I wanted to do then was earn some money. I didn't have the facility for learning then, didn't like it much and that set me back years.'

Everything in our society points to the young as being the generation whose object in life is to have a good time. Seen in this light and coupled with the marriage stakes, education is merely a barrier to achieving the desirable goal, as Penny McGuire recalls:

I think I was particularly passive as a young girl and just floated. I left school with ten O-levels and it's inconceivable now that one wouldn't have thought of further education of some sort but I think I just did expect to get married and have children. I wanted to have a 'nice time' and couldn't wait to get out of my girls' boarding school.

The problem about falling by the wayside in a system which assumes continuous linear progress is that failure to reach certain goals at certain prescribed times can induce a feeling of failure beyond the merely educational. Thus a person who fails at 11+, then at CSE or O-level, possibly never reaching A-level and beyond, consequently has a feeling not only of intellectual failure but probably of general inferiority all round. For one thing this may not necessarily be true and is illogical and wasteful in the extreme, coming moreover at the beginning of a person's life and setting a pattern of limitation which it may take a considerable time to break.

So many individuals emerge from their schooldays with totally undiscovered potential; partly due to the system, partly to the apparent inappropriateness of extended formal learning for adolescents. For women especially, this initial sense of failure is compounded since they are seen as unreliable by employers because of pregnancy and child-care demands. They are thus less likely to be chosen for in-service training or sandwich courses and their opportunities for continuing education are consequently further limited.

The real irony in the situation for both sexes lies in marriage. Formal education appears to favour men: choice is more real within it and marriage and sex can be viewed as activities alongside rather than instead of other options. It is then assumed that they go into a job, which in time is meant to support a wife and family, and there is suddenly no choice and little opportunity on the whole for change. Women, on the other hand, often inhibit earlier choice at school by following their 'natural' devices and desires – they get married, or at any rate have children. Some women may be in the position to choose whether or not to work outside the home within marriage, but nowadays are probably in the minority.

The course of most women's lives is such that they have more room in which to manoeuvre later on than most men, despite being bound on a domestic treadmill. For one thing, change is in-built in the daily round through the development of their children. Further, many women discover as they grow older that aggression has a place in achievement and while this may have been taboo in youth, it can later prove to be a boon. A form of maturity can develop as a result of marriage and having children, but it seems likely that rather than being integral to the core personality of a woman this is something necessarily acquired in one particular direction. Marriage therefore fulfils the basic requirements of being female in our society: being someone – a wife and mother – and doing something by virtue of being that someone. But both identities are conferred in the first place, not necessarily learned or internalized. Experience of both can lead many women to question fulfilment in the domestic role, this questioning subsequently providing the basic motive to extend their horizons.

The case for statutory provision of further and higher education which extends beyond the present youth-oriented system hardly needs emphasizing. Many men and women would undoubtedly benefit by leaving the constraints and unrealities of school somewhat earlier, with the option of being able to return later in adulthood. Formal education which catered for adults with job and domestic responsibilities would often be more appropriate and relevant than extending the school-leaving age.

Maturity for women is quite often achieved abruptly during their middle years when they find they have sole responsibility for themselves and their children through the break-up of a marriage. Recognizing their educational immaturity often for the first time during mid-life, many women seek courses of the Fresh Horizons and NOW variety in further education colleges, which will help them back on to some kind of academic learning basis; they need a form of educational bridge between school and higher or professional training courses. In theory, women mainly seek more education in order to get better jobs: the reality of a recession may doom this to failure. But the initial impetus for pursuing education can inspire them with a delight in the intrinsic value of the experience, which in turn may prove to be of greater and more lasting value.

Courses aimed for women planning to go back to work or simply to extend their personal horizons, stretch far beyond the purely educational in a formal sense, which is shown by comments from women attending a NOW course as to why they embarked upon it:

CAROLE: I haven't worked for a number of years and that's why I'm here to try and find something to do to support my children.

SHEILA: I'm thirty-five, married with no children. I worked full-time until last year. I'm now working part-time. I can either live like a cabbage or look to the future and think what my potential might offer. Also, before I came here I found I could cope with a one-to-one relationship but I got into a panic if it was a group circumstance. Coming here has re-established my confidence which I had lost.

DIANNE: I'm thirty-three and I just want to gain confidence to go out and get a job again because confidence is something you lose.

Lack of confidence was a topic which was explored earlier, but in this context education is often seen as a means of re-establishing it. Sometimes a woman feels her lack of a core identity is reinforced as children grow older and personal inadequacies are underlined by comparison. The increasing education of her children shows up the inadequacies of a mother's learning but at the same time points the way towards rectifying the balance. Education in this light seems to supply all the missing answers.

Motivation to pursue the discovery of potential must surely be enormously high in adulthood when the cost of doing so can be more clearly assessed. One of the costs is likely to be increased feelings of guilt about the family because a woman is doing something which apparently concerns only herself. Orienting oneself towards personal achievement, however much the gain can be assessed to benefit one's family, needs enormous courage and support. Some women find they can only take the plunge with the backing and example of close friends, as Pat Hull discovered: 'For years I'd also thought about doing a degree but was frightened by the thought. When a good friend had applied and went to do a course, it gave me a push.'

For other women the spur may be a basic resentment at feeling left out or behind through lack of education. This was the motivation for Penny McGuire, who began an A-level course 'because I felt I had to do something about my education. I'd always read a lot but my education was non-existent. I'd felt intellectually inadequate as an academic wife . . . if I hadn't been quite so relaxed I might have done these things rather earlier.'

Because formal education tends to be associated with the young, generally speaking, return to school may also signal return to a kind of second adolescence. Many women curtail their true adolescence quite abruptly by embarking on marriage and motherhood, giving themselves no time to explore their own immature aspects which are, in effect, the growth points towards greater maturity. Inevitably there is the possibility of a clash between what could be seen as a form of personal consciousness-raising and domestic harmony. Sometimes this can lead to the break-up of a marriage; in other cases the resulting conflict may bring about greater accommodation between the partners. For some women it proves impossible to reconcile the two aspects;

when Kelly Anderson took a degree, she felt it 'was a disadvantage living in two worlds, as I didn't get any discussion which the youngsters had'. Unable to discuss her work at home, she 'missed a lot, which was unfortunate'. While keeping the balance *is* exceedingly difficult, it can be made easier if a woman's partner is understanding, but in Kelly's case, 'My husband didn't regard my going to college as profitable although all my grant money went into the house; it was just something I was doing, something to amuse myself. I knew it wasn't. It was desperately important to me.'

Whereas a child is likely to receive some parental encouragement, for an adult this may not only be lacking but the enterprise may be actively resented. Also it is probably true to say that adult egos are a good deal more fragile than those of the young in a formal teaching situation, needing proportionately more encouragement and an approach which takes account of this difference. In a roundabout way, the break-up of a marriage may provide a woman with the encouragement she needs to take up education; she may eventually realize that marriage has stultified much of her potential and its dissolution provides the spur, as Eileen Curry found:

> I started to explore myself while I was working at the college and thought I'd try O-levels to see if I was any good. So I did and got A grades. What I realize now is I was competing with him, proving I was just as good. I did A-levels, then thought right, I'll show him, I'll do a degree.

An ironic twist emerges about women and education in later years, at least for some. Many, many women do battle with their husbands over their part-time earnings which are so important to their morale but often a source of irritation to full-time earning partners. When the state confers a grant on a woman not only does it confirm that she is worthy of receiving it in the first place, but also it is often more financially rewarding than her previous part-time jobs.

It is not easy to return to school as an adult; even if the institution has a more highfaluting title like 'college', it must still evoke memories of earlier experiences. Some institutions have a better image than others in terms of the help they offer to mature students. Nearly all the women interviewed who had returned to education considered polytechnics rather than universities. Pat Hull's reasons are typical: 'I'd always thought in terms of polys rather than university because I felt they were less intimidating, more accommodating to mature students. If I failed it wouldn't seem to be so much of a failure and I felt I had a better chance of getting in.' However, we cannot assume that all women who pursue education in their middle years do so entirely because they feel they lost out earlier on, having become ensnared by the 'bright lights' of marriage and motherhood. Though it seems likely that many women do act for this reason, for others the situation is different.

Education always has been the means of changing direction, both professionally and personally, for men and women. It is now becoming an increasingly recognized change for women to make, more usually when their children have become less demanding. What is still not the norm is to recognize that many women need to start almost from scratch rather than just continuing on. In many instances formal education is effectively being taken up for the first time, school being a distant and not very productive memory.

Some women take the opportunity to pursue their studies while they are at home with young children. Judith Bicknell describes why she did so: 'When I stopped work I started the Ph.D thesis because I wanted something to keep my mind active while I was bringing up children and something which would bring in some money via a grant.' Professional courses taken during the middle years may do considerably more than increase expertise, in the sense that they provide a salutary break from home. Elizabeth Knight's two courses produced more spin-off than originally envisaged; the first provided an excuse 'to be away from the humdrum of marriage' during the week and in fact improved the relationship, but the subsequent course 'made me assess my life . . . I thought to hell, am I going to put up with this for the rest of my life or am I going to do something about it?'

However, women who go on professional courses, possibly for the first time during their middle years, may find the consciousness-raising aspect at odds with the reality which faces them on their return. Returning to school or to work, possibly after a long break from either, women can bring a kind of proselytizing fervour which is unacceptable to those who have slogged along without pause. There must be a difference in expectations which needs necessarily to be reconciled, as Eileen Curry discovered following an Industrial Society course which she found very stimulating:

> I wrote a report for the firm when I got back, suggesting one or two things which could improve it and they were taken up! I liked the work – it gave me a high if you like, but it was a bit of a come-down after that, having to wait until the company's reconstructed.

The difficulties involved in attempting courses and the domestic upheaval that undoubtedly results may erode the value of tackling them in the first place. Highly motivated though most women are to try something new in terms of work and education, they can still use their families as an excuse for dropping out and not completing what they started. However, dropping out can add another dimension to a personality, bringing more realism about what can be attempted both personally and within the confines of work and domestic arrangements. More often than not, it is not outright failure so much as a mistake in the first place, learning which may prove useful in other ways. Women in particular need reminding of this because their confidence is so often fragile and easily beaten down.

But does education during the middle years and beyond fulfil all or at least some of the expectations women have of it? Is it a reliable yardstick which measures the years before it was attained and the years after?

Going to college for the first time later in life can be a matter for regret when the experience is set against that of younger people. When Kelly Anderson took a degree she found the course fulfilling but 'I did feel I'd missed out on the social life in the sense that I should have done it when I was younger and learnt more from the experience.' However she would recommend anyone else to go ahead.

On the other hand, some women thought they had played a part in joining the youth culture and no longer felt 'has-beens' as they had at home. Liz Ahrends, for instance:

I felt a little part of the world of the late sixties when I began studying again, part of that splurge of youth culture, and I didn't feel it odd or contradictory. Maybe it's now when I know I'm going to be fifty in two and a half years' time, to be still feeling that I'm on the verge of that young world, that's odd. I feel that soon I'm going to have to accept middle age, meaning from about fifty onwards, and I'm going to find that hard to do.

Some women discovered a second intellectual peak such as they had not experienced since school. Motivated as never before, their academic achievements were greater, as Jenny Kent describes: 'I went back to college for a diploma which related to my teaching and did better academically than I'd ever done before.'

Finding better work after further education may prove harder now during the recession, but even if this does not materialize as planned, the choice may be greater. Work subsequently obtained may not prove as satisfying as hoped but the tool of learning acquired in the education process may prove to be more valuable in the long run. Pat Hull sums up this point: 'Reading for a degree now gives me the opportunity to learn what I want to which I never did at school. Whatever degree I have, it allows me to get into a job at a different level whatever the job may be.'

To change attitudes always takes time and having embarked on this women of the middle generation have much to contribute. For one thing, by their continuing example of taking up and pursuing education beyond the customary age, they may help to abolish that peculiar differentiation between student (implied as young) and 'mature' student (anyone beyond the pale of twenty-five or so). Surely a student is a student is . . . and to distinguish between the two is to place an imbalanced emphasis on education for the young. As more and more so-called mature students take up education throughout life, it will become a commonly accepted pattern of living rather than one demanding special provision and enormous personal upheaval.

This chapter began by considering adolescent sexuality and its influence on education for the young. Indeed, St Paul recognized that 'it is better to marry than to burn'. Whether or not we take that euphemistically if our education system could take more account of the distractions which sex can cause in youth and make statutory provision for continuing education later in life, very many people – women especially – would feel fewer of their youthful years were 'wasted'. We cannot all follow the same pattern of progression and many women develop later than customarily expected. By creating new patterns for change and development through education, those in their middle years may help to bring about the possibility of more continuous personal fulfilment for both sexes.

11
Love . . . Sex

> It's love, it's love that makes the world go round.
> Anon.

Love is a very confusing word in the English language, quite apart from the confusion it causes in the human breast. The Ancient Greeks ordered things better by having different words to distinguish between different aspects of love, like Eros and Agape, but we have only one. This chapter explores love in relation to sex, which could be covered in some respects by opting for something nice and safe, like 'emotional life'. However, that seemed too broad a spectrum, while a chapter on sex alone was, oddly enough, too limiting.

Part of the confusion arises because love and sex are so frequently bracketed together. Until recently of course, it was not possible to envisage having a sex life unless in connection with marriage, which in turn came to imply love. The causal link was thus established, often quite erroneously. Another difficulty is the word 'sex' which is often used as a shorthand version of 'sexual intercourse', is often confused with gender and just as frequently ignores the fact that we are all sexual beings, whether or not actively so. As if all this was not sufficiently confusing, the myth that love and sex belong exclusively to the young is now being exploded sky-high. We are actually beginning to realize and accept that not only do we have a sexual identity from the cradle to the grave but we can also be sexually active for almost as long.

So where does that leave sex and the middle-aged woman today: floundering between the so-called permissiveness of the sixties and the straitlaced mores of her earlier youth? In fact, with the social climate becoming generally more honest and open about things sexual, it is likely that individuals in middle life are better able to come to terms with the true nature of their sexuality without the pressure for conformity which existed even twenty years ago. (Here we are concerned with the vast majority of people, not the privileged few who were and always have been in a position to buck the system, whether openly or with discretion.) As a woman enters her middle years, she has probably gained some degree of experience and confidence in herself and can feel there is an element of choice about how she conducts her emotional and sexual life. How that understanding is gained depends in part on youthful experiences: whether, for instance, love and sex were inextricably entwined with the notion and/or fact of marriage or whether there was some freedom to mature sexually and emotionally outside this relationship. Dreadful pitfalls exist either way, not least the confusion between love and sex which can arise out of limited experience of either. The middle-aged woman of today belongs to the first generation of women on any scale who have experienced the practical possibility of separating love and reproduction because of the widespread availability of efficient contraception. This is not true, however, for all.

The conditioning of generations past – that to have a sex life at all involves marriage – was unlikely to be removed by the promotion of a packet of Pills. The link between the two continues to persist and in some quarters appears to be encouraged with vehemence as a means of shoring up the forces of good against those of decadence. Once the point of social development had been reached where a girl was free to choose her partner, she often did (and does) so on the basis of sexual attraction – to pursue that to its logical conclusion generally meant marriage and of course still does for very many women. As Linda Thornber said of her marriage, 'You had to get married then'. The Rhett Butler philosophy – 'A good girl to marry and a bad one to have fun with' – persisted quite strongly amongst both sexes and had fairly obvious repercussions later once the initial attraction had faded. During Julia Mitchell's five-year courtship she never slept with her future husband: 'Any sex in my life was reserved for diversions from that courtship when we had break-ups.'

It was thus alarmingly easy for two individuals to find themselves locked in a permanent union which then became infinitely more complex because of sexual inexperience. There always has been – and curiously enough still is to a great extent – a strange anomaly about marriage: it is considered a 'good' thing for the relevant partners to consider wisely and well before they embark on it, but not 'nice' for a girl to have had more previous sexual experience than her partner – nor indeed to have had any at all. Experience in most areas of life is held to be valuable, except when it comes to sex and women! It seems logical that once an individual can differentiate and appreciate the differences between sex and love, more satisfactory relationships are likely to result. Penny McGuire solved the problem in this way:

> My parents sent me – I say it like that because I seemed to have practically no will whatsoever looking back, was just like an absorbent sponge – to secretarial college, where everyone seemed to be husband-hunting. You certainly didn't fuck around, which I did rather secretly. I don't regret falling into bed indiscriminately because I feel I sorted all that out rather early on as part of the process of growing up, however painfully.

The desire to experiment and experience is particularly strong in youth in all manner of ways. Without this happening, not only does the grass appear infinitely greener if one's own patch seems to grow a little scrubby over the years, there is also the lurking suspicion that in some way one might have missed out by opting for the one man/one ring syndrome without testing the field beforehand. On what basis can you choose a permanent partner without true choice in the first place?

On a superficial level, it makes life far easier to categorize people and to know, if not at a glance, who and what they are. Social commerce is patterned by the age and gender of the individuals involved: we tend to communicate differently with a small child of three and an aged granny of eighty-three, for instance. We categorize an individual's sexual proclivities further, into heterosexual – the norm, because it is assumed to be the sexual inclination of the vast majority – and homosexual which until recently was considered not simply deviant but downright 'unnatural' as well. Those with bi-sexual inclinations or any others, were likely to exist in some greater state of confusion because society was unable to box them into a neatly acceptable group. However, conforming to the pattern of the dominant group is especially strong in youth and realization that this was not the path of one's true inclinations may not come about until the middle years. Helen Ness, for example, felt that:

> Being cut off from my family (while I was at university) brought out a strong streak of conformity in me which wasn't there as an adolescent. What was marriage all about? Had I conformed for the sake of approval and to the detriment of my personality because I was aware that I'd been a very naughty girl in the past and mustn't ever do that again?

The reappraisal which, as has been previously discussed, can come about through sheer duration of a marriage, may produce reactions like those of Julia Mitchell ten years after marrying her first husband: 'Sometimes I thought that maybe I shouldn't have got married, maybe it was not men I wanted but women . . .'

As we considered in an earlier chapter, marriage does provide emotional security for very many people. Moreover, having the undivided love and attention of one person may well provide a launching point for many other areas in life, as Sheila Dainow found.

In all the interviews, apropos of marriage, no one mentioned love as such in that context, though many referred to emotional dependence on the relationship. This suggests not so much lack of an emotional life within marriage as the inappropriateness of the word 'love' to describe it. Maybe the love of a marital partner has a different dimension, generally speaking, from that which exists pre- or extra-maritally. Perhaps love as a word best describes that emotion not included within marriage?

Several women emphasized the emotional importance of their husband's continuing support – and sometimes approval – in their working lives outside the family. For June Barry its importance is such that '. . . so if it really came to the crunch and his life was shattered because of my job, I would give it up. But I'd fight hard before I did that.' Other women implied this was important, but had not recognized the extent to which they were dependent on a husband until he was no longer there. After Christine Merton's divorce, she 'felt totally stripped: I felt completely unprotected . . . Suddenly I lost my status.' Recognizing the effect of this emotional dependence, some women fear it while at the same time enjoying what it brings, which is how Jean Shrimpton feels about 'having found something I treasure so deeply, it frightens me to death'.

The duration of a marriage can bring not only reappraisal of the relationship but also greater dependency and less inclination to break free. Perhaps this is especially true of someone who, like Julia Mitchell, marries again after the break-up of the first marriage – as she says:

> When we got married I said that I couldn't be sure that it would be for ever. How can one say that? We have an unspoken agreement that something could happen, though the reality is such that as the years go by, you depend more on one another. I don't know if an opportunity presented itself which I felt I had to take and which meant parting from Charles, whether I could actually do it.

Presumably habit is and has been the answer for many a longstanding marriage – that and the assumption that having 'got the ring', a woman should not ask for anything more or better. Given the lack of pre-marital sexual experience many couples have, the degree of incompatibility within marriage could logically be quite high. Until recently, it has been women rather than men who have subjugated their sexual needs for the sake of harmony within the family home, mainly because their opportunities to alter the situation have been far fewer. Also, some women collude with themselves, maintain the *status quo*, like Elizabeth Knight and her attitude towards her husband's extra-marital affairs. She now feels this was cowardly, but at the time 'I felt I was protecting the children, my mother, my marriage and something was better than nothing.'

A reluctance to explore sexual incompatibility within a partnership must also suggest that one partner at least is sacrificing a vital aspect of being alive for the sake of a marriage. If the woman is the more sexually active of the two, like Eileen Curry for example, she is the more likely to accept her lot because her conditioning in relation to marriage is that much stronger than that of her husband:

> I'm a very physical sort of person. I couldn't have a relationship unless I fancied him physically. I did fancy Jim but I don't think he was particularly sexual. At university he was aware he wasn't out chasing the birds like all the rest and he went through a crisis whether he was homosexual or not. I'm quite a randy character and things were fine for the first few years . . . Then it came about as if I was being rationed and I always made excuses for that – one of my biggest faults, making excuses. In about seven years it was an absolute fiasco.

After seeking medical advice the situation improved – but only for a short time. Soon 'we were back on "ye old routine" and I more or less accepted this was "me lot" and I had to put up with it. I was never one to look around and couldn't sleep with someone just for a screw.'

Sex can remain an unspoken issue between a couple so long as each partner keeps to his or her prescribed place. When a woman launches out into a career later in life, her husband may experience pangs of sexual jealousy because she is part of an unknown world over which he has no control and from which he possibly feels excluded. This of course ignores the reality that many women are excluded from a husband's world of work and have to accept the fact that he could be presented with endless opportunities for sexual conquest which are not comparably open to them.

On the other hand, a woman may find her husband's reaction adds a certain *frisson* to the relationship, confirming her desirability to others and giving her a feeling of self-confidence.

By the time they reach their middle years many women feel that they have missed out on the love stakes in some way. Age, coupled with the feeling that they might not be desirable for much longer can make them far more romantically inclined than younger women, in which case these years can bring desperate last-ditch longings to have their desirability as sexual beings confirmed. Love, as we have seen, is generally associated with the young and therefore by implication with the beautiful – not entirely a matter of the eye of the beholder, more in the nature of the media's image. Women who find themselves on their own during middle age can feel a prey to unwanted sexual advances; one way of avoiding these is to cultivate, to all intents and purposes, a non-image, which is how Linda Thornber reacted in deciding, 'it was safer to be a mother figure and not be sexually attractive. It was easier to be a fat lady because no one expects much of you. Men don't want you if you're fat and they think you don't want them.' Conversely, romantic love is likely to enhance the beloved's image whether or not it conforms to the popular one, as Mary Baker found: 'It's partly because of this other man that I like my body now. He confirmed it all for me a little while ago when he bought me something far too small and I asked whether he really thought I looked like that!'

Shulamith Firestone has an interesting idea about romanticism that 'it develops in proportion to the liberation of women from their biology'. This is a highly debatable point since efficient contraception, while obviously desirable, does remove the element of risk and excitement which is surely part of romanticism. Without pursuing the argument endlessly, what could be more romantic than pre-Pill *Casablanca*? In P.D. James's opinion, those who fall deeply and romantically in love, are lucky in that the decision whether or not to marry is virtually made for them.

In many ways, falling in love when one is older is bound to be more shattering and overwhelming than in youth. We are not conditioned to think of love in this context and when it happens to a woman later in life, she may feel that it should have occurred earlier and she has wasted all those years. At the same time, age brings home more forcibly the tragi-comic aspects of it all; Linda Thornber fell in love for the first time at thirty-eight, in a way she had always thought belonged only to books, but the man was married with three children. She says, 'It's too late' and he is still with his family, but the hope is there that her once-in-a-lifetime feeling does have a future, no matter how far ahead.

Conformity has its own built-in support system if only in terms of numbers – more are doing the same thing at the same time. To step out of kilter can invite censure, which yet hides grudging admiration and even envy. We are conditioned to think that lovers should be approximately the same age, possibly allowing the man a few years' lead otherwise the woman is accused of 'cradle-snatching'. The reverse, however, is still not regarded as acceptable. Older women who fall in love with younger men may well feel constrained by their age to some extent: because they are flouting the conventions, they are inhibited about acting as they really feel. When Elizabeth Knight fell in love with a man twenty-four years younger than herself, 'There were times when I felt my age was a great obstacle.' She had 'terrible feelings of insecurity' and experienced difficulties with both her own and James's peer groups.

The changing social climate has made it easier to fly in the face of convention, although it still demands enormous courage and conviction to follow through a situation which is generally regarded as odd. Age can, however, have a distinct advantage, by enabling a woman to rely on her instinct and intuition in giving her confidence to go ahead. As Elizabeth Knight commented, 'It's a gut feeling . . . Instinctively I knew my relationship with James was right.'

Conventions, like rules, have always existed to be broken. What is different for those now in the middle years is the sheer span of choice available to greater numbers. The convention in the youth of women who are now middle-aged was that sex was an activity which took place not only between marital sheets but exclusively between members of opposite sexes. This view still holds good for very many people, but maturity may lead some individuals to doubt its application in relation to their instincts and feelings. Helen Ness illustrated the confusion which can result in this case:

> An area I find hard to separate is physicality and sexuality. Maybe sex is something you turn on if you want to. I don't know where sex starts because it has something to do with an element of choice and a lot to do with personality and energy you pick up from somebody. I've always been clear if I fancied a man and quick to pick that up. That's why I was thrown when I discovered how I felt about Pam.

The middle years can also bring recognition that heterosexual activity is an insufficient outlet for sexual expression, when a woman realizes that sexual relationships with women are equally important. This happened to Jenny Kent, who recognized her need when she was thirty-five but did not want to end the happy relationship with her loved and supportive husband:

> I suppose I'd had fantasies about women from about nineteen or so and had a crush on a woman at one point. When I think about it all now it's very amusing because it was all couched in terms of heterosexuality: she would sweep me off my feet exactly like a teenage romantic novel. Nothing came of this fantasy though I was in a total turmoil about it, no one knowing except me . . .
>
> Then I did just find myself in a situation where I was infatuated with another woman . . . Not only was she very much younger, only nineteen, but the balance of power between us was very unequal as I was in a very much more powerful situation than she. The whole romantic notion of love conquering all was still very much with me and so I went into a relationship with her because of the intensity of my feelings.

Some women pursue a deliberate policy of 'women only' in as many aspects as possible, in extreme cases regarding men as contaminants who should be avoided. For women now in the middle generation, the possibility of pursuing both a mixed-sex social life and a completely separate and female one is an entirely new departure – an option unlikely to have been available in their youth. Like fashion, the choice is nowhere greater than for the middle-aged woman who was born into more sexually restricted times and has matured in an increasingly sympathetic and generally tolerant social climate.

While appreciating the logic of lesbians, by the time they reach their middle years, many women recognize that their heterosexual conditioning is too strong to overcome and that – like Bernice Rubens – they have related their sexual appetites in one direction too long to be able to change.

For some women, de-conditioning themselves from the married state of emotional dependency appears rather easier. In the case of those who married relatively young, putting husbands and home before all else, their loss impels a new perspective. Some cannot envisage a life without a permanent partner and simply change their domestic situation, as do many men. Others are able to view the break-up of a marriage as an opportunity to explore their potential through work for instance, to the general exclusion of men who, having come first, subsequently come to occupy a very secondary place. Since Eileen Curry's divorce, her priorities have shifted in this way:

> The divorce has affected my relationship with men though; they're very secondary in my life and not important. I don't wait for anybody any more. I've got boy-friends but if there's a choice between work and a weekend away with one of them, it'll be the job first. There's no way that men are going to be number one again with me.

It is easier now to make this kind of choice, whereas previous generations of single and divorced women had to contend with enormous social stigmas and personal hardship; no wonder women in these situations remarried, if they could. That women need not be emotionally dependent on one man and can survive without marriage as a backdrop to their lives, represents a great social advance.

What seems to happen to very many women who find themselves alone after some years of marriage, is that they experience a strong desire to reaffirm their sexual and emotional identity which has so often been eroded through the break-up. After years of seeing themselves as X's wife and Y's mother, they discover that divorce provides an opportunity to explore the exact nature of their sexuality. Not only do women have to adjust to more equal relationships with men but they need to confirm to themselves that they are sexually desirable individuals, as Eileen Curry illustrates:

> I went out with this man who was married and looking for an emotional attachment because things weren't too good with his marriage either. I used him sexually on a purely physical level. I went off the rails with one man instead of several, which was great for me and he delighted in me being so sexual

because it hadn't been like that for him for n years.

The combination of limited sexual experience before marriage and the subsequent break-up of the partnership may also cause many women in their middle years to experiment sexually, as they might have done in adolescence had this been possible. A period of experimentation appears to be necessary before they can come to terms with their sexual and emotional needs. More often than not this is a 'trial by fire' impelling but not necessarily enjoyable. Looking back, Annette Wagner considers she made many mistakes in her reaction to the single state. She felt 'ravenous to catch up on what I'd missed' and 'had no moral sense whatsoever, no principles at all'. It took her some years to realize the importance of principles and to develop selectivity; she is not proud of that period in her life but feels 'it was one of the things I had to go through in order to find out about myself'.

Julia Mitchell also discovered the unsatisfactory nature of temporary relationships and recognized the need in herself for a permanent one with a considerably older man, following a time of being 'totally immoral, almost wild'. That women no longer perceive the need to repress their sexual and emotional needs represents an enormous social advance. Two or three decades ago, divorced women probably felt too bowed down by the horror of the divorced state to consider how they might satisfy purely personal needs outside marriage.

Though the presenting symptom of marital break-up for many women may be (amongst other things) sexual frustration, it seems more likely that Erikson's 'search for identity' lies at the heart of the matter. Often marriage can inhibit and suppress aspects of personality which are only discovered when dependent ties are broken. To emerge as a woman independent of a former marriage necessarily demands a period of self-examination and experimentation outside those original boundaries.

A different facet of this search for identity arises when a life-style is completely changed, as when Marion Burman left her convent after thirty years. Her experience of personal relationships with men was restricted to those of early youth — not so different from many others who marry young and settle down with limited experience of men other than a husband. It was crucially necessary for Marion to find out in the first place whether she could establish a 'normal' relationship with a man, having denied herself the possibility of finding out while in the convent. She had some short, unsatisfactory affairs 'which were rather shoddy somehow' but provided 'the experience of what it was like to have a close relationship with a man'. Feeling intuitively that she was 'normally attractive' she 'desperately needed that to be reinforced'. An additional problem in her case was her previous identity as a nun rather than a person.

Having 'played the field', a woman is more logically capable of deciding how she wishes to conduct her sexual and emotional life on the basis of some experience. For Annette Wagner at this stage, it was a clear decision against any more prosaic relationships: 'I want a relationship which is all fire and great things like that – even if it's only for a day or two. That's fine and I'd rather that than have someone around all the time.' Other women in similar circumstances may be confirmed in their need for a permanent, reciprocal relationship which is likely to be the more precious because it has been discovered later in life. Marion Burman eventually 'decided what I really wanted and needed was marriage'. She joined a marriage bureau and met her present husband straight away: 'I feel terribly fortunate now and realize some of the things I missed. I have companionship and the love of someone who cares about me in a special (sort of) way.'

A woman who regards the break-up of her marriage as a personal failure may then doubt the possibility of any reciprocity in a relationship with a man. Middle-aged women today do have the choice of being emotionally independent if they wish, and are freer to admit this than they once were. Eileen Curry has decided:

> I'm not prepared to let any man get to me, nobody gets me body and soul now, not even wholeheartedly body – there's always a little bit for me. I hate being in love, it's utter misery and I feel better on an even keel. Sometimes I feel split in two: a part of me wants to be a Victorian creature with a great protective husband and another wants to stick up for herself. On the whole the split is towards the independent lady. The price of being kept is being a domestic woman and I can't do it. I'm not like that any more . . . I'm quite happy on my own.

The risk of becoming emotionally scarred again may be so great after a marriage break-up that some women dare not attempt other relationships with men for some time. Possibly they hide behind the quite genuine reason that they cannot subject their children to the risk of being rejected by a 'stepfather', but basically they may lack the confidence to try. Lack of confidence in oneself as a desirable woman seems to be a common factor which many share and as Elizabeth Knight says 'I need reassurance all the time.'

Apart from families, there is possibly no other factor as capable of producing conflicting emotions as one's sexual life. While it can enrich some relationships beyond all measure, it can also destroy, confuse and degrade others. Some would argue that there has been little quantifiable progress for women in their sexual and emotional lives and that real choice is still not open to all. In answer to this, we need only consider women now in the middle generation who, having tried one path towards emotional fulfilment and found it wanting, have been able to change to another without fear of any social stigma. 'Fast', 'loose' and 'scarlet' are no longer words which are used to describe female sexual behaviour; they have lost their sting in a society which is gradually moving towards greater sexual and emotional freedom in relationships. Such terms can only have meaning when there is one fixed code of practice, and advances in the past twenty years or so have demonstrated that there is no one path for everyone. Moreover the opportunity is now available to create new patterns of life in this respect which may be radically different from those adopted in youth. Far from being moribund and the exclusive prerogative of the young, sex and love for the middle-aged may well represent a new lease of life. A woman who has acquired the confidence and certainty to know what she wants from a relationship and to pursue it, is helping to create a social climate which is more conducive for both sexes to achieve fulfilling and enriching relationships.

12
Effects of Change on Partners

Stay as sweet as you are . . .
Don't let a thing ever change you.
                     Popular song

Change can be either horribly upsetting or wildly exciting – depending on your point of view and whether you are doing the changing or receiving its backlash. For the woman who sees her primary role to be in the home and directs most of her energies towards the welfare of her husband and family, the changes which occur are mainly those evolving slowly around the growth of children. A wife who has little involvement beyond the domestic presents no threat to her husband while the *status quo* is maintained, and is possibly his confidante and emotional buffer against the slings and arrows of his work. However, there is little opportunity for such a wife to find relief from her own stresses and tensions in the home. Because most men are the main bread-winners, they may see it as more important to deprive their families of their presence: substituting income for absence. Women, on the other hand tend to feel their presence is more important and that to deprive the family of it is not only to risk their displeasure but to fly in the face of what is right and proper. Until recently, it has not seemed to be important for a woman to acquire an identity outside the home, whereas this is seen to be essential for a man.

Many marriages exist on a basis of inequality not unlike that of a parent and child – but unlike that relationship, of a permanent nature. Where the major bread-winner is the husband, this is often felt to give him the right to take decisions on behalf of all his dependants, regardless of how his wife is contributing in other ways. To question this arrangement will not only upset the *status quo* and produce conflict, but may also be regarded as entirely unreasonable and even damaging. Nevertheless, following an initial reaction of outrage, the challenge may come to be seen as ultimately beneficial and liberating to all concerned.

As we have already considered, the sheer duration of marriage brings its own form of reappraisal, whether overtly or not, and there seem to be two other main strands which can also contribute to change within the relationship. During their middle years many women begin to discover hitherto latent potential within themselves; they may direct these energies straight into a job or else take up formal education before channelling them into work. Either way, once a woman launches out with herself as prime focus, there are likely to be repercussions for her husband and family. Once she starts to take off, she is bound to feel an impelling need to catch up on what she fears she has missed.

But what about the husband who may well feel he has not had the opportunity to discover what he has missed because his nose has been firmly fixed to the bread-winning grindstone on behalf of his family? He may feel justifiably aggrieved and even jealous.

Let us first consider education and the part it plays in bringing about change for women in relation to their husbands – this may well be a preliminary to other, greater changes between them.

Evening and part-time day classes have always provided a source of formal education for men and women who have other responsibilities and commitments during the day. Kelly Anderson started making changes by going to evening classes and when her husband raised objections, 'I said I was going anyway, which was the first time I'd done anything he didn't really want me to.'

On the face of it, an evening class hardly appears to constitute a great threat to a marriage, yet it does provide a challenge to a wife's traditional place and in the process, upsets the 'natural' balance. For a man who is contented as things are, there is an underlying risk that he will be made to feel inferior by a wife who apparently wants to achieve more through education. That she defies his wishes is evidence of independent behaviour over which he has no control. To assert this independence via education suggests a woman is trying to 'better' herself, which in turn may make a man feel he is not – or will not be – good enough for her.

If evening classes are regarded as a threat because of what they represent, how much greater is the threat posed by a degree course, especially to someone who neither has a similar qualification nor feels the need or desire to acquire it. The very nature of what a degree now stands for can make a husband feel intellectually inadequate by comparison. Sometimes the threat appears so great that it cannot be challenged openly within a marriage. When Kelly Anderson later went on to take a degree, her husband appeared co-operative on the surface, but she later discovered he had confided in a relative his fear that she would 'blossom out into an intellectual woman and leave him behind'.

No one can win in this situation. A gulf inevitably develops between husband and wife when something which is part of daily existence is actively ignored by both in the home context. A woman will feel she leads a schizoid existence between college and home and inevitably resent that she is losing out; there is no opportunity for one activity to enhance the other. Her husband may justify his wife's activity to himself by belittling it, thinking of it in terms of something to 'occupy' the little woman – and anyway, he could probably do it himself if he wished. Neither partner then has the active support and encouragement of the other. But if a woman suspects her husband feels this way in the first place, she may hesitate to bring it into the open for fear of diminishing his sense of self-worth even further. On the other hand she can become so absorbed by the new horizons opening up for her that she virtually attacks her husband and marriage for not allowing her to experience this sooner. As a result of reading 'sociology at a very radical place' Liz Ahrends changed from 'someone with ordinary political commitments' to 'this lefty feminist which was very different . . . I went about it very stupidly: constantly on about it to the family. My husband had to adjust to my ideas, learn what they were and had to put up with me constantly on about it.' She feels that:

> He wanted to be sympathetic and felt, maybe, the sense of the arguments but at the same time, got a bit fed up with me. Our marriage went through a very difficult time. You can see, looking back, all the steps leading up to it and to do with my taking off. There was I, moving away faster and faster and maybe too aggressively. I wasn't sensitive enough, didn't do it well enough.

Adolescent fervour in middle age may well be rather hard to cope with and not at all conducive to peaceful co-existence, especially since life probably goes on as it always did for the husband and his work.

Perhaps less drastically, some women find that by extending their horizons through further education they are no longer so accepting of the *status quo* as they once were, as Sheila (NOW) explains:

> Just by coming here, to some degree I've reverted to the kind of wife I was when my husband first met me. I'm not so much a 'yes wife' as I was. My job must always come second to his job because it's in his mind that it's something for me to do. I've either got to be devious to get my own way or knuckle down and be a 'yes wife'.

What seems a common pattern in many areas of achievement by a married woman who has not received continuing support for her enterprise from her husband, is his pride and pleasure (and possibly relief?) in her ultimate success. Having tolerated the exercise, it is then often difficult to say openly what he feels: the pride remains as indirectly expressed as was the resentment. When Kelly Anderson got her degree her husband was thrilled and gave her a gold pendant, 'But it didn't mean a thing, because I needed help and support over the three years, not now. Then I thought, how ungrateful.'

Formal education does have one great asset for a fearful husband in that it comes to an obvious end. Having jumped one hurdle, honour is satisfied and the possibility of another in the same direction may not seem as horrendous. A husband may then feel that his wife should return to the previous *status quo*, as when Kelly Anderson's husband wanted her to work in his vicinity. Not only would this put her in the position of being where he could keep an eye on her – 'and he would' – but she wished to make better use of her degree qualifications.

A man may feel undermined simply by the suggestion that his wife wants to have a life outside that which she shares with her family. If she has not worked at all since she had children and to all intents and purposes seems happy in her domesticity, to be confronted with the idea that she is not satisfied may make him feel that he has in some obscure way failed her. When June Barry was unsettled and unhappy following their move, 'Don found it very difficult because he felt as if I was blaming him, that he had failed me in some way – and Barrys never fail!'

A woman who has been at home for years has in effect given her 'all' to her family: to suggest that she remove part of herself from their service in order to service others outside the home, could be seen as tantamount to a betrayal. Since the daily routine established custom and habit, a man may be unable or unwilling to realize why his wife has become dissatisfied with her domestic role. He may be so convinced that she is wrong that the only way to prove it is to let her try. Considering his own knowledge of the outside world of work and his wife's relative lack of it, he may convince himself that he has some sort of superior 'know-how' which ignores her intense motivation to work. For example, when June Barry was put on the short list for a job, her husband appeared to think 'that justice had been seen to be done and we could all go back to how we were before'. Once she had started work, he was like many husbands who, having become accustomed to their wives being available whenever required, resent competing for attention and suffering encroachments on what they consider their rightful time.

Some men do still regard their wives as personal possessions who should therefore be available at all times. Joy (NOW) found her husband's reactions to her work very hard to cope with:

> I was working for the local council when I was in my first marriage and my husband then couldn't accept I worked overtime and wasn't there to cook him a meal, in spite of the fact that I rushed home and put something in the oven before

going back to the office. It got to the point when he was punishing me for any extra work I did, including voluntary work. He's now admitted, only last year, that he immobilized my car so that I couldn't go out. He got this complete obsession that other than when I was being paid to work, I was his wife and his wife alone.

A man who cannot appreciate why his wife needs and wants to work, on the basis that he can provide *all* her wants and needs, probably sees himself in the role of protector. His wife may well be dispelling this myth precisely at a time when he is going through what is sometimes called 'the male menopause' – a period of personal and professional reassessment. June Barry feels that her husband's reactions when she first went back to work were complicated by middle age and considers ' . . . men are much worse than women during that period'.

Having to cope with an apparently aberrant wife at a time when he most needs her undivided attention, may well seem an unnecessary and additional burden for a husband, which he resents having to bear. There is obviously an inherent risk in any marriage that if both partners have work outside the home, they could be in the situation of making invidious comparisons between the partner and their colleagues. Eileen Curry experienced the difficulties caused by this factor:

> Working at the college was the best and the worst thing that could have happened as it turned out. Suddenly I was surrounded by staff who were thinking, intelligent, interested in world events and interested in other people's opinions. It was a very stimulating atmosphere. Then I'd come home and cook a meal . . . and Jim'd sit and we never had a conversation. I wanted him to talk to me but I think he felt he couldn't give me what I wanted . . . I think he felt a little inadequate. I used to put a lot of creativity into the meals I cooked and spend six or seven hours in the kitchen doing a real splurge.

Such comparisons can obviously occur at any time, but the later it happens and the longer marital roles have had time to crystallize, the harder it is bound to be for both. To have an economically reliant wife is to know where she is and probably what she is doing – and she is certainly unlikely to constitute a professional threat. A husband may feel that the only advantage of having a working wife is more money – a comment which several women made of their spouses' attitudes.

A wife who has stayed at home for years has given her husband a fairly circumscribed idea of her capabilities. Launching out later on may shatter his entire concept of her and will obviously require considerable readjustment on his part. The reaction of June Barry's husband will probably strike a chord with many other women: 'He was fascinated in spite of himself. Amazed that anyone could take me seriously and regard me as worthwhile to employ.' She feels that having been an only child he had never had to step aside for anyone – always having had things done his way made adjustment more difficult despite his efforts.

Change brought about by a wife and mother going out to work will certainly alter the pattern of daily life. The new activity will inevitably seem more exciting than the one which has been continued year in and year out by the major bread-winner, hence a husband's resentment at having to take a back seat when he was accustomed to being the only runner.

In addition to feeling left out or pushed to one side in his family by the novelty of his wife's job a husband will feel further excluded because he is not part of her work any more than she has been of his. His primacy as head of the household can therefore be challenged from a number of directions; also there may be an element of sexual jealousy involved once a woman leaves the 'protection' of her husband and family. This experience is likely to be all the more acute for husbands who see their wives as their exclusive property.

The trust which exists between husband and wife is open to greater challenge and is more vulnerable now that the basis of the working relationship has changed. While appreciating that there is nothing he can do to forbid or prevent his wife from working in this day and age, a husband may nevertheless act quite childishly to protect what he sees as his own interests, as did Joy's (NOW) husband when he immobilized her car. Justifying what he does in terms of protecting his wife from the ravages of the world, a man can try to extend his role as husband into her working life, causing not only humiliation but resentment in the process; this was certainly how June Barry felt when her husband insisted on collecting her from work. She also found that sexual jealousy may extend into professional jealousy when a wife's success appears greater:

> In some ways, I think he thinks I've achieved more in my job than he has in his, because for a time I think he felt he hadn't got the recognition he either wanted or deserved. He felt very vulnerable because I was achieving that recognition and he wasn't – a lot of male pride came into that.

Negotiating a new marital balance when one partner is altering her previous role in the marriage can be very fraught and delicate. A husband may well feel displaced if (until his wife's return to work) he has been solely responsible for earning the family's living and if any rewards were going, they should be rightfully his in terms of precedence if nothing else.

Should working roles be reversed as a result of redundancy as opposed to choice, many men feel emasculated. They have relatively little experience of being 'kept' in the sense that women have been conditioned to accept the state. Sheila (NOW) describes how her husband felt in this situation: 'He can't cope with me having a job because we need the income. He was unbearable when he was out of a job and we lived on my money. I don't think I could ever bring my husband to terms with my earning an income which we needed.'

A woman who 'makes it' in the eyes of the world, contrary to all her husband's expectations or wishes, may receive his reluctant admiration but probably not an outright acknowledgement of her ability. In time, as a greater number of women become as successful in their paid employment as in their unpaid work at home, and a stronger precedent is established, more men may come to feel proud of their wives' work and able to understand the value of the liberation it brings them. In theory at least, the middle years for a man could be precisely the time to alter the pattern of his own life by virtue of the changes his wife has brought about for the entire family.

Education and work are two obvious ways in which a woman can accomplish change in her life, both of which require adjustment within a marriage. Marriage itself evolves over time, and the middle years are likely to produce a trigger from one direction or another which challenges reassessment from either or both partners. Having 'accepted' her husband's many affairs during their marriage, Elizabeth Knight found that he showed a strong adverse reaction when her younger boy-friend moved in with her, despite the fact that they were already parted and she had told him she would not return to him.

Regardless of all the different changes a woman can opt to bring about in later life, she will almost inevitably become a different person from the one her husband married. Irma Kurtz sees the pitfalls as considerable for someone who, for example, decides at the age of forty to opt for a career and change her husband's comfortable home life; not everyone would agree with her assumption that 'Deep down what she's rebelling against is that union and that's part of her pattern of revolt', but probably few would deny that '. . . however bitter and neglected she felt, her husband's going to miss the old person she once was. . . . he can't be expected to live with a new person in the old house.'

Mary Baker feels she has changed a great deal, in her opinion for the better:

> I put a hell of a lot on Tim by being childish and I leaned on him tremendously. Now he says I'm not the same person he married. He doesn't like the tough side of me. But I'm very proud of being tough because I really admire what I'm becoming. I like myself and I never really liked myself before. Recently I said I would leave Tim if our marriage wasn't going to work and I would never have said that before because I felt I couldn't upset him.

Sheer habit may not always be a positive factor in a marriage, but it can lead the partners to believe there is a great deal worth preserving and therefore to work towards joint accommodation within a new – and possibly even more valuable – framework. It is very sad when the exact opposite occurs and habit reduces the possibility of adapting and changing the old framework. So often it seems that when one partner changes, this is not seen by the other as part of the growth of the marriage as a whole but as something unsettling and upsetting. Yet change in one or more directions by one partner does not necessarily mean that the eternal verities they share are altered as well. June Barry's marriage underwent considerable change over about five years as a result of her work; she now has more self-confidence and the decisiveness essential to her job has spilled over into her private life. She is aware, though, that she is not the same person, and 'Don had to get used to living with a different person in many ways.'

Fear that a woman may grow away from her marriage as a result of changes she is making, is probably one of the most common feelings a husband can experience. A wife may also feel this to be an inevitable consequence, which can either make her hesitate to embark on new involvements or else accept that she is likely to communicate with her husband even less than previously. Kelly Anderson, for example, finds that her degree course has made her 'a bit afraid of my marriage going by the board. I can't talk to my husband. I never have.' In her case communication was never very good and has now more or less ceased.

Many wives do establish a new accommodation with their husbands, as has been observed. Others acknowledge that they have outgrown or no longer share anything with a partner. Generally women recognize the fact that they are accustomed to daily change, which is a factor their husbands do not experience. They also appreciate that the marriage which provides a base for their lives is essential to their continuing emotional security and are prepared to help their husbands adapt to the 'new' women they have become. Perhaps the innate difficulty in this situation is that underneath the surface many women consider they are merely fulfilling potential of which they always knew they were capable. Their husbands may have had no such inkling. Possibly a woman considers the changes she is making will regenerate rather than destroy her marriage, bringing it a new lease of life at precisely the time this can be most enjoyed.

Marriages which have existed always on a more equitable basis are probably less likely to find change in one partner either unnerving or unsettling – it can be seen more easily as part of a pattern of growth and the partners will be mutually supportive of one another. It is interesting that while many individuals recognize that the human species as a whole has acquired an innate capacity to adapt in order to ensure survival, many others cannot apply that ability to their personal relationships. Yet the conflict which inevitably arises out of change can be immensely productive, bringing about a closer and more equal partnership. On the other hand, it can of course blow it wide apart, exposing incompatibilities which are too deep for new accommodation to be reached; that in itself can be far from negative in the long run, though shattering in the short term.

There is only a thin line between a quiet life and one which is so dull as gradually to extinguish all creativity and excitement. Change is immensely challenging, and it is sad that so many of us immediately leap to the assumption that it will be for the worse. The more we can do away with fixed roles for ourselves and regard change as the key to creativity, the more enjoyable life will be. It is only in recent years that women have had the opportunity to bring about change in all aspects of their lives, so on the whole men have had little time to adapt and become accustomed to the different ideas with which they are being confronted. Obviously some women do trample over their partners in their urge to 'find themselves', but most adopt a far less aggressive approach because they know that to do so is to cut off their noses . . . Once women have established change as a customary development in their lives, it will no longer be seen as so threatening to their partners but will simply be the norm.

13
Friends

'Friendship is a disinterested commerce between equals.'
Gay, *The Good-Natured Man*

Friends play an important part in most people's lives, and are a virtually essential ingredient in helping to bring about change. Not only are true friends continuously supportive and encouraging but because of the nature of friendship they form part of the fabric of existence, maintaining a stable background when the pattern is in the process of altering and changing shape. They also provide another dimension to the love and care which families cannot always give.

Changes in the attitude to family life have had their spin-off with regard to friendship. Generally speaking, for previous generations blood relations always took precedence of importance over friends, but now the situation is no longer quite so clear-cut. One of the effects of criticizing the function of the traditional family has been to displace its absolute supremacy over friends, who now fulfil many of the roles once occupied by the extended family. Many individuals would now claim that friends are as important to them as their families – perhaps more so, given the element of choice which exists for one and not the other. The importance of friendship for women who are bringing about change in their lives is therefore an essential aspect of the picture.

There has always been a separate community of women existing alongside that shared by both sexes: one which is characterized by the lack of contractual commitment. Often it has constituted a form of defence against the male-dominated world outside, concerning itself with the small, meaningful matters which help to stabilize and integrate a community – being a 'good' neighbour, running fêtes and bazaars and keeping an eye on things in general. Helen Ness's neighbours were of great support when she came out of hospital: 'The friends I had as neighbours were amazing: looking after the children during the day so that I could sleep when I was so exhausted. Someone else came round with a quiche when I came out of hospital . . .'

Paradoxically, that separate community of women may be both less and more exclusive than traditionally it once was. In many ways, now that women tend to be less excluded from traditional male preserves, they are more free to seek the support of both men *and* women. On the other hand, there are some women who consciously wish to exclude men from as many areas of their lives as possible, and the community of women in this sense is far more politicized than formerly. For Jenny Kent, 'My involvement with the Women's Movement has also led me to a social life involving women only. I like the idea of a woman-orientated existence though I'm not anti-men. I have very little social life with my husband, though that developed that way a long time ago.'

Why are friends of particular importance to women contemplating change? In effect, what *are* friends? Penny McGuire suggests that friends are friends because they provide a reflection of oneself:

> Women friends do provide the opportunity for you to go into the minutiae of emotional life because they're good listeners – probably you choose friends precisely for that. They're amateur shrinks in a way and provide a service which would otherwise drive your partner up the wall. I suppose it's like talking to your reflection. Perhaps we choose friends whom we realize will be uncritical of us and take us as we are. That's not possible in a relationship with a man.

Some women suggest that the essential service of mutual

support provided by friends is not felt to be so necessary by men, and many mentioned the importance of having female friends who complement the relationship a woman has with her partner. Christine Merton, for example, needs 'a balance of friends and loved ones. There are areas where I need to talk to friends of my own sex.' She feels that fear of being thought homosexual may have inhibited heterosexual men from making personal friendships in the past, and that wives can do a great deal to encourage friendship including that between fathers and sons.

On the other hand, there are wives who find in a husband everything they want in a friend. When an intense relationship like this remains undiluted by friends of either sex, there can be difficulties when the woman changes her role in marriage and the family by taking up interests which to some extent preclude them; both partners then experience a rough and lonely time until a new accommodation is reached. By sharing with friends the dependence which would otherwise be placed solely on one partner, the burden is lessened and possibly enhanced. However, the couple orientation of our society can make it harder to maintain friendships, as Helen Ness found until she reached the situation where, 'Now I'm no longer bound up with babies and so on, I feel freer to make contact with friends over the past few months, people feel more aware that they're important to me and therefore I am to them.'

Ironically, at precisely the time when friends may most be needed – during the break-up of a marriage, for instance – some women withdraw their support. Not only can the marital break-up provoke comparisons with their own situation and highlight cracks in a relationship which they would rather ignore, but people whose social lives are ordered and established do not wish to cope with single, unattached women. When Bernice Rubens separated from her husband she experienced virtual hostility from her friends, which she attributed to the different perspective into which this put their own marriages.

There are times when friends may turn out not to be friends – such as when one does not conform to their ideas of what one should be or should be doing. Elizabeth Knight feels that: 'Throughout my life I've evoked jealousy in some female friends. Maybe it's because I'm so enthusiastic. It makes them feel guilty. I think perhaps when you're thirty-five to forty, you're meant to knuckle down and be sedate.' Linda Thornber discovered that all her social life disappeared with her marriage. At times such as these many women have to start from scratch and in so doing develop strong friendships they might not otherwise have contemplated; Linda now has a very supportive sisterly relationship with Carol and feels circumstances produced a unique situation: '. . . she was there at the right time and the right place'.

So far, the assumption has been that close friends rather than acquaintances are an integral part of everyone's life. However, making friends assumes a reciprocity which some people feel they can neither offer nor have the wish or need to share. Jean Shrimpton has often felt the need for a good friendship with another woman, especially when there have been problems in her personal life, 'but so far, it's never quite worked out'.

Women may become 'loners' as a result of a damaging experience in the past. Annette Wagner became disillusioned and wary after being badly let down by a woman friend, and also feels that the 'front' of invulnerability she puts up in order to avoid pity probably deters others. Recipient of what she considers 'disastrous advice' during the highly traumatic period before parting from her husband, she has got into the habit of not discussing her problems.

Friendship implies involvement, which in turn implies risk. Combined with a natural inclination to stand back and observe, the risk factor may make some women reluctant to take the plunge, while at the same time being aware that they are in some way missing out. Linda Thornber endorses this in saying, 'I don't put a lot of effort into relationships. I like to watch.' She thinks 'there's something lacking in me when it comes to personal relationships. I know people but I have no friends, never have had. I pretend not to mind but I think I do, being so lonely.'

Even women who are without close female friends are now more aware of a wider 'sisterhood' which exists 'out there': a network which can offer practical help and advice beyond the domestic. This is friendship in the widest sense of the word and is much valued by Nancy Roberts who believes that, 'If we help one another, we can make it at any age, it's never too late.' On the other hand, the fact that this network operates in so many ways – Women's Aid, Women in Print and so on – may make women who do not consider themselves in any sense part of the

Women's Movement, feel excluded from what's going on. The women's sphere has expanded from purely parochial to national concerns and exists on many more levels than formerly. Some of those interviewed suggested women as a whole were less competitive and more co-operative than they once were, recognizing the need to affiliate in order to bring about change in the social order.

More specifically, friends are especially important to single parents – not that the latter constitute a new phenomenon, but until recently they existed in a state of virtual purdah and may still do outside urban areas. While they are no longer likely to be cast to one side by their families, single-parent units do not fit neatly into the established order and need to rely on supportive friends who can offer practical assistance in terms of sharing child care, babysitting – even financial help – and also dilute the intensity of the one-to-one relationship between parent and child. Pat Hull wanted her own friends to be her daughter's too:

> I felt that if we had been friends with someone, they should keep up that contact for Emma's sake, even if they moved. It was quite irrational I know but I was very conscious that without friends, there was no dilution of resources outside myself. That's why it's very important to share the house – apart from babysitting which is tremendously important. Friends were very kind as I was very pinched financially.

Many women find the 'psychic' support which others offer more continuously satisfying than that which a partner provides. Presumably this is one of the reasons why men have always foregathered in pubs and clubs. Sheila Dainow's female friends 'have always played an enormously important part in my life' and at times 'my relationships with women have been more fulfilling than those I have with men'. She feels that if her stable relationship with a man came to an end she might opt to live with a group of women rather than searching to replace it, and emphasizes, 'I really don't think I could manage without the women friends I have because it's to them that I turn when I'm really despairing in a way that I don't turn to Cyril . . .'

In Bernice Rubens's opinion, it is in their middle years that women are particularly supportive of one another 'because they're all going through the same experience and because they are ashamed of what they might term failure, particularly if it's marriage failure'. She is convinced that, 'When women reach forty or so, the greatest thing they can do is to seek other women friends and that's a sure beginning, for the strength of united women is enormous.'

Some people choose a more communal way of life which provides a continuing and ever-present network of friendship. This has been Lee's experience: 'Thirty years ago we were a group of women who thought of ourselves as feminists having the communal support of one another. There was not a time when we could say "now I'm free of the children" because we could arrange that often and in a way that was good for the children too.'

Many of us will identify with those women in the process of change who want to rediscover and explore the selves they were before marriage and children changed them and their lives. Helen Ness's friends helped her to build up a picture of herself: 'In taking stock of my situation, it's become very important to make contact with old friends from the past, some of whom I've known longer than John. I need to build up a picture of myself that's not just as a married woman but as someone who exists apart from that.' This is another aspect of the feelings expressed by June Barry when she first began to contemplate change: 'I had this great urge to be me.'

Many women gain courage from the support of their friends when they embark on a totally new way of life. Marion Burman, for instance, was sustained in her difficult decision to leave the religious life by another sister who left the convent at the same time. Jane Worthington found help in a slightly different way, when she embarked on a professional course: 'I don't think I could have done this without a friend. With Liz I could try on the role of talking about sociology outside the college and that reinforced the idea of myself as an intelligent, rational person. You can practise on one another.'

Friends may well provide the final push which a woman needs to embark on something new and frightening. No matter how compelling the motivation to launch off she may still hesitate – endlessly weighing up the pros and cons without coming to a conclusion, as did Pat Hull: 'For years, I'd thought about doing a degree but was frightened by the thought. When a good friend had applied and went on to do a course, it gave me a push. But I was still frightened I would fail and then there'd be nothing left.'

Most of the women who were interviewed talked about their female friends; a few talked about fraternal feelings they had for men; only one said she was more comfortable with men than with women. The vast majority echoed Sheila Dainow's sentiments about the difference between male and female friends, that women are more comfortable to be with and that 'having an intimate relationship with a man which isn't sexual is very difficult. Sex is never irrelevant in a relationship with a man and it can be with a woman.'

It is an interesting paradox that alongside the development in self-help, individualistic solutions to life and living, there has also been a parallel growth in co-operative enterprises. The Women's Movement has and does exert considerable influence on women – even those who do not actively identify with it – because it emphasizes the importance of affiliation for all. Friends have always played a supportive role in most people's lives, but today that sense of friendship can be extended to assist others in similar situations even though the individuals involved may not be known to one another. A widespread network of organizations exists to help other women, not just through active concern with problems but in the true spirit of amity. Friends are no longer peripheral to the family unit; and to a great extent its meaning has expanded to include them and it is through their unstinting support that many women gain the strength and courage to make changes in their lives.

14
Being Alone

This 'fear of being left empty' and, more simply, that of 'being left', seems to be the most basic feminine fear, extending over the whole of a woman's existence. It is normally intensified with every menstruation and takes its final toll during the menopause. No wonder, then, that the anxiety roused by these fears can express itself either in complete subjection to male thought, in desperate competition with it, or in efforts to catch the male and make him a possession.

Erik H. Erikson, *Childhood and Society*

What a terrible indictment of the female sex! The quotation contains much that is unfair, but disregarding if possible the link between menstruation and being alone, the main point seems to hold true for very many women. Just why women should find it harder than men to be on their own is likely to be a matter of nurture rather than nature. Many of those who find themselves alone, by circumstance rather than choice, adjust not only competently but with enjoyment. After all, a picture of the solitary state is conjured up far more readily by single gents with string bags of shopping than by their female equivalents. Moreover, given the disparate life spans of men and women, females actually have far more practice, historically speaking, at coping on their own.

However, there is more to being alone than at first meets the eye, not only in terms of what is involved but what is actually meant. One can be left on one's own after marital break-up, which implies not living with anyone else; or on one's own with children after marital break-up, in other words without adult company but not strictly speaking alone. Then there is loneliness, which means being without anyone who cares for you: a state which can exist equally within or outside marriage. Also the loneliness which is an inherent part of being human. Finally, there is independence: that elusive state which suggests a form of self-sufficiency and implies capability of being on one's own, having worked out dependency problems.

Many wives who bring about change in their lives face from the outset the prospect of being left on their own. Divorce may well be the price they pay for the achievement of their independence, but that does not necessarily mean being bereft of all close relationships. Being alone has come to mean the state of being without a partner or without family. What it does not suggest is that numerous women lacking one or the other are far from alone by virtue of friends and acquaintances.

Undoubtedly many women do have a particular problem about being on their own, at any rate in the earlier years, for which marriage can in part be blamed. Much of the orientation of their lives is towards being part of a couple, hence the whole focus is not on being an individual but on becoming half of a pair. Being alone is thus viewed as a transient state prior to being coupled, therefore according to P.D. James, 'The prospect of being alone is something they never face or train themselves for, either psychologically, physically or economically.'

Most women have very little practice at being on their own – and in some cases do not perceive that the opportunity is there. Social attitudes and expectations impel them towards dependency on a man, which for many becomes a substitute for personal growth for a good many years, if not for ever. To Irma Kurtz, being alone is 'the most painful and important thing to have done, to be absolutely on your own with nobody who needs, wants or calls on you. You learn a lot.' She feels that, 'Being on your own is the most strengthening thing there is: recognizing if anything's going to happen, you're going to have to make it happen, there's nobody else.'

The Women's Movement has produced some contrary spin-off effects with regard to being an independent, capable woman living on one's own. Many women would see this as the most desirable state to achieve and struggle to attain it, but middle age may bring a realization that this is a struggle you would rather give up: you come to terms with your dependency needs and recognize they may be what is now considered of the old-fashioned variety. Nancy Roberts had always considered her emotional dependence to be a drawback – 'Then I thought, why should I have to learn to live by myself?' She now accepts that she is happier with someone around: 'Now it's as if I'm finally sympathizing with myself and can stop criticizing myself all the time.'

One of the problems about being part of a couple is trying to visualize what it is like to be on one's own. Many women have suggested that marriage not only inhibits personal growth but by implication, distorts perspectives. In effect, it is almost impossible to imagine the positive side of living alone when this has never been experienced. Simply living with another person over a number of years and growing accustomed to the comfortable familiarity of the marital home may in itself make the thought of striking out alone not exciting but terrifying – the exact reverse of the way many adolescents feel about leaving the parental home. Mary Baker feels there are certain obstacles in her path:

> You learn to love comfort more in middle age. Playing roles is easy, you can't get clear of them. I can't leap into the role I have in my girl-friend's house when I'm at home. It takes real courage to jump from being a childish lady married to an older man, to being a woman in London looking after her kids by herself.

'Alone' being such a chilling word, the image of a solitary woman without the comfort of the family to which she has grown accustomed over time, may also act as a deterrent. Jenny Kent echoes the feelings of many women who were interviewed in wanting to explore the extent of her dependence on her husband and family, having never had the chance to find out whether she could survive on her own. On the one hand she has 'a tremendous need for privacy but once you have children, that's it: the opportunity's no longer there'. Yet on the other, 'I'm held back . . . as well by the fear that independence could be a disaster. I might be a pathetic creature in a bed-sit and in achieving this, I might be sacrificing something which is solid and good.' These conflicts probably explain why many women stay married, because as Elizabeth Knight expresses the situation: 'It's easy to sit back and do nothing – rather frightening to do anything else. Home, family, everything jogs along gently. It's a big thing and very traumatic to suddenly break up a marriage and be completely independent. Sometimes it's better to have somebody than nobody.'

So many aspects of being on one's own are initially foreign to many women's way of thinking; coupled with the sheer difficulties of coping with children without customary male support, this inhibits some from ever taking the plunge. Julia Mitchell thinks most women underestimate their capacity to cope and thus remain in a compromise situation, not realizing that 'the so-called damage to their children might not be as drastic as they think'. She believes moreover that, 'Some women never realize the extent of their compromise, which is even sadder. I've got a lot of sympathy for women who do realize it but can't take the hassle of breaking out on their own.'

While the lure of being an independent individual may be considerable, this is counterbalanced by an inability to see how to cope with dependence on other people. Liz Ahrends, for example, 'would like to be strong enough to survive alone but I'm not sure about it because in the end, people need people. What is awful is dependence and it's that which screws up relationships. One needs emotional support and you can define your needs.'

Many women are deterred from breaking free from unsatisfactory marriages by the fear that with the loss of a partner, they will lose all close human contact. In effect, a woman on her own may be more than alone – she may be lonely. P.D. James describes the need to be needed, to know one is important to someone else's happiness, which is an essential part of the human condition and comments:

The real loneliness must be for women who haven't this and it must be very real and very frightening. I don't think it necessarily need be a husband or a child. It may be a best friend or a parent. The ultimate loneliness is to know there is no one in the world who would really be very much worse off if you didn't exist, no one who looks to you for their needs. So that in a sense we are organized in pairs. I think it is difficult for any human being to live entirely alone and if he does, it can be a rather selfish existence.

Women who are on their own without the support of friends or family must inevitably suffer from a form of shock after having lived for some time as part of a couple. Linda Thornber has found the process of adapting very hard but refuses to compromise: 'I don't like the idea of staying on my own, I don't belong on my own. I wouldn't advocate this loneliness. I wouldn't say to a woman of thirty-eight, go on and try it.' She considers that 'being alone is an art because it's very depressing and writing has been an antidote'.

The grief and aching sense of loss which comes with the death of a partner is really a subject on its own which merits more attention than can be devoted to it here. All women who find themselves on their own when they have not chosen to be, for whatever reason, probably pass through a period of mourning what has been lost until they can adjust to their new situation. This is a time during which an individual has to come to terms with what is past and look ahead to what lies in the future. When Eileen Curry's husband left, she 'went on a pilgrimage up to Newcastle, living in the past because I was in a really morbid state and they'd been happy times and the future didn't look too bright'. Finally, she came to the crisis point when 'I realized the past ten or eleven years were dead and I could either sink or swim'.

Women who find themselves without the protection of a man, to which they have grown accustomed over a period of years, may feel particularly vulnerable; Christine Merton's divorce in her late forties left her feeling 'tremendously insecure' and she 'took about seven years to heal'. Her emotional shock was compounded because she had never taken a job before nor dealt with the practical 'business' side of running a household. The sharing of all tasks and responsibilities in the home, which is now more common, does have the advantage of alleviating the totally bereft feeling experienced in these circumstances.

Given that so much social activity is organized around couples, this too may end with a marriage, increasing a woman's sense of isolation just at the time she most needs the support of friends. Added to this, a mother may feel guilty because she thinks she is depriving her children of a parent and this accentuates her feeling of being out in the cold. Despite this, children may provide the impetus to keep going because there is no choice but to go forward. Coming to terms with living alone after being married must inevitably lead to reflection on that marriage; from the new vantage point of independence, many women realize for the first time the extent of their previous dependence. Several women admitted they might be rationalizing the advantages of the single state; nevertheless Annette Wagner is quite certain that she is 'perfectly content by myself', and no longer feels she needs anyone else on a permanent basis. For her, 'There are great satisfactions being independent' which outweigh the disadvantages.

As with marriage, habit sets a pattern. Coupled with age, women who found themselves alone during their middle years admitted they would probably find it difficult to live with someone else. Bernice Rubens, who started to live alone at the age of forty, is probably typical in being 'hooked on living alone now though it cost me a great deal to learn how. I'm not sure it's all that natural to live by yourself and a certain area in me regrets that I'm no longer fit to live with anyone else. The first year was really hard . . .'

Perhaps in reaction to a feeling of failure about a broken marriage, some women may even take a perverse pride in emphasizing that they would be impossible to live with, after years of being on their own. That apart, there are some occupations particularly suited to a solitary way of life, writing especially.

Many women who had grown accustomed to being on their own implied there was a danger of becoming too self-absorbed – just as they had once been too concerned with their family's affairs to the detriment of their own. They suggested there was a danger of losing a sense of perspective when living alone. However, a great many others found that living on their own was the making of them, and Christine Merton is one of them. Divorce in the late forties left her feeling totally unprotected – 'Suddenly I lost my status' – but she subsequently 'took up studies in ceramics and sculpture and grew from that. A combination of many things – awareness, confidence and so on – made me become a more total person . . . I'm happy now and, if I can carry on, that's fine. I don't want any more.'

The conflict between independence and marriage continues: is the achievement of one incompatible with the other and in order to achieve independence, does marriage have to go by the board? As we know from harsher forms of conditioning, what can once be learned can later be unlearned. So often talking about women alone refers to women without a partner, which is to ignore the network of support now generally available. Age in any case brings increasing recognition of the fact that all human beings are ultimately alone – thus the cyclical nature of birth and death takes on new significance.

The great advantage which all women share today is the knowledge that marriage does not *have* to provide the ultimate antidote to loneliness, or indeed to any other aspect of living. It can and obviously does satisfy vast numbers; that it no longer *has* to do so is a freedom which many more women of all ages are beginning to realize. This is not to detract from the courage it takes for a woman to launch out on her own with the possibility of being without the partner to whom she has become accustomed. Human beings are infinitely adaptable: women particularly so. Being alone after being married may well involve relying heavily on one's own resources for a time, but it need not necessarily entail being solitary. Finding the courage to be resourceful is the elusive key which, as we have seen, more and more women are discovering.

Postscript

Conclusions tend to sound like chemical formulae – to arrive at a specific conclusion here would imply that there is a finite end to making changes in the middle years. In fact, the one conclusion we can reach is that this is merely the beginning.

More and more women are viewing their middle years from the 'half a glass full' standpoint rather than the 'half a glass empty' alternative. Today's social climate not only enables women to be more aware that a way of life established in youth need not necessarily be the way they wish to function later but also affords them the opportunity to act on this. It would be false to suggest that all women, or for that matter all men, are fulfilling their potential as they could and ideally should do, but headway is being made on a scale larger than ever before which must be encouraging for everyone.

As the book progressed I have become increasingly conscious that it has not been possible to do justice to all the material on which it was based. Each chapter deserves more exploration and expansion than is practicable within this particular brief. It can only be a beginning, a hint of the shape of things to come.

Optimistically, this book will become outdated and part of social history before too long, simply because women generally will have established themselves as individuals capable of participating in the business of living at all times and on all levels. When headlines referring to 'the first woman in space' or 'the first woman scaffolder' no longer appear, we shall know that women have achieved that position as an equal – though different – half of the human race.

At no time has it been suggested that change is easy or even that everybody wants to make changes in their lives. Often the greatest changes of direction go unmarked and unnoticed by others because they are intensely personal, involving fresh ways of thinking and new attitudes to life. It is my fervent hope that men and women who feel dissatisfied with their lot – whatever this may be – can take courage from the example of others in this book and realize that changes can be made if they are really determined to bring them about. Only one flash of intuition is needed to recognize alternative ways of setting about things; then a start has been made.

It takes courage to live life to the full, let alone to attempt changes. If we aim to achieve the fine balance between selfishness and self-concern, we can learn to make the best of ourselves while striving to ensure it is also the best for others. Elizabeth Knight sums it up perfectly:

> I would say to anybody, to do what they want to do. The only person you can please all the time is yourself, with regard to other people and their fears. You can only do what is right for you. Life is for living and you only have one of them.

Bibliography

Adams, Carol & Laurikietis, Rae, *The Gender Trap, 1: Education and Work; 2: Sex and Marriage; 3: Messages and Images,* Quartet/Virago, 1977, revised edition 1980

Ardener, Shirley (ed.), *Defining Females. The Nature of Women in Society,* Croom Helm, 1978

Beauvoir, Simone de, *The Second Sex,* Penguin, 1977

Bernard, Jessie, *Women, Wives, Mothers,* Aldine, 1975

Berne, Eric, *Games People Play,* Penguin, 1977

Boston Women's Health Book Collective, *Our Bodies, Ourselves,* Simon & Schuster, 1976

Chown, Sheila M. (ed.), *Human Ageing,* Penguin, 1972

Clausen (ed.), *Socialisation and Society,* Little Brown & Co., 1968

Comfort, Alex, *The Process of Ageing,* Weidenfeld & Nicolson, 1965

Dalton, K., *Once a Month,* Fontana, 1978

Delamont, Sara, *The Sociology of Women,* Allen & Unwin, 1980

Dowrick, Stephanie & Grundberg, Sybil (eds.), *Why Children?* The Women's Press, 1980

Erikson, Erik H., *Childhood and Society,* Penguin, 1973

Figes, Eva, *Patriarchal Attitudes,* Panther, 1972

Firestone, Shulamith, *The Dialectic of Sex,* The Women's Press, 1979

Fiske, Marjorie, *Middle Age – The Prime of Life?* Harper & Row, 1979

Fransella & Frost, *Women, On Being a Woman,* Tavistock, 1977

Friedan, Betty, *The Feminist Mystique,* Penguin, 1979

Gavron, Hannah, *The Captive Wife,* Penguin, 1970

Gordon, Linda, *Woman's Body, Woman's Right,* Penguin, 1977

Gould, Roger L., *Tranformations – Growth and Change in Adult Life,* Simon & Schuster, 1978

Greer, Germaine, *The Female Eunuch,* MacGibbon & Kee, 1971

Groombridge, Joy, *Connexions: His and Hers*, Penguin, 1978
Janeway, Elizabeth, *Man's World, Woman's Place*, Michael Joseph, 1971
Kenny, Mary, *Woman by Two*, Hamlyn, 1979
Klein, V. & Myrdal, A., *Women's Two Roles*, Routledge, 1968
Levinson, Daniel J., *The Seasons of Man's Life*, Alfred A. Knopf, 1978
Liedloff, Jean, *The Continuum Concept*, Duckworth, 1975
Mackenzie, Midge, *Shoulder to Shoulder*, Penguin, 1975
Merton, Broom, Cottrell (eds.), *Sociology Today*, Basic Books, 1959
Mill, John Stuart, *The Subjection of Women*, Everyman, 1970
Miller, Jean Baker (ed.), *Psychoanalysis and Women*, Penguin, 1978
Miller, Jean Baker, *Towards a new Psychology of Women*, Pelican, 1979
Miller, Lurie, *Late Bloom*, Paddington Press, 1979
Mitchell, Juliet, *Women's Estate*, Penguin, 1971
Mitchell, Juliet, *Psychoanalysis and Feminism*, Penguin, 1979
Mitchell, Juliet & Oakley, Ann (eds.), *Rights and Wrongs of Women*, Penguin, 1976
Montagu, Ashley, *The Natural Superiority of Women*, Allen & Unwin, 1954
Morgan, Elaine, *The Descent of Woman*, Corgi, 1974
Neugarten, Bernice L. (ed.), *Middle Age and Ageing*, University of Chicago Press, 1968
Novarra, Virginia, *Women's Work, Men's Work*, Marion Boyars, 1980
Orbach, Susie, *Fat is a Feminist Issue*, Hamlyn, 1980
Richards, Janet Radcliffe, *The Sceptical Feminist*, Routledge, Kegan Paul, 1980
Rowbotham, Sheila, *Woman's Consciousness, Man's World*, Penguin, 1976
Ruddick, S. & Daniels P. (eds.), *Working it Out*, Pantheon, 1977
Sharpe, Sue, *Just like a Girl*, Penguin, 1978
Sheehy, Gail, *Passages*, Bantam, 1977
Stassinopoulos, Arianna, *The Female Woman*, Davis Poynter, 1973
Tolson, Andrew, *Limits of Masculinity*, Tavistock, 1977
Williamson, J.B., Murley, A. & Evans, L., *Ageing and Society*, Holt, Rinehart & Winston, 1980
Wilson, Elizabeth, *Women and the Welfare State*, Tavistock, 1977
Wollstonecraft, Mary, *The Rights of Woman*, Everyman, 1970

Davis, Ann E., 'Whoever said life begins at 40 was a fink or, those golden years – phooey', *International Journal of Women's Studies* Vol. 3 No. 6 Nov/Dec 1980 pp. 583–9

Dix, Carol, 'Paradise Regained', *Guardian*, 20 January 1981
Greene, J.G., 'Stress in the Phyllosan Years', *New Society*, 18/25 December 1980
Nicholson, John, 'The Shrinking Stereotype of Sex', *New Society*, 18/25 December 1980
Oakley, Ann, 'For Love or Money – the unspoken deal', *New Society*, 18/25 December 1980
Polan, Brenda, 'Some Mothers do have them', *Guardian*, 5 February 1981
Stott, Mary, Women's Page, *Guardian*, 15 September 1977
Wandor, Micheline, 'Where to Next?' *Spare Rib* No. 105, April 1981
Warnock, Mary, 'Why are Adolescent Girls so Awful?' *Guardian*, 17 August 1981